Methodology and History in Anthropology

General Editor: David Parkin, Fellow of All Souls College, Oxford

THE LIFE OF PROPERTY

House, Family and Inheritance in Béarn, South-West France

Timothy Jenkins

Berghahn Books
New York • Oxford

First published in 2010 by

Berghahn Books

www.berghahnbooks.com

©2010 Timothy Jenkins

Library of Congress Cataloging-in-Publication Data

Jenkins, Timothy, 1952-
  The life of property : house, family and inheritance in Béarn, south-
west France / Timothy Jenkins.
     p. cm. -- (Methodology and history in anthropology ; v.21.)
  Includes bibliographical references and index.
  ISBN 978-1-84545-667-2 (hardback : alk. paper)
  1. Ethnohistory--France--Béarn. 2. Kinship--France--Béarn--
History. 3. Family--France--Béarn--History. 4. Property--France--
Béarn--History. 5. Inheritance and
succession--France--Béarn--History. 6. Béarn (France)--History. 7.
Béarn (France)--Social life and customs. I. Title.
  DC611.B373J46 2010
  944'.716--dc22

                           2010007286

British Library Cataloguing in Publication Data
A catalogue record for this book is available from the British Library

Printed in the United States on acid-free paper.

ISBN 978-1-84545-667-2 (hardback)

CONTENTS

Ainsi se déroulait dans notre salle à manger, sous la lumière de la lampe dont elles sont amies, une de ces causeries où la sagesse non des nations mais des familles, s'emparant de quelque événement, mort, fiançailles, héritage, ruine, et le glissant sous le verre grossissant de la mémoire, lui donne tout son relief, dissocie, recule et situe en perspective à différents points de l'espace et du temps ce qui, pour ceux qui n'ont pas vécu, semble amalgamé sur une même surface, les noms des décédés, les adresses successives, les origines de la fortune et ses changements, les mutations de propriété. Cette sagesse-là n'est-elle pas inspirée par la Muse qu'il convient de méconnaître le plus longtemps possible si l'on veut garder quelque fraîcheur d'impressions et quelque virtu créatrice, mais que ceux-là mêmes qui l'ont ignorée rencontrent au soir de leur vie ... la Muse qui a recueilli tout ce que les muses plus hautes de la philosophie et de l'art ont rejeté, tout ce qui n'est pas fondé en vérité, tout ce qui n'est que contingent mais révèle aussi d'autres lois: c'est l'Histoire.

– Marcel Proust, *Albertine disparue*, Éditions Gallimard 1954
(pp. 356–7).

Then, in our dining-room, appropriately lamp-lit, there began one of those long conversations in which the wisdom not of nations but of families takes some event, a death, an engagement, an inheritance, a bankruptcy, and putting it under the magnifying glass of memory, brings it into relief, separating out the elements, taking a step back and viewing in perspective from various points in space and time such things as the names of the dead, successive addresses, the origins of wealth and its subsequent history, transfers of property – things which, to those who have not lived through them, seem to be arranged on a single plane. That wisdom is inspired by a Muse best ignored for as long as possible if one wants to keep some freshness of impression and creative power, but met with towards the end of life by even those who have neglected her ... the Muse which has collected up everything the higher Muses of Philosophy and Art have rejected, everything that is not based on truth, everything that is simply contingent but which also reveals other laws: the Muse of History.

PREFACE AND
ACKNOWLEDGEMENTS

This is a work of cultural and historical anthropology which is both a European ethnography – containing materials on politics, law and gender – and, at the same time, is structured around analytical, theoretical and comparative considerations that contribute to the history of ideas. The four chapters which make up the core of the book were originally delivered as the Evans-Pritchard lectures in Oxford in 2001. I have subsequently rewritten them whilst retaining the content and ideas expressed in the lectures. Pressure of other work has delayed their publication. I have added to them two further chapters, written subsequently, which illustrate and expand upon the argument of the lectures, and some brief concluding remarks; together, they provide a coherent whole.

The subject of the book is an anthropological investigation of the nature of property using materials gathered in the French Pyrenees. Taking the long-term continuities of a particular way of life in the foothills of the French Pyrenees, it relates that form of life to a broader framework, considering this relationship both in terms of what impinges upon the local from national and more cosmopolitan interests and – more originally – what the local contributes to those wider interests and outside gaze: how the local shapes national identity. In the case of Béarn, the continuities are carried in local forms of property and inheritance, which are borne witness to by legal materials that go back to the twelfth century. These are traced through archival (legal-historical) work and their contemporary expression explored through ethnographic fieldwork. Their contribution to wider political and sociological concerns is discerned through detailed readings of the work of the nineteenth-century sociologist Frédéric Le Play and that of the twentieth-century sociologist and theorist Pierre Bourdieu. These chapters frame the ethnographic and historical account; together they demonstrate the claim that the life of property in Béarn is a good deal more complex than one might imagine, and influences matters a good distance beyond the local. The book therefore combines ethnography and intellectual history.

It is the product of a long period of reading, fieldwork and archival research. My initial fieldwork, between 1977 and 1980, was spent in Paris, Toulouse and then Béarn, and my earliest interests were in the Occitan language movement and in the life of the farms on which that language was spoken and passed on. Whilst doing this fieldwork I was supported first by a Philip Bagby Studentship from the University of Oxford and then by a research grant from the Social Science Research Council.[1] Over the next fifteen years I made a number of short visits to Béarn; I was only able to return for a prolonged period in 1997 with the help of a British Academy Grant[2] (and also a grant from the Bethune-Baker Fund of the University of Cambridge) when I gathered much of the material presented here, in particular researching – in the Departmental and other archives – cadastral records and registers of births, marriages and deaths from the Revolution onward, and household censuses from the latter part of the nineteenth century; reading the ancient laws and commentaries and notarial archives and records; and investigating aspects of local political life. I was greatly assisted at this time by the Departments of History and Geography at the University of Pau. The materials and arguments presented in the lectures owe much to this more recent visit, but build upon a longer period of engagement that began in the late 1970s.

They also draw upon the teaching I received between 1973 and 1976 in the then Institute of Social Anthropology at Oxford (now the Institute of Social and Cultural Anthropology), which set my broad intellectual interests. As the heart of the book originated as a set of lectures dedicated to the memory of Evans-Pritchard, it is worth saying briefly what I owe to the Institute and to him. I did not meet Evans-Pritchard, for I entered the Institute as a Diploma student more or less the day he died, in September 1973, but his presence was strongly felt and his influence permeated my anthropological education and that of my contemporaries. In retrospect, I can identify certain strands to that education that remain effective. First, he introduced us to the importance and excitement of intellectual history: put simply, the demand that you should know where your ideas come from. At the same time, he created something of a cult of writing clearly and of integrating theory into description. We found these tasks difficult at the time, but that is where the ambition to do both stems from. He also pointed to certain series of specific authors or traditions; not only to the best sociologists, Durkheim and Mauss, and – as is well known – the French and Scottish Enlightenment philosophers, but also the British legal historians, Maine and Maitland, whose interest is by no means yet exhausted. And in terms of ethnographic thinking in the strict sense, Evans-Pritchard was exemplary for the consistent way in which he privileged the question of the scale at which human meaning is constructed. This is the most general way of expressing his sure handling of such delicate matters as motivation and accountability, freedom and time: in short, the way he identifies the 'middle distance', between the too-abstract and the too-concrete, in which human lives are created and lived out.

This book is concerned with precisely such interests, and with such a 'middle distance', for its immediate subject is house, family and the transmission of wealth in Béarn. None of these three terms is transparent in the sense of giving up its meaning easily and each will have to be mapped out, in part through paying attention to the etymologies of these ideas, when some legal history will have to be taken into consideration. Given this complication of what at first appear to be simple ideas, it would perhaps be sensible to offer a thread to hold on to: if there is a single theoretical concern underlying the whole, it is an investigation of the concept of 'property', which is a key in our world to human being and order, to personality and politics, to extent and duration – a concept, therefore, with wide implications. And the investigation is both given body and consistency – and set limits, or restricted in scope – by its location, for it arises out of nearly thirty years of intermittent research in Béarn.

Because of this long and fragmented period of research, my debts both personal and intellectual are too many to be acknowledged in full, and indeed are too varied for me to be aware of them all. I am most grateful, first of all, to the electors to the Evans-Prichard Lectureship for their confidence in appointing me, and to the Warden and Fellows of All Souls for their hospitality during the period of the lectures. I also owe a good deal to the British Academy for its earlier timely grant, and to the members of the Departments of History and Geography at the University of Pau for their welcome and practical assistance. Further, my long-term research would have been impossible without the various persons – scholars, hosts and others – who received me so kindly and did so much to help me in Paris, Toulouse and Béarn. I would like to record the names of four of these Occitan scholars who have since died: Jean-Claude Dinguirard, Christian Anatole, Roger Lapassade and Michel Grosclaude. I am endebted too in a long-term fashion to my contemporaries and teachers at the Institute in Oxford; among those colleagues I wish to thank Paul Dresch, David Parkin and Wendy James in particular for their encouragement and friendship, and also to record my gratitude to my supervisor, Edwin Ardener (1927–1987), under whose guidance I first went to France. Peter Glazebrook has read and commented upon the manuscript, particularly from a lawyer's perspective, and I am grateful too to Émile Perreau-Saussine and Joel Cabrita for their comments. I have been particularly helped by the detailed suggestions put forward by Jacob Copeman and the publisher's anonymous reader. Last and in a different way, I wish to thank my family for their companionship and support in the research and writing of this book; they have participated in the interests explored here in the closest fashion, especially my wife, Diane Palmer.

Two chapters have been published before; both have been edited and reframed for inclusion here. Part of chapter 5 was published as 'Mariage, héritage et évolution social dans un roman gascon: *Los tres gojats de Bòrdavielha* de Simin Palay' in *Ethnologie française* 36, 2006, and is reprinted with permission of the publisher, Presses Universitaires de France. The final, definitive version of the article that appears as chapter 6, 'Bourdieu's Béarnais Ethnography', has been published in the journal *Theory, Culture and Society* 23(6), 2006 © SAGE Publications Ltd. It is republished by permission.

Cambridge, January 2009.

Notes

1. The project was 'A Social Anthropological Study of Two Ethnic Minorities in Modern France', May 1979, ref. HR 6349. See Jenkins (1981).
2   British Academy Research Grant APN 5740.

INTRODUCTION

This book reflects a prime concern in contemporary social anthropology, as well as perhaps the major interest of the discipline to a wider audience, which is that the study of small-scale ethnographic practices can cast light upon larger-scale political and historical phenomena. This is true not only in the areas social anthropology has traditionally concerned itself with but also in contemporary Western Europe, where such a demonstration is perhaps more startling; here, too, knowledge of the detail of local, even domestic, forms of life from a specific region illuminates features of national debate and policy, raising the important issue of to what extent national, metropolitan life is an expression of local forms and concerns. One might look to such local forms to explain, for example, aspects of the elusive but real characteristics that distinguish the various national politics of the different European nations. Local, historical and ethnographic categories appear in the seemingly alien forms of cosmopolitan life, 'alien' because apparently generalized, non-time-specific, and belonging to a metropolitan culture. The claim advanced here is to redress the balance, for until recently humanities and social science accounts have tended to emphasize the influence of wider concerns and perspectives – particularly state powers – on local life, considered as a passive object. Essentially, European ethnography was considered as a salvage operation and as a record of the inevitable defeat of local life. Close ethnographic study, however, draws attention not only to the powers of resistance to a metropolitan gaze of the local, but also to the latter's power to show initiative, to set agendas and to shape concepts that both control the impact of wider forces on local life and also create patterns of activity that are then given wider application, that are taken up and transformed at a national scale, or sometimes even at a wider, European, level.[1] Contemporary anthropology has focussed in particular upon the interactions of ethnographic categories and state powers, but other forms of life – cultural, intellectual and economic, for instance – are also implicated.

This book presents a case study read from this perspective, which illustrates these processes in some detail and therefore offers one kind of model for writing European ethnography that should be of interest beyond the confines of the discipline, in particular to historians, political scientists and historians of ideas. This case study is set in Béarn, a former province in the south-west of France, and its focus is with what is termed 'the life of property'. It is concerned with the forms of ownership of property and its transmission in this region, with the continuities and mutations of these forms, and with their influence and transformations at other scales (such as local politics), with their serving as unconscious frames and models for other concerns in the region, and with their 'being used to think with' both by sociological interests and by political interests at the wider, national level. It tells a complex story, drawing upon varied sources; in order to keep the different parts in proportion, and despite the detail offered, each of the first four chapters in particular represents only a sketch map that could have been turned into a monograph. Their purpose together is to play their part in making the argument concerning the life of property.

The study begins with the 'discovery' at a national level of these Béarnais or Pyrenean forms in the nineteenth century; with on the one hand their contribution to sociological theory, first in the guise of the 'stem family' and later in that of 'family strategies', and on the other hand with their deployment in contemporary political debates about social reform with respect to political, economic and cultural issues. The second chapter examines the question as to what were the local forms of life and continuities that permitted this discovery, and turns to consideration of regional legal and notarial materials, taken as evidence simultaneously of certain culturally specific resources, of the longevity of these resources, and of the transformations these resources have undergone, not least through the introduction of the Civil Code. There emerges a clear pattern indicating how both 'traditional' and 'modernizing' possibilities are generated simultaneously, permitting both flexibility and adaptability whereby the new is assimilated on the basis of the old, or long-term forms prolonged through the adoption of new ways[2]. The third chapter, which is based on fieldwork and the use of comparative ethnographic materials, examines contemporary (late-twentieth-century) local life, focusing on peasants. It considers the playing out of the categories discerned in the fine detail of the everyday lives of both men and women, in both the farming and the non-farming community. As well as describing continuities, two examples of radical change and development are considered within this framework – the introduction of new agricultural technologies and the consolidation of land holdings – and the long-term pattern of adaptation to the new contributing to the prolongation of older forms, detected initially in the legal forms, is sketched. In the fourth chapter, the focus is widened again, to see how these local forms impinge at other levels, first considering the place of such an account with respect to two contemporary anthropological ideas, inalienable possessions (Annette Weiner) and house societies (Lévi-Strauss), and second reviewing matters of local politics with respect to issues of legitimacy, authority and power, expressed in particular in land sales and land use. Local government is largely concerned with questions of the utilization of property and the mobilization of local identity for economic ends, and therefore offers a complex exemplification of local categories interacting with wider concerns, some of which concerns bear the marks of earlier encounters with the region. In this instance, contemporary political, economic and social policies applied and exploited in the region bear traces of earlier debates about the nature of civil society to which the discovery of the Pyrenean family contributed.

These several readings of the same phenomenon from various perspectives add up to a fairly complete overall description of what I have called the life of property in Béarn, its plural dimensions and the causalities they contain, the forms of continuity it achieves in interaction with wider frames and, because of its adaptability, its elusive nature. This kind of phenomenon is met with in contemporary theory under the term 'hybridity'[3] but, as these materials show, it has a long pedigree. This life of property takes the form not of a continuing essence to be expressed in different materials but rather of a series of overlapping strands, a life contained in a pattern that structures a sequence of encounters at very different social levels. This case study therefore offers a fine example of the forms of continuity of local life, of the generation as well as the integration of new forms, and of the contribution local life can make in this way to national culture, through the transfer of forms and accepting them back transformed.

This description is supplemented by two further studies, deploying new kinds of evidence. The first of these (chapter 5) offers an ethnographic reading of a Gascon novel by Simin Palay, *Los tres gojats de Bòrdavielha* (1934). The novel operates at several levels. It offers materials on the habits and customs of nineteenth-century Béarnais society, with the central themes of marriage, property and inheritance in a farming family. It also contains a detailed account of the various psychological dispositions and motivations associated with the local categories, which are absent or secondary in many ethnographic accounts, and which give clues about how aspects of the modern world may find their roots in the local social order. On this basis, the novel contains a fine description of the complex interactions of this indigenous world with the wider society through legal and political events. It therefore contains an indigenous view of history and social change, which may give new insight into the processes of modernity, and which can supplement existing historical and ethnographic accounts of the region. This account repeats the lesson of the first four chapters, emphasizing the local generation and reception of the new, showing how a local, ethnographic society does not simply suffer history but also participates in it.

The other study (chapter 6) uses comparable materials to make the complementary point, concerning the contribution of the local to wider categories. This study concerns the place of Béarn in the work of Pierre Bourdieu, an important contemporary sociologist. Bourdieu was born in Béarn and conducted fieldwork there, publishing the results early in his career, in 1962. He returned twice to that fieldwork in articles which developed several of the central concepts, concerns and approaches deployed in his major writings, in particular, the concepts of marriage strategies, symbolic capital and symbolic violence. Moreover, later in life he reflected increasingly on the place of biography in the construction of both social and sociological knowledge, invoking his autobiography as a key to explaining his ideas. These articles on Béarn therefore form a privileged body of material for understanding Bourdieu's *oeuvre*, providing access to the link between biography and theory, and a means of grasping what is at stake in what he terms a 'reflexive sociology'. The aim of this chapter is threefold. First, it considers the contribution of Béarnais material to the development of Bourdieu's thought. Then, it offers a critique of his use of that material from the perspective of an anthropologist who has worked in the region, and who is familiar both with the kinds of materials and also the earlier accounts on which he was drawing. And last, it indicates ways that Bourdieu's reading of the local materials influences the character of his wider theoretical concepts. This material offers a detailed contemporary example of how the local categories with which we are concerned contribute (once again) on a national – and indeed international – scale.

These two further studies therefore add to and illustrate the central concern of the book, the complex and enduring expression at many levels of local categories initially concerning residence, kinship, marriage and the transmission of wealth, but which expand to engage with questions of the state, law, local languages, farming techniques, politics, economics, demography and so forth. The last chapter offers a summary of these concerns, relating property and a certain understanding of history. Ethnography is a way of engaging both with the complexities and with the historical depth of modern European life: the 'life of property' is a clear illustration of this claim.

Notes

1. This is an approach exemplified in European anthropology by the work of Michael Herzfeld; see, e.g., Herzfeld (1992).
2. I regret that Dominique Bidot-Germa's work on medieval notaries in Béarn (Bidot-Germa 2008) came to my notice too late to be taken into account.
3. See Latour (1991).

Chapter 1

THE DISCOVERY OF THE
PYRENEAN FAMILY

I

Béarn is a former province in the south-west of France, lying between the crest of the Pyrenees to the south and the flat Landes region to the north, with the French Basque Country to the west, and the former county of Bigorre to the east. It consists of a mountainous part to the south; the mountains are cut by rivers or *gaves* (the local term) into four valleys, descending to form fertile plains in the north; and between these two parts the foothills lie. Since the Revolution, Béarn together with the Basque Country make up the Département des Pyrénées Atlantiques, formerly the Département des Basses Pyrénées.[1]

The single most important social organizing principle in the French Pyrenees is 'the house', a complex value encompassing dwelling, property and family.[2] Through the common subscription of its members to the aim of ensuring its perpetuation, 'the house' orders the transmission of property, both material property – land, chattels, and money – and immaterial property – such as status and name. It controls flows of labour, wealth and blood (through relations with neighbours, inheritance and marriage). And it shapes the fate of each of its members, both those who remain and those who are dispersed. 'The house' therefore creates continuity over time, and there is evidence both of the historical depth of the principle in the region and of its successful adaptation to change.

Such complex social phenomena are most commonly apprehended from an outside perspective from a single angle: in this case, the transmission of property through what has been called the 'stem family', or *la famille-souche*. One member of the family in each generation both inherits the property in its entirety (known locally as *la casa* or *l'ostau*), and at the same time succeeds to the authority to be head of that house (becoming *cap d'ostau*). The family property – not only the house, the land and its wealth, but also such less tangible goods as authority, reputation and status – is thereby transmitted intact from generation to generation.

This mode of transmission is accompanied by a characteristic mode of cohabitation: the household consists typically of the farmer and his wife, plus the heir and his (or her) spouse and children, together with any unmarried members of the farmer's or the heir's generation, and any servants or hired hands. It also follows that there is a strong differentiation within a generation between the heir and the non-heirs. Despite the apparent emphasis on the family, this is an example of a social form that maintains one kind of moral unity, the house, at the expense of another, the group of kin: property is protected against dispersal, as is authority, but kin are not.[3] Inheritance in both property and status is restricted (to one person in a generation), and the marriage of non-heirs entails, first, their (variable) compensation, sometimes in dowry form, for not inheriting and, second, their departure from the family home.

Property in this sense is a moral fact: beyond the material objects such as soil, buildings, equipment, livestock or money, it has a life and force. For it organizes, on the one hand, the life possibilities of all its members: their status and their fate, whether they stay to work locally or emigrate, their marriage opportunities, and so forth. And, on the other hand, the property is the key to local life: through reputation and local geography, it organizes the neighbourhood, through customary rights and duties with respect to shared labour and common land, and local politics, through a variety of concepts, including that of 'eligibility' or the capacity to be elected. In short, property and its transmission is a 'total social fact', which we have to explore in order to understand.

II

There is also, clearly, an external dimension to be considered in all this. I suggested that such a 'total social fact' tends to be grasped from the outside from a single angle, in this case, as an example of the genus 'family'. Two things are worth noting. On the one hand, a local society such as that in the Pyrenees is by no means passive in the act of being

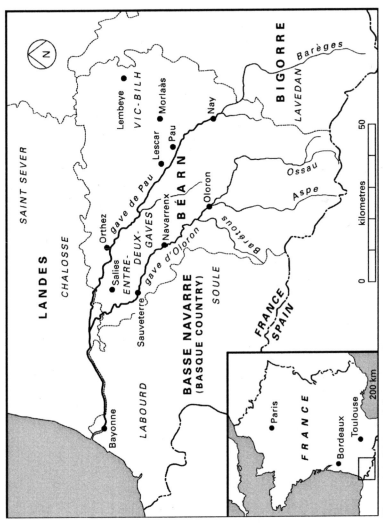

Figure 1.1: *Béarn and the surrounding region*

apprehended: it is concerned – to speak figuratively – both to present aspects of itself to any outside enquiry and, by the same token, simultaneously to conceal other features. Local phenomena survive in an interplay of what Herzfeld calls self-presentation to, and self-concealment from, a metropolitan gaze.[4] Yet despite that, on the other hand, the local society does not choose how and when it becomes an object of interest, or control when an outside agenda finds an object located in some aspect of local practice to help it think through a specific problem. Investigation of 'the house', as a form of the life of property, needs therefore to take into account both indigenous activities and the outside gaze, for together they constitute its existence over time.

For this reason, in this chapter I shall investigate the 'discovery' of the Pyrenean family, for it both introduces us to the complex, layered history of the notion, and at the same time draws our attention to the nature of the processes at work, not least to the fact that neither party in the encounter is left unchanged.[5]

The process might sound obscure when put like this, but it has practical consequences. I can point to my own experience in selecting a place in which to carry out fieldwork. Although the choice of a site appears largely contingent, in fact a certain constraint comes into play. My itinerary led from Paris, where I first made contact with the regionalist movement constructed around the southern dialects known as Provençal or Occitan, to Toulouse, working with scholars concerned with that language and its literature, to Béarn, where I lived in a market town and upon farms in its vicinity, seeking to find out how the movement 'earthed' in the world of indigenous patois speakers. On the farms, my focus of intellectual interest shifted from the language movement to questions of land inheritance, but the geographical trajectory too was not taken without hesitations, which are traceable in grant applications and subsequent reports. In retrospect, indeed, I was sleepwalking, and awoke to find myself in Béarn.

Because of my interest in the language movement, I was directed from Toulouse to an area which had a local tradition of interest in the dialect – of writers, lexicographers, paremiologists and so forth – and where the patois spoken was supposed to be better preserved, more frequently employed and less influenced by French, than in the surrounding areas. I say 'supposed' for both the speakers of the local dialect in question, and those of neighbouring ones (and indeed, some people who do not speak the patois at all) will tell you that this precise region is where the 'best' patois is spoken. I found, for example, that patois speakers in the area easily understood my wish to learn their dialect, while those in other, neighbouring areas advised me to move on to the local centre. I cannot tell whether it is objectively the case that the patois in this area is better preserved than elsewhere. What is important is that the area selected itself, so to speak, and that it seems that a local tradition of writers who use their dialect raises its value, both in the eyes of those speaking it and further afield. Even my range of choice was determined by the phenomenon that I originally came to study.[6]

This process of refinement and selection of research area is of course a common enough experience of fieldwork. And practical considerations determined my final choice. Béarn has a strong continuing tradition of writers in the local language, and my settling there was determined by my contacts, extending from Toulouse, with the active local language movement, Per Noste, and the friendship of a school teacher, himself an activist, who introduced me to the families of certain of his pupils. They, in turn, passed me on in due course to other families. In this way, I reached deep into the countryside, learning the language spoken on the farms, and my interest developed to encompass the way of life I found.

It is worth remarking upon a second curiosity. Having been drawn to the area, and indeed the precise locality, by a series of metropolitan concerns – the militant movement and the production of a literature – it is striking that I discovered a distinctive form of life to match them – essentially the specific mode of transmission of property and a structure of the family – although this has extremely little to do with the militant or literary movements. We might suspect on these grounds alone that registrations made from without are by no means independent of local categories and institutions. My own trajectory, with its air of sleepwalking, is an illustration of this causality. So too is the existence of a cluster of remarkable studies of this coherent way of life, of which I learnt subsequently. I mention only the most distinguished, in their reverse chronological order (the most recent first): the works of the anthropologists Georges Augustins and Pierre Bourdieu, the rural sociologist Henri Mendras, the linguist Gerhard Rohlfs, the historian Henri Lefebvre, and the social reformer Frédéric Le Play.[7] The sheer number of good studies of the region is itself a social fact requiring explanation. I shall concentrate in this chapter upon the last mentioned, Le Play, for he is the person who 'discovered' the Pyrenean family, and this discovery usefully displays most of the dimensions of our problem.

III

Le Play (1806–1882) was a contemporary of de Tocqueville (1805–1857) and Comte (1798–1857). He began as a mining engineer and statistician, but early on turned his attention to the conditions of the working class, this latter interest falling into two distinct phases.[8] The first was a long period of journeys and direct observation, which lead to a series of monographs. In his forties, however, he became a public figure under the Second Empire (1851–1870), filling official roles and creating an organization dedicated to the promotion of 'social prosperity'; in this period, his texts concerned proposals for social reform. Broadly speaking, the interest he showed in the conditions of the working class is characteristic of the post-Revolution, Restoration period, and the preoccupation with social reform representative of a widespread reformulation of this concern after 1848.[9]

Both phases are of interest to us. The monographs were the first empirical studies of European workers' families. They were organized systematically upon a threefold basis, with preliminary observations concerning the family, followed by the family budget, and a third part – termed 'social constitution' – which supplemented the data with observations on the local economic conditions, associations, historical traditions, relations between workers and employers, and ecology. These studies were undertaken between 1829 and 1855, and were published as *Les ouvriers européens* in the latter year.[10]

Le Play sought collaborators and formed an association, la Société internationale des études pratiques d'economie sociale, which published monographs[11] between 1857 and 1885 in its own journal, *Les ouvriers des deux mondes*. The monograph of particular concern to us resulted from research conducted in 1856 by Le Play at Cauterets, in the Hautes Pyrénées, which was published the following year in the first number of that journal, an essay entitled 'Paysans en communauté du Lavedan'.[12]

In his second phase, Le Play became an advocate of social reform, publishing a series of books from 1864 onwards, employing the materials he had collected and the classification by which he had organized them, in order to promote certain political and social concerns. This series began with *La réforme sociale* (1864), and went on to consider the question of the organization of labour (1870) and then of the family (1871).[13]

Le Play's work therefore began under the Restoration and the July Monarchy (1830–1848), came to fruition under the Second Empire (1851–1870),[14] and was prolonged into the Third Republic (1871–1914). Given this longevity, it is easy to misdate his work, as Catherine Silver has pointed out,[15] and to miss his striking originality. Silver also tries to separate out the value of the empirical work from the later concern with social reform, on the grounds that the political motivations of the latter have served to discredit and hide the scientific achievements of the former. It is not clear, however, that this separation can be made, for the underlying sociological classification was already clear in the typology organizing the monographs in 1855. Certainly, in the case of the monograph on the Pyrenean family at Lavedan, the separation cannot be made, for it comes at the juncture between the two periods, and it gains an increasing, and increasingly central, role in the later work. It was the product of Le Play's final period of fieldwork (to employ an anachronism), building upon twenty-five years' experience in making these surveys. At the same time, it allowed him to make his discovery, that of *la famille-souche*, the stem family, which became the key, not simply to a classification of family forms, but also to proposals regarding social prosperity. This centrality is made clear by the subsequent republication and evolution of the piece.

The monograph in question was reprinted in full as the second part of *L'organisation de la famille* (1871), the book's full title being 'The organisation of the family: the best model, as indicated by consideration of all peoples and historical periods' (*le vrai modèle signalé par l'histoire de toutes les races et de tous les temps*). Here the monograph was given the title 'la description du modèle ou une famille-souche du Lavedan en 1856', which indicates its change in status to being a catalyst for theory.[16] It was reprinted again in 1877, in the second edition of *Les ouvriers européens*, this time as 'Paysans à famille-souche du Lavedan (Béarn)'.

In brief, the Lavedan monograph is the empirical catalyst that permits the precipitation both of a sociology of the family and of a project of social reform. All three elements – empirical study, sociological typology and political project – have had their consequences and effects that endure to this day. In order to understand these, we have to examine the elements and their relationship in Le Play's work, where it emerges that the political project is the key both to the broader sociological classification and to the specific discovery of the significance of 'the Pyrenean family'. I will look in the first place at Le Play's sociology of the family, and in the second at the political context in which it was put to work. I will then allude to two parallel cases before considering the specific case study of 'the stem family in Lavedan'.[17]

IV

Le Play makes the family the basis of social order, linking authority and transmission of property in an account of family stability.[18] I offer two initial comments: first, the identification of the family as the elementary unit for all social phenomena is compatible with a statistical approach, as is Le Play's unique interest in 'workers'' families (among which he includes peasants, nomads, artisans, as well as the working classes), for they are the most numerous in society and nearest to subsistence. Second, it follows that the monographic method is the key to a general sociology; as Le Play says: 'the description of a worker's family will ... draw in all the essential elements for the constitution of society'.[19] Le Play takes both these emphases from Bonald, whom we shall consider briefly below. There is a matching, therefore, between family form, with its modes of authority and continuity, and social form.

Le Play elaborates this principle and offers a classificatory scheme of human societies according to three types of organisation of the family. These three types are the patriarchal family, the unstable family and the stem family. In the first type, the patriarchal family, all the sons marry and remain within the paternal household. This form associates up to four generations, and favours the transmission of customs and habits from the old to the young. Periodically, swarms leave the parent community to set up like communities. This regime, to be found in pastoral communities in Asia, is intellectually conservative and has an authoritarian tendency, and it can give way to corruption, oppressing individuals in a variety of ways.[20] The second type, the unstable family, is the opposite in some respects of the patriarchal family, for the children of either sex leave the parental home as they become self-sufficient; the parents begin as an isolated couple, become such again, and die so. Such property as exists is divided equally among the heirs. The ills of such a regime are clear, not only with respect to property, but also the transmission of knowledge and morality, and such associated issues as authority, and care for the weak and elderly. Examples of this type are found in modern, industrial society. Between these two types, characterized by the weight of tradition and the community on the one hand, and by excessive individualism on the other, lies an intermediate type, the stem family, which avoids the excesses and unites the advantages of both. In this third form, one of the children marries and lives with the parents, in community with them, perpetuating a traditional way of life, carrying on the family business. The other children in due course set up elsewhere, founding a new house, unless they prefer to remain unmarried and stay in the parental house. In this way, parental authority, virtue and tradition are sustained and properties and businesses are not divided, but, at the same time, individuals are generated to be at the service of modern society – enterprising, open to the new, but not alienated or anomic individuals.

This analysis certainly has a conservative, though not reactionary, flavour, and when we turn to the corresponding analysis of social forms, we might anticipate that Le Play will match family forms with different societies in a tripartite classification – something along the lines of ancient patriarchal society (Old Testament Jews plus Greeks and Romans), the Ancien Régime and modern, post-Revolutionary society corresponding to the patriarchal, stem and unstable families respectively – and so set up a politically charged opposition between on the one hand the ills of modern, urban, post-Revolutionary society and on the other an Ancien Régime that combines moderation and the orderly transmission of property with innovation.[21]

But this is not so. In fact, he contrasts the patriarchal, pastoral families of the east, seen as being essentially without history (despite their occasional swarms) and of great antiquity, with the evolution of the unstable family in the west and in Gaul in particular, which he links to history and development. He associates the unstable family with the development of hunter-gathering, for hunting is individual; it destroys communal habits as young couples break away from their parents. These small units may unite into clans in order to defend territory, but the unstable form persists even when settled agricultural life develops: hence, he deduces, the Gaulish qualities of strong leaders and heroism combined with an incapacity to form an enduring nation. Le Play links the unstable states formed between the Loire and the Rhine with the persistent individualism of this family form, manifested in such diverse matters as the division of goods and land, quarrels over inheritance, restriction of fertility, rivalry between heirs, and neglect of the elderly and weak. The ills of modern French society, apparently the recent fruit of Protestants, *philosophes* and revolutionaries, in fact have deep peasant roots.

Le Play concludes (in his introductory chapter to *L'organisation de la famille*) that there is a geography of family types in France: he points out that, in addition to the unstable family, to be found in the north, there are examples of the patriarchal family in the mountains – the Alps, Jura, Vosges, Auvergne, Vivarans – and in the large prairies of the central plateau – the Nivernais. And in addition, among these enduring social resources, there is the stem family, to be found in the south-west. Le Play's family sociology, with its emphasis upon forms of authority and transmission, is therefore a good deal more subtle and 'situated' than one might have anticipated. The ideological elements which are unmistakably present – a speculative genealogy of modern ills and their potential cures – are underwritten by a historical geography of inheritance patterns that is both impressive and fruitful.

Le Play suggests that the stem family is the best form of organization of the family because it achieves four ends. First, it assures the rapid succession and fecundity of generations by the early choice of an heir – Le Play was convinced that an heiress was often preferred – and the early habit of marriage. Fertility has been a French preoccupation since Montesquieu's *Lettres persanes*.[22] Second, this family type, by associating successive generations in the same household, perpetuates the traditions of work, honour and virtue: he indeed suggests that it is the reputation of the family vis-à-vis their neighbours which constitutes their true wealth.[23] Third, it confers the benefits of this form of social organization upon all the useful classes of society: it is equally well suited to peasants, tenants and rural workers as it is to more wealthy families, and at the same time as perpetuating businesses and trades it supplies skilled workers to agriculture, industry and the army, as well as to the magistracy and government. It is a key, therefore, to social flourishing.[24] Last, and developing this point, this analysis bases an alliance of interests in society not upon feelings of conflict and passion, but of respect and affection: it expresses a vision of a harmonious society, quite unlike the dominant features of the history of France in Le Play's lifetime. It suggests a basis for the polity other than class interest and conflict.

These claims integrate the sociological and the political, even if in a rather abstract model, and they are able to do so because the family has been identified as the key to social order. In making this move, Le Play is heir to Bonald, who points to 'social relations' as the principle of intelligibility of modern society, explaining both present disorder and its potential remedy.

As a final remark on Le Play's family sociology, it is worth emphasizing the role played by inheritance in the definition of the causes of order and disorder in society.

Le Play's social dialectic plays around the alternatives of privileging kin or sustaining property intact (and with the latter, custom, tradition, and symbolic as well as material wealth). Once there is a pressure upon land, he claims, patriarchal families easily break down into unstable families, and it is hard under either of these regimes to establish a common good, for families, clans and individuals exploit their neighbours, and personal and public order, chastity and polity, are the losers. In general, with a lack of soil to be cleared, one has to resort to social institutions to resolve these social questions.

The key social institution is inheritance, the orderly transmission of property, with its necessary consequences in the sphere of authority. These consequences are first within the family, expressed in the right or otherwise of the father to leave his property as he will, but then within the local society and the wider social order. Paternal authority, focused in the right of testamentary freedom, is mirrored in relations between employer and employee, between ruler and subjects and, finally, between God and man.

Such a set of topics introduces Le Play's careful evaluation of the Ancien Régime, itself standing as a product of feudalism. A regime that combines chastity and primogeniture in families can sustain a common good between the classes of society, he claims, with local reciprocal obligations of service, rights and duties organized in a hierarchical order supplying public stability and peace. This common good was associated with an unprecedented prosperity, and Le Play cites Arthur Young on pre-Revolutionary Béarn.[25] Furthermore, the precise cause of the fall from this state of well-being is identified in Revolutionary legislation concerning inheritance. And this brings us to the context of Le Play's interventions.

V

Because social order and family order are interdependent in this perspective, it is possible to act upon society, the state and the solidarity of institutions by acting upon the family, and at the same time to explain the current state of society by attributing responsibility to the earlier actions of the state upon the family. The form of the family is linked, therefore, to legislation, and the current state of society depends, to a great extent, upon family law, in particular, the laws of inheritance.

As we have seen, social authority is linked in the stem family with integral transmission. But, Le Play insists, this stable form is the product not of law, but of custom: it is, indeed, accumulated and proven 'best practice'. It offers a model of social stability, but at the same time it has been undermined by Revolutionary legislation that favours the unstable family. In *La réforme sociale*, Le Play details the attacks written law has made upon custom.

Le Play never refers to the ancient written customary laws of Barèges and Lavedan,[26] but portrays Pyrenean customs as a set of practices of great antiquity, which were contested since the Middle Ages by legal specialists, who in this way anticipate the activities of the Revolutionary lawyers. (We shall touch upon this material in chapter 2). Custom is therefore something deeper and less artificial than law, containing the habits and institutions of a people that have assured their lasting well-being.[27] It may however need to be defended by law. Written law comes from without, relaying the authority of rulers, modifying the impulse imprinted by custom and habit.[28]

However, and once again, this contrast is not simply a mythical opposition between a natural order of custom and the movement of history in the form of law, for Le Play situates the opposition geographically. He not only finds the stem family in the south-west, but he also draws upon contemporary legal arguments concerning the juridical resistance of the south to the unification of French law, a unification attempted first in Revolutionary law and then in the Civil Code.[29]

The focus of argument in the Revolutionary period concerned the effects of the laws of succession upon authority within the family and, in particular, the law of 7 mars 1793, which abolished the power of testamentary freedom in direct line, giving all heirs an equal interest in the parental property – and at the same time, abolishing all distinctions between elder and younger, male and female, land and chattels, patrimonial and acquired goods.[30]

A measure of reaction to this extreme egalitarianism followed, and testamentary freedom was partially restored by the promulgation in 1803 of that part of the Civil Code relating to successions,[31] particularly articles 913 and 919. The former maintained the regime of equal division in cases of succession *ab intestat* (meaning in the absence of any will),[32] but abolished the equal rights of illegitimate children.[33] Furthermore, it allowed a person to dispose freely of a portion of their property, by gift or by testament. But, critics claimed, the effect of this regime was nevertheless similar to that of 1793: it promoted individualism, for at least half the property in every case is divided equally between heirs, and it therefore undermined the authority of one generation over the next by confining the power of the testator.

From these symptomatic claims, we can read off Le Play's criticism of the multiple ill effects of the Revolution. The promotion of individualism, the countervailing strengthening of the state, with the loss of middle ground, the undermining of tradition, the splitting of properties, the destabilizing of populations, even the rise of class antagonisms and of hostility to religion, may all be seen as due in part to failures in legislation concerning property law, and their consequences upon the family.[34]

Le Play's approach, although stimulating, is based of course upon a double reduction, first of society to the family, and second of the family to the laws of succession. But as such it lends itself to a political project of social reform. In his reformist mode, therefore, Le Play's strategy was to look towards the re-establishment of paternal authority through the restoration of testamentary freedom. This was not reactionary in the sense of counter-revolutionary, but rather an attempt to correct a failure of the Civil Code to achieve its ends, for it was conservative in intent.

Le Play's project was taken up under the Second Empire and, although unsuccessful, was only the most broadly argued of a number of attempts to reform the laws of inheritance. These attempts displayed a variety of motives. Merchants and manufacturers deplored the influence of the laws upon the character of their children, creating a sense of expectation rather than obligation, and upon the social situation in their workshops. Agricultural reformers were concerned with their effects in terms of the destruction of farms and the dispersal of family members. And, of particular interest to us, southern jurists were confronted locally with the challenging of settlements, and nationally with the overturning by the Court of Appeals of decisions reached by lower courts in the south. I am particularly indebted here to the work of Louis Assier-Andrieu.[35]

These challenges, and the overturning of local judgments at a national level, focused around a particular legal point, which could be interpreted precisely in terms of increasing individualism and diminishing authority. In brief, the property was evaluated at the point when an heir was identified – usually upon marriage – and the non-inheritors compensated. In the case of three offspring, the father could give the heir the disposable share of the property – one quarter – and a share in the remainder equal to that given the other siblings – a further quarter. To retain the property intact, the other two siblings had to renounce their share, and receive in return monetary or other compensation from the heir, over an agreed period, usually to be completed at the father's death. However, at the death of the father, the division could be contested, or renegotiated, as a revaluation at this stage could prove to be to the advantage of the excluded siblings who, in effect, would take a share in any value that had been added to the property by the heir's labour, prudence and good management.

The attitude the courts took on this question of renegotiation depended upon the relative weight given, on the one hand, to the individual interests of the excluded siblings and, on the other, to the continuity and viability of the farm. The interests of the kin group and those of the property were opposed. The southern courts tended to find in favour of the latter, favouring the valuation made at the time of the heir's marriage agreement; the Court of Appeal, however, favoured valuation at the moment of the death of the parent.

It is this conjuncture of contested land inheritance linked with wider questions of authority in society that gave political force to Le Play's sociology linking the family and social stability, and which is focused in the discovery of the Pyrenean family. The notion has an exact genealogy: it replies to these precise questions.

VI

Before outlining Le Play's monographic account of the stem family, I wish to discuss briefly two parallels indicating some wider dimensions of the intellectual context of Le Play's work. The first is the work of Louis de Bonald (1754–1840), a social theorist from the generation earlier than Le Play. During the Revolutionary period, Bonald developed a sociological account of the importance both of authority relations and of intermediate institutions; and in the course of this produced a sociology of the family that in many respects anticipated Le Play's writings. Sainte-Beuve indeed refers to Le Play as a 'rejuvenated, progressive and scientific Bonald' (*Bonald rajeuni, progressif et scientifique*).[36]

Bonald's account classifies three types of family on the basis of the presence or absence of divorce, which is considered as an expression of relations of authority; and links these types to a corresponding series of social forms. The series consists of patriarchal, imperfect and perfect societies, a gradual perfection of nature through history, exemplified by Jewish, Roman and Christian societies, and corresponding to family forms marked by the power of repudiation, divorce (or symmetrical repudiation) and non-dissolution respectively.

We might note, first, that Bonald regards human social life as constructed, not given, and throughout his work is concerned with the various relations between authority, education and tradition; second, that in this account, political society and domestic society are mutually implicated; third, that Bonald discusses the relations between these two societies as either harmonious ('constituted') or disorderly ('unconstituted'), thus creating a single motor to drive a theory both of progress and decline; and fourth, that he sees legislation as a key to adjusting those relations – as well as giving an account of why legislation might have a particular role to play in the contemporary period. This last is, of course, a sociological question of continuing importance.

Bonald also, more specifically, offers an account of the decline of modern, perfected society under the influence of the Reformation, the *philosophes* and the Revolutionaries, whose ignorance of the natural constraints inherent in human organization led first to disorder, and subsequently to remedies that contained more of the same kind of poison.

Bonald elaborated his thought in a number of works, including one entitled 'On Divorce', published in 1800 and written in response to aspects of the proposed Civil Code.[37] He also published in 1826 a pamphlet entitled 'De la famille agricole, de la famille industrielle, et du droit d'aînesse'('Concerning the agricultural family, the industrial family, and primogeniture'). In it (as Nisbet notes) he rehearses the essence of Le Play's argument,[38] claiming that primogeniture (*droit d'aînesse*) is the only means to perpetuate families, social order and states alike. Abandonment of the principle (and of the power of substitution) has led at the level of the family to the destruction of paternal authority and family loyalties, the division of farms and businesses, pauperism and the destitution of the elderly. At the social level, the change has led to rural populations moving to the towns, where the values of consumption, fashion and luxury mix with poverty and immorality, licence and crime. At the state level, it is associated with social disorder, class conflict and a loss of polity, the need for conscription and a lack of any solidarity, whether with land, business or any wider project. Bonald also notes the role lawyers play, with their emphasis upon private interest, whether their own or their clients', in disseminating these effects, and comments upon the different reception of these republican laws in the north and the south of France. He concludes that a recipe for social stability would be a regime of inheritance that concentrated landed property and dispersed movable property (allowing more persons to become landowners); yet this is the opposite of what is happening.

It is important to note that while divorce had been legalized under the Revolution and Empire, it was abolished under the Restoration, on 8 May 1816, 'in the interests of religion, morality, the monarchy, and families'.[39] Some critics credit this abolition to Bonald; divorce was only legalized again by the Naquet Law of 1884 – which was attacked by Action Française[40] in Bonaldian terms. When Le Play was writing, marriage and inheritance were the issues rather than divorce.

This is true for the other parallel to which I wish to draw attention: to wit, Honoré Balzac (1799–1850), whose novel writing (1829–1848) is contemporary with Le Play's early period. There is no question here of direct influence; rather, a major strand of Balzac's work is a meditation upon the effects of the Civil Code's provisions with respect to the transmission of property, and especially upon the fate of women, who – with the division of property – have become the carriers of wealth while at the same time remaining – because of the indissolubility of marriage – under the tutelage of either their father or their husband.

Balzac's views evolved over his lifetime.[41] He started by sharing the Saint-Simonian view that the Civil Code disadvantages women, and considered the impossible paradoxes of liberty and education: how can a woman gain intelligence and awareness without experience? And how can a woman be given the freedom to gain experience, without being vulnerable to exploitation, folly and ruin? Balzac developed, however, a more nuanced view of the capabilities and powers of women: both of virtuous women, who effectively become the head of the family, and of uncontrolled and adulterous women, who become agents of destruction. Interestingly, both categories hold the written law in contempt. He covered the range of options with a certain systematic thoroughness, and integrated the interplay of effects at the familial, social and state levels with a skill that has not been surpassed, at least by any sociologist.

One critic (Faillie) concludes that this reflection upon the 1804 Code and responses to it has largely been superseded by the introduction of permission to divorce, and perhaps Balzac in this respect belongs to a past epoch. Nevertheless, in Béarn, the transmission of property intact remains of such importance that divorce is effectively not an option among property-owning families, and therefore, in my view, a certain Balzacian atmosphere persists. I will touch on this in the third chapter.

VII

The argument so far is that the discovery of the Pyrenean or stem family is 'overdetermined', as the Marxists have it: it is the product of, and solution to, a set of pressing social, political and legal questions, which together comprise a meditation upon French identity and its history, the threats to it and the resources to meet those threats. It is therefore a sociological object of some complexity.

Le Play found his example, which became so important as its significance emerged, in 1856: a family called the Mélouga who lived in Cauterets in the Hautes Pyrénées. The household consisted of fifteen people, one of whom was a domestic servant. It comprised the widower of the deceased mistress, the present mistress (his daughter) and her husband, together with their seven children, the eldest of whom was the designated heiress. The other adults present were a brother and a sister of the deceased mistress, and two brothers of the present mistress, all unmarried.

The household fulfilled all Le Play's requirements, including the transmission of property through women. The property had passed through two successions since the introduction of the Civil Code without being divided up; it appeared therefore that custom had so far resisted the law. Tradition continued to be transmitted by the association of generations, the property was supported selflessly by the unmarried non-heirs, and in return the elderly and the weak were protected. The principle of the system was its moral force, Le Play claimed: each member saw the advantages of preserving the patrimony intact, and therefore subordinated him- or herself to this aim, thereby maintaining the authority of the head of the household. Nevertheless, he concluded, the system was under threat, as its geographical, linguistic and economic isolation diminished through the encroachments of communication, education and the law.

One part of the interest of this case study lies in the dynamic situation in which Le Play invokes it: the family is simultaneously threatened in fact, and yet in theory offers a political remedy, if willed, to a series of disorders of which its threatened existence is a symptom. But another part of its interest lies in the fact that empirical follow-up studies of the same family were conducted by followers of Le Play: by Emile Cheysson in 1869, 1874 and 1884, with the story later summed up in 1907 by Bayard in an article entitled 'La famille détruite par le code civil. L'agonie des Mélouga'('The family destroyed by the Civil Code: the death-throes of the Mélougas').[42]

Cheysson pointed out that increasing pressure was exerted through an increase in population and the expansion of tourism (Cauterets was a spa resort), which offered alternative ways of earning a living and raised property prices. In 1865, one of the heirs excluded in the division of 1835 contested the compensation, demanding a new valuation. This led to four years of expensive litigation; the original settlement was upheld at the Court of Appeals, upon the grounds that the family property could not be divided without undergoing considerable depreciation. Le Play himself, at that stage a Senator and Counsellor of State, intervened in the appeal.

The combination of expense and dispute undermined the economic and moral basis of the unity of the family, so that the settlement in the next generation was also contested; in 1874, the property was divided, with the eldest daughter being privileged. In fact, the new heiress bought back the land from all but one of her siblings, but any unreflective notion of obedience to a common project was gone. Moreover, each successive repurchase demanded both new financial commitments and new financial costs, again weakening the household's economy.

Indeed, the combination of the actual costs and the potential threat of a future challenge to the division, together with the high prices land was now fetching because of the fashion for Cauterets, caused the heiress and her husband to sell the farm and its lands, and settle in a new, small house in the town. The Mélouga family was therefore without property, and the heiress's mother was without any permanent home, being passed between a sister and a charitable carer. It constituted an apparently perfect case study illustrating both sides of Le Play's thesis – in its end demonstrating the ill-judged effects of the Civil Code upon what he calls the 'social authorities': those distillations of custom and practical wisdom to which we need to have recourse to rediscover social stability and a common purpose. The discovery of the Pyrenean family is at heart a meditation upon the nature of civil society.

VIII

The particular conjunction of legal, political and sociological interests has passed. But Le Play's work continues to have its influence. The broad classification of patriarchal, unstable and stem families, to which, if he did not invent it, he gave shape and substance, is found in many forms. The stem family, too, has enjoyed enduring attention and application in both historical and ethnographic materials.[43] And the monographic method, with the associated detailed descriptions, has been influential more recently in the conception of 'family strategies'.[44] Le Play not only identified the Pyrenean family as an object of interest but also contributed a good deal towards the wider intellectual contexts in which it would be repeatedly rediscovered.

His transparently reformist aims have undermined his sociological reputation and resulted in his relative neglect, at least in terms of attribution. This is unjust, for there is a good deal of sophistication in his thinking.[45] But it is also worth noting that Le Play's political concerns similarly have persisted, though transformed.

The discovery of the stem family was perceived as a means of promoting social harmony over and against the limitations represented by either the undifferentiated patriarchal family or the individualistic unstable family. The resources at stake in this discovery continue to be of interest to any group of social reformers who on the one hand accept that the form of the family may have implications for the form of the state (and vice versa), and on the other hand are trying to steer a path between forms of monolithic authority and those of unregulated competition. Le Play is part of that tradition which defends intermediate institutions as a necessary third party standing between the state and the individual, and he has been a resource to those thinkers attempting to find a third way between state authoritarianism and market liberalism. He has therefore had followers among left-wing Catholic social theorists as well as among the intellectuals of Action Française; and because of this double legacy, his ideas fertilized some of the corporatist thinking of the Second World War Vichy regime and re-emerged in certain 'European' ideas. He is a resource for any policy seeking a way between socialism and capitalism in their barer forms, and may realistically be claimed as one of the sources for current European Union social policy.

Le Play and his 'moment' therefore go a long way to explaining my sleepwalking path that led me to Béarn and the fact that I could find a recognizsable local way of life when I got there. It is a way of life that exists at several levels of 'memory': local, national, and even international, and is expressed in many different forms, domestic, agricultural, intellectual, legal and political.[46]

But the matter does not stop there. I would point to two puzzles to conclude this chapter. First, Le Play does not have all his facts right. Indeed, almost everything he discovered can be contested, including the significance of the stem family. So what is the local life to which we are pointed? And second, there is the acute question of why we can still study phenomena of the kind he identified. After all, we saw the last of the Mélouga. How is it that I, similarly, could not only find a distinctive way of life, but also repeat a hundred years later the unhappy experience of observing, over a period of twenty years, a family coming to an end on its property? We are confronted, in short, with the form of existence of a local way of life, and the nature of its continuities, a form which includes the mode of 'being about to disappear' – which any account of property must take into account.

Notes

1. See Tucoo-Chala (1970: 5–7).
2. On 'house' societies, see: Lévi-Strauss (1991), Carsten and Hugh-Jones (1995), Augustins (1989), and Augustins and Bonnain (1981, 1986).
3. Cf. Augustins (1989).
4. Herzfeld (1987).
5. Cf. the essay 'Comprehending Others', in Ardener (1989: 184).
6. See Jenkins (1981: 2–3).
7. Augustins and Bonnain (1981, 1986), Augustins (1989), Bourdieu (1962a), Mendras (1976), Lefebvre (1990), and Rohlfs (1977).
8. Following Chenu (1994: 3).
9. Cf. the thesis of Georg Lukács (1989).
10. Frédéric Le Play (1855). The first edition of 1855 comprised 36 monographs; the second edition, published between 1877 and 1879, ran to 57 monographs.
11. Le Play published *Instruction sur la méthode d'observation dite des monographies de famille* in 1862.
12. *Les Ouvriers des Deux Mondes*, Paris: Société internationale des études pratiques d'économie sociale, 1857–1885. Le Play's 'Paysans en communauté du Lavedan' appeared in volume 1, part 3 (1857), pp.107–160.
13. Frédéric Le Play (1874 [1864]) *La Réforme sociale en France, déduite de l'observation comparée des peuples européens* (5th edition, 3 volumes); Le Play (1870) *L'organisation du travail, selon les coûtumes des ateliers et la loi du Décalogue, avec un précis d'observations comparées sur la distinction du bien et du mal dans le régime du travail, les causes du mal actuel et les moyens de réforme, les objections et les réponses, les difficultés et les solutions*; Le Play (1871) *L'organisation de la famille, selon le vrai modèle signalé par l'histoire de toutes les races et de tous les temps*.
14. After the brief Second Republic from 1848 to 1851.
15. Silver (1982: 6).
16. See Chenu (1994: 8).
17. It is worth making clear that I have read a number of Le Play's works, but not all of them; I have read the three volumes on social reform, and the two volumes on the family, and I have looked at the six volumes of *Les ouvriers européens*. But I have also relied upon a number of modern critics and scholars, among them in particular: Assier-Andrieu (1984), Chenu (1994), Papy (1995) and Silver (1982).
18. In this exposition I draw in particular upon Assier-Andrieu's (1984) account.
19. *Les Ouvriers européens*, 1879, 2nd edition, volume I: 237 – cited Assier-Andrieu (1984: 496).
20. There are echoes here of Montesquieu on patriarchal societies – see Montesquieu (1989[1748]).
21. Not to mention the opposition of atheism to Christianity.
22. The heiress might marry at eighteen to twenty, producing offspring until the eldest offspring in turn marries and is named heir, in this way giving an almost unbroken continuity of children. Le Play associates the topic of Pyrenean 'feminism' with questions of chastity, dowry and the influence of the wife; cf. Goody (1975).
23. Cf. Bourdieu (1962a). See also chapter 6.
24. It is of course a little less clear in its diagnosis concerning unskilled, propertyless workers and the place of mass industry: Le Play is not Marx.
25. Arthur Young (1929[1792]: 47–63); see in particular the section concerning Béarn (pp.53–54), cited in chapter 3.
26. See Ourliac (1979).
27. Le Play (1871: 112).

28. Assier-Andrieu comments on the one hand that this contrast derives from an impoverished version of Montesquieu's thought upon the virtue of ancient customs and the genesis of laws, and on the other that it is taken up by Charles Maurras as the distinction between a *pays réel* and a *pays legal* (which we may gloss as the authentic and the legal nation respectively). Assier-Andrieu (1984: 502).

29. This north/south opposition was mobilized by Maurras among others – *que le Midi continue à suivre sa coutume* (cited by Assier-Andrieu) – and taken up by Vichy.

30. It should be noted in passing that these revolutionary laws suppress distinctions, simultaneously freeing individuals, strengthening the state (which is supposed to represent the identical will of every – good – citizen), and destroying intermediate institutions (which are, according to Hobbes, parasites in the entrails of the state).

31. 29 germinal an XI/29 avril 1803.

32. Law of 8/4/1791.

33. Cf. law of 4/6/1793.

34. Again, see Assier-Andrieu (1984).

35. See ibid.

36. Sainte-Beuve (1867, 9:180).

37. Bonald (1864[1800]).

38. See Nisbet (1952); see also Klinck (1996: 200–207).

39. See Phillips (1988: 189).

40. A political group founded in 1899 with an agenda of 'integral nationalism' – cf. note 28.

41. See Faillie (1968).

42. These contributions are included in Le Play et al. (1994[1857]).

43. One might mention the early examples of Homans and Habbakuk. For a critical approach, see Verdon (1979); for a recent ethnographic example, see Rogers (1991).

44. Both through Scott and Tilly's reworking of Le Play's material, and through Bourdieu's work on the Béarnais family: Bourdieu (1972a). For general criticism of the concept, see Moen and Wethington (1992), and Viazzo and Lynch (2002).

45. I would then treat with caution Durkheim's accusation – in *Les règles de la méthode sociologique* (Durkheim 1988[1894]: 119ff.) – that the monographic method was insufficiently sociological, although recognizing Durkheim's desire to distance himself from Le Play's reformist programme.

46. Work on the social forms of memory began with Maurice Halbwachs (1968[1950], 1952), and later took on definitive form with the three volumes of *Lieux de mémoire* (Nora 1981–1992). As Ho Tai (2001) discusses, the concept of social memory has lost focus as it has enjoyed success among historians. For an anthropological account, see Connerton (1989); and for an exemplary French ethnography deploying the concept, see Zonabend (1984[1980]).

Chapter 2

CONTINUITY OVER TIME: PATTERNS OF LAND INHERITANCE

I

Le Play, in discovering the Pyrenean family, placed continuity in tradition and custom, which he opposed to the law (and, more particularly, to the efforts of lawyers), and traced back to a time immemorial, for he invoked a Basque substrate. As Ourliac points out,[1] Le Play shows no sign of having studied the local *coutumiers*, or bodies of local law, for example those of Barèges or Lavedan or, indeed, of Béarn: as a result, his notion of custom is rather vague. At the time he wrote, editions of all three had been published,[2] although, in the case of the *Fors de Béarn* (published 1841–1843), the edition had such severe limitations that it could only be used in an emblematic fashion. At the same time, it is clear that the primary evidence for a continuing local form of life lies in this body of law and its practice, whatever the difficulties of interpretation, and it is to this evidence that I turn in this chapter.

I shall make two preliminary comments. In the first place, bodies of law constitute at best indirect evidence, particularly upon such matters as marriage and the transmission of property. These everyday matters are rarely treated, and only under exceptional circumstances. Laws and legal rulings emerge from untypical cases. Legal texts, taken as material pointing to practice on the ground, therefore need careful evaluation. However, other pertinent matters may emerge from them, not least the capacity of legislation to create new social possibilities, to 'fabricate persons and things'.[3] And then, in the second place, the most valuable materials are to be found not in legislation, decrees or judgments, but in evidence of local practice, embodied in notarial records of agreements that were seen as legally binding. So this chapter falls into two halves: I will look, first, at the significance of certain aspects of local customary law, and second, at the notarial evidence and its evolution over time. Together, they constitute a case for a long continuity of a form of local life, one centred upon the transmission of property. Moreover, it is a way of life that has always had to co-exist with competing forms and threats, and, too, with an outside gaze that both interprets and prescribes its possibilities.

II

France has long been considered to have been divided in the pre-modern period between the regions of customary law, in the north, and written (Roman) law, operative in the south. This may be called the 'Montesquieu effect'.[4] This division was given scientific form in the work of Jean Yver.[5] However, neither region is homogeneous, and Poumarède,[6] following Yver's method, has shown both that the south-west has customary law of its own, and moreover that there is a geography of customs within the region. In particular, he has demonstrated a boundary between the law of the Garonne region on the one hand and Pyrenean law on the other. Within the latter, the custom has been single inheritance in each generation, accompanied by the designation of the heir usually within the father's lifetime, no division of land, and dispersal of non-heirs upon marriage. Custom in the basin of the Garonne River to the north, however, is in marked contrast; there has been equal inheritance, the rights of the eldest and the principle of masculine privilege were both unknown, fathers could neither disinherit nor advantage a son, and, in the case of a second marriage, both families shared in the inheritance.

The documents concerning these local customs date from the twelfth century. Given the antiquity of the evidence, there are two kinds of theory proffered to explain the local differences, both of which need to be set aside. (Neither in fact offers an explanation, but rather consists of a displacement, distracting attention from the lack of explanation by a gesture in the direction of a supposed but untheorised cause.) The first explanation invokes material causes, the relative scarcity of land, or geographical isolation as determinant of forms of inheritance and of their evolution.[7] Single inheritance in the mountainous region to the south is explained by the relative paucity of land and, at the same time, by the conservatism of isolated communities; the mountain conserves 'the oldest juridical notions'.

The broad extent of the Garonne plain, to the north, is, in contrast, 'open to the circulation of men and goods', and 'welcomes new ideas'. Yet this combination of physical need with cultural constraint in a geographical determinism, which echoes Montesquieu's climatic causalities, is refuted by the evidence of differentiation within each area. In the region of Pyrenean law, absolute primogeniture – that is, irrespective of sex – was the rule in the Lavedan and the Barèges valley. The Béarnais and Souletain (Basque) customs likewise maintained the right of the eldest in the mountainous parts and in serf households, but introduced the principle of masculine inheritance in the case of noble successions. And the customs of Saint-Sever and the Chalosse attempted to reconcile the rights of the eldest with the principle of equality.[8] Law, especially that concerning the family and succession, is not the product of chance and need, but is a social fact with its own processes and reasons, both of creation and of development.

The second kind of explanation is to attribute the differences to a contrast in the ethnicity of the original populations. In this case, reference is made on the one hand to the upper Palaeolithic Franco-Cantabrigian civilization, which corresponds in extent to the ancient Basque tongue, and on the other to the ethnic diversity produced in the sixth century BC by Iberian incursions, whose populations occupied the good agricultural lands in the plain and forced the indigenous populations south into the mountains. The hypothesis therefore places the original contrast between two systems of inheritance in an opposition between Basque and Iberian substrates. Yet such a displacement effectively removes any possibility of a historical or sociological explanation. It is a myth, although none the less effective for that, for there are radical contemporary claims on this basis to a Greater Euskadi, or Basque territory, which stretches from the mountains to the Garonne, and thus embraces all of present Gascony or the Aquitaine region. I shall propose a different account of the logic of the objects of Béarnais practice in due course, based rather upon evidence from the *Fors*, the local legal texts.

III

The term *for* was originally used over a wide area, corresponding to the Visigoth kingdom, designating exemptions, customs and liberties. It then came to be applied to the documents that defined and granted these concessions, and then to the texts as the written, corrected and augmented products of a developing system of justice, which were assembled into a collection.[9] In this latter sense, the *Fors* became the expression of an identity, with a long subsequent history.

We are concerned at the moment with the early history of the *Fors* of Béarn, and I shall sketch the context of the making of this compilation.[10] This is preparatory to considering the broad structure of the *Fors*, and its sociological significance.

The ethnic and linguistic diversity of the wider region, alluded to already, was born witness to by the Romans, who termed the south-west province Novempopulania, 'the land of nine peoples'. It was considered unsophisticated in comparison with the long-settled and romanized province of Narbonne. If there is a tradition to be discerned in the earliest materials, it is one of repeated opacity, an independence from such centres as existed and their powers of documentation.

In the period of the Great Invasions, the south-west was dominated by the Visigoths, whom Clovis destroyed in 507. The Franks never settled the region, however, and between AD 561 and 584 Vascons from south of the Pyrenees crossed the mountains, establishing the Duchy of Vasconie in 602, over which the Merovingian kings had only theoretical sovereignty. The eighth and the ninth centuries remain obscure (as the saying goes). Charlemagne created an ephemeral kingdom of Aquitaine upon returning from Spain; a Duchy of Gascony was founded around 860, which, whilst remaining in the same dynasty until 1032, became effectively independent of the Carolingians and the first Capetians. During this period of consolidation, a number of domains were created within the Duchy by the play of inheritance, division, marriage and alliance, and some of the marginal regions, including Béarn, succeeded in freeing themselves from the authority of the Duke. In 1058, the Duchy of Gascony passed to the House of Poitiers, and became part of the Duchy of Aquitaine, so entering into broader streams of history.

I might make a broad point: we are dealing with a certain kind of history, that of an absence of any primary ordering. And I would claim that an anthropological approach is suited to studying the cultural effects of being at the edge of places historians can study, places that are brushed by the movements documents bear testimony to, but not directly represented therein, except by their impress or shadow. This is another way of saying that local particularity is in some aspects a play of self-representation and self-preservation of a place under an intermittent 'metropolitan' gaze, and that any description of Béarn has to take this feature into consideration. In a historiographical perspective, it means such areas frequently bear the traces of earlier, 'tribal' cultures – *gentes* is the nineteenth-century label – and are defined by kinship and other ethnological relations.

But there are two more specific factors to be taken into account. The first concerns the relations of local law to Roman law. The myth of the juridical unity of the lands of written law was an article of faith to historians for generations.[11] The view has been subsequently attacked, with the suggestion that southern populations distrusted rather than welcomed Justinian's law, and that this distrust was expressed in a movement of recording customs.[12] From the thirteenth century on, a great number of charters were compiled, which have provided the basis for contemporary legal history.

These debates both draw upon and feed more contemporary oppositions, such as those – at different times – between the Civil Code and local practice, between Roman law and Germanic custom, between civilization and culture, and between European law and national practice (just to give a *tour d'horizon* of the last two hundred years). But the account, in terms of its proper historical context, needs to be nuanced. The revival of Justinian's law began in Pavia in the eleventh century and developed in Bologna, which became the centre of legal training in Europe, epitomized by Peter Stein[13] as leading a movement in legal thought 'from force to argument'. In the early twelfth century, the new learning spread to southern France, to the Rhine valley, and thence to Montpellier and Toulouse. A Provençal translation was made, *lo Còdi*, and a Béarnais version is included in the *Fors*.

Stein however is concerned to point out that no courts corresponded to the practice of Roman law:

> Church courts applied common law to such matters as marriage and personal status; the courts of feudal lords applied feudal law to questions of landholding; the traditional community courts applied the local customary law to claims for compensation for wrong-doing. What the civil law supplied was a conceptual framework, a set of principles of interpretation that constituted a kind of universal grammar of law, to which recourse could be made whenever it was needed.[14]

Civil law was therefore neither an outside imposition nor a political threat; rather, it offered an intellectual solution, a recourse when the law of other courts proved deficient. So, in the case of conflict between bodies of law, the local situation determined whether local custom or Imperial law prevailed. It also served as a model: when local law was set down in writing, 'those responsible turned to the civil law to provide organising categories and organising principles'.[15] In considering the Béarnais material, we shall see the force of Stein's position.

The second factor to be taken into account concerns the specific power relations between the Viscount of Béarn and his subjects which provided the occasion for the compilation of the *Fors* of Béarn. The recent editors of the texts suggest that the collection dates from between 1393 and 1428, when the authority of the Viscount was diminishing and the influence of the Assembly of the Estates increasing.[16] The Assembly – the Etats de Béarn – was formed in 1391, to safeguard and guarantee the liberties and usages granted over time by the viscounts, and subscribed to by each new Viscount. The *Fors* therefore emerge in this period under the auspices of the Assembly, recording old concessions, duly augmented, and creating a tradition that was recast in the middle of the sixteenth century into a New *For*, under the double authority of the Viscount and the Assembly of the Estates.[17]

The texts we have therefore display several strata: subsequent judgments and decrees overlie earliest practice. The influence of Roman law, as has been suggested, was essentially to supplement and order, not to replace, the older provisions; it appears in the definitions of forms, grounds for adjournment and modes of proof, the exposition of reasons concerning fact and law, the admission of appeal, and the creation of the office of judge, with authority to conduct a trial.[18]

At the same time, there is a potential for conflict. Roman ideas permitted the Viscount to claim sovereign authority, for example in matters of appeal, which gave form and expression to a power struggle with the Barons (in the form of the *Cour Majour*), leading – in the view of the editors – to the reassertion of ancient rights and freedoms and the compilation of the *Fors*. The *Fors* are prefaced by a mythic account of the 'election' of the first Viscount, and also, in the key manuscript, a chronicle of events concerning the Viscounts of Béarn between 1308 and 1331. These prefatory texts have been put to work in other situations, far removed from their original purpose.

IV

I want briefly to consider the broad features of the *Fors*, because certain issues emerge which have a bearing upon the longevity of the form of social organization with which we are concerned, even though family law is not a major focus. Study of the *Fors de Béarn* has been enormously aided by the edition produced in 1990 by Ourliac and Gilles: before their work, with its clarifications and hypotheses, chaos and darkness reigned in this area.[19]

The *Fors* brought together texts relating to local customary law, in use at the time of the compilation, and complementary texts – sources, commentaries, and judgments – which were held to have similar authority. It therefore served simultaneously as an assemblage of custom, a legislative code, and an official tool of practice.[20] It includes privileges granted by the Viscounts, extracts from viscountal regulations and decrees, court judgments that have made law, tariffs, works of learned law, and procedures.

Setting aside the complementary texts, the *Fors* has two major parts. First, the General or Ancient *For*, which was applicable to the territory where the Viscount of Béarn exercised authority. And second, the *For de Morlàas*, which was initially a charter of settlement granted to that town, and then applied to other important settlements and rural communities that invoked it. Added to the latter were the judgments applied to and reinforcing the Morlàas charter, termed 'judgments of the High Court which pertain to the For of Morlàas' (*jugats de la cour majour qui son de for à Morlàas*). And in addition to these texts there were also charters granted to the high valleys (Oloron, Ossau, Aspe and Barétous), which were in large part modelled upon the General *For*. There are, in brief, two foci: the General *For*, and the *For de Morlàas*.

The General *For* operated everywhere when officials of the Viscount were concerned. It contains the more conservative and earliest law, charters defining the relations between the Viscount and his nobles (pre-thirteenth century), procedures relating to hostages and truces, the feudal and manorial rights of the Viscounts, the Viscount's rights concerning roads, lodgings, law enforcement and taxes, a series of fines payable to the Viscount (prior to 1221), and an early set of legal decisions. Subsequent judgments and decrees are arranged around the older provisions, which are termed in some manuscripts 'a heading from the old *For*' (*test de for anciaa*).

The judgments applying the law come from the Cour Majour, the Barons' court, and contain developments of the law from the twelfth to the fifteenth century. These often include procedural regulations as well as the provisions of customary law. Viscountal decisions having force of law are also transcribed; for example, those in 1251 establishing the exercise of criminal justice in Béarn, instituting the courts, procedures, officials, sanctions and compensation. And, important to our purposes, with respect to civil law, the establishment and control of notaries. The Cour Majour instituted sworn notaries in the towns and *bourgs* of Béarn in 1256.[21]

The *For de Morlàas* set up a jurisdiction for, and granted privileges to, the population of a new territory. The charter was granted at the end of the eleventh or the beginning of the twelfth century, and was confirmed in 1220. After this date, it was applied to other communities. Later judgments of the Cour Majour were added, and it is among these judgments that we find such provision as we have concerning civil law: both family law and contract.

Both topics show evidence of the influence of Roman law, although potentially in contrary senses. The suggestion of the modern editors is that, in the case of family law, Roman law must have posed a threat for any such matters to have been committed to writing, that marriage and inheritance is the business of custom, and that such indications as we have point to a diversity of customs.[22] All the evidence points to the inalienability of the house and its property, which is to be transmitted intact between generations. However, as already mentioned, the degree of choice concerning the heir varies. The *For d'Ossau* speaks of absolute primogeniture, irrespective of sex; the *For général* of primogeniture accompanied by male privilege. In noble houses, there is no division; if there are no sons, the eldest daughter inherits. The judgments accompanying the *For de Morlàas*, however, discuss equal division among the daughters under these circumstances. A possible conclusion is that there is a contrast between, on the one hand, a conservative, customary tendency, and on the other, a greater emphasis – supported by Roman law – upon individuality and flexibility. In the latter case, the authority of the head of the family becomes an issue, for a father has the power to favour or disinherit a child; in contrast, the conscious or arbitrary authority of the father is ill served by the customary designation of an heir.

Other areas of flexibility with respect to the disposal of property emerge in these judgments. As we would expect, division of property is excluded, except in the extreme cases of debt or ransom. Nevertheless, cadets – non-heirs – may be granted a share or portion of the property, but it is not completely alienated. The lineage, in the person of the heir, has to agree and has a right of recovery. In these cases, the tension between the rights of the property and the rights of the kin is strongly expressed. This expression is given clearest form in the dowry: property is transferred between houses upon marriage, but with the provision that the dowry should be returned if no offspring result, or returned in part if a widow with children remarries. Property does not attach to persons, although it creates many of their possibilities, but belongs to houses, whose rights may persist over two generations. There are therefore distinctions to be made between property descending through male and female lines.

Beyond such matters, there is a second issue: the disposal of acquired goods, in distinction to inherited property. This question too refers to the discretion and authority of the parents. From the thirteenth century, wills became common, permitting the father to dispose of acquired goods, and to impose duties upon the heir, notably to endow younger brothers and sisters. Once again, there is a contrast, between a conservative rural law that determines the rights of the house over all of its component members, and a more malleable urban law, influenced by Roman law, that favours individuality and flexibility, raising the authority of the father and the concerns of the kin against the apparently more archaic custom.

This contrast is also implicit in the topic of contract. Morlàas and Oloron were market towns, and as such associated with commerce, roads, questions of security, and money – and, too, with the fate of non-heirs. Concerns included buying and selling houses, weights and measures, more speedy justice, debts, contracts, written (as opposed to oral) agreements, and the role of witnesses.[23] The influence of Roman law indeed spread beyond the realm of commercial law: the reform of criminal procedures, the institution of the notariat, the imposition of written evidence and the admission of rights of appeal are all evidences of learned law.

One needs to be cautious in interpreting this evidence. For it is not the case that the new law applied in the towns permitting more 'modern', individualist behaviour, and that the old law, with its collective personality, applied in the countryside. Rather, both bodies of law, or tendencies, existed simultaneously, and either could be appealed to; each law could be invoked in the other jurisdiction if appropriate. That is why not only are there clauses from one body cited in the other (doublets), but also why they are sometimes accompanied by different decisions. This fact contributes greatly to (what is to us) the confusing appearance of the texts, which were practical legal documents, employed by practitioners, and contributes, too, to the merit of the recent edition, that resolves these difficulties by identifying their purpose.[24]

We might conclude that here we have, from the thirteenth century, in the reaction to the introduction of Roman law, evidence of a characteristic pattern, a conservative and apparently archaic body of family law coexisting with a body of more radical law. Together, they form a total structure, which permits the continuing existence of a way of life by projecting flexibility, individuality and change onto the town. Custom is neither timeless nor prior, but exists under an appearance of being so, alongside and interacting with written law. Each forms part of the definition of the other, as its 'other'. This structure is sustained within an assertion of local identity (or of liberties) that both recognizes and binds the Viscount, and is simultaneously the product, and the mastering, of a developing historical situation.

V

There is one more question to be posed, concerning the possible origin of the customary forms, but I will delay offering an answer. Instead, let us turn to a consideration of the evidence concerning marriage and succession contained in the notarial records, which constitute a much clearer and more detailed ethnographic record of local practice than does the written body of customary law.

The value of the notarial records has been evident since the work of Pierre Luc, who in 1943 published an account of 'rural life and juridical practice in Béarn in the fourteenth and fifteenth centuries'.[25] This book constitutes a break with previous writings, which had consisted in treatises on family law, drawing in large part upon the Reformed *For* of 1551, with references back to earlier practice.[26]

Luc is not only the sole effective source concerning Béarn for the period, utilized repeatedly by later authors in their comparative, wider-ranging studies, but also a model for subsequent social historical work upon property transmission in the region.[27] Moreover, it constitutes a work of reference for local educated persons, with respect to current practice. When I expressed my interest in studying local land law, I was told to read Luc not only by the leading historian of the region, and by a local second-hand bookseller (who made me a photocopy of his example of that rare work), but also, most significantly, by a local notary. Luc is considered to be the basic account of local inheritance practice; this testimony carries within it the entire question we are confronted with, as to the nature of the continuities of local life.

Luc offers us evidence upon the life of property, both with respect to forms of inheritance and to marriage regimes, and it is worth giving the broad outlines, not least because they occasionally remind us of other, non-European systems (to which I will allude in the fourth chapter).

In this material, the crucial distinction concerning the nature of property and its transmission is between *acquêts* and *propres*, between goods that have been acquired and may be disposed of at will, and goods that have become family property and can only be transmitted according to strict rules. This distinction, which is at the heart of Béarnais conceptions of property, can resemble others, such as that between chattels and real estate, or movable and immovable property. But its key is the contrast between alienable and inalienable possessions, or between personal and house property. It is this distinction that organizes men and things, and makes possible, as secondary matters, money, exchange and the transfer of ownership. It underlies and permits the expression of what we would call the economic forms of life.

The documents therefore distinguish goods from the point of view of whether they may be alienated: there were those things coming from the patrimony, upon which the lineage had rights – termed the right of recovery, or the right of return – and things which had been acquired, and which the acquirer might freely dispose of.[28] Just as there appear to be two types of law, and two jurisdictions, there are two kinds of property.

Acquired goods were of little importance in the early texts, and legal interest in their disposal focused upon two exceptional circumstances: at what stage did acquired goods become family goods, and what was their status in the case of death where there was no will or formal grant? The evidence is that two transmissions (three generations) served to convert acquired goods to family goods, and that the rule of inheritance *ab intestat* was equal division, at least among non-noble families.

With respect to family goods, in contrast, succession *ab intestat* served to indicate the role of primogeniture (or single inheritance). All the family goods, house, land and livestock, were transmitted to a single heir, with a portion (unspecified in terms of amount or proportion) reserved for the other children. In normal practice an heir was named, with whom the head of the family associated himself in signing any legal documents, and who was treated in a fashion distinct from the non-heirs. The choice of the heir was not, however, automatic. The normal order of succession could be modified, and this, Luc states, was an expression of the collective authority of the house through the will or formal grant of the head of house. Cases of renunciation by the heir make this clear, where primogeniture is trumped by deliberate, meditated strategy. The system worked upon a basis of authority granted to the head of house, together with the acknowledgement of and subscription to a common good by the members of the household.

Selection of the heir was made formal at the institution of a marriage contract, and confirmed, if necessary, by a will. If the head of the house died prematurely, he might suggest a child as an heir, but more often left the choice to his spouse and executors. The purpose of the will was rather to distribute any acquired goods. From the point of view of inalienable property, the crucial document was therefore the marriage contract. If the customary order of succession was modified, the validity of this depended on the renunciation of the customary heir – or on the promise of the person instituted to obtain that permission upon the other's majority, or return to the district. The most frequent substitution was of the eldest daughter by a younger brother. Other motives for renunciation included emigration, entering holy orders, illness or disability, or a refusal of responsibility.

Associated with the strong differentiation of kinds of goods, therefore, there is also strong differentiation within the family, between the sexes, between generations, and between siblings. Before the marriage agreement, the father might use his authority to require the heir to renounce. Once the agreement is made, the father and the heir are in a sense bound together; they have common interests. At the same time, once the heir marries, there are new obligations: another family has interests in the marriage, and the heir is tied by new obligations to his wife and future children. The marriage agreements therefore also refer to a regime between the father's and the heir's generation: either the father retains authority, although he cannot alienate or mortgage the land without the son's consent; or the father retires, demanding certain guarantees and rights; or – rarely – the farm is temporarily divided between the two, each part being worked separately until the father's surrender of the land or death.

Strict inalienability of property restricts both the authority and the freedom of the head of the house who, at the extreme, becomes simply an expression of the interests of the lineage and the heir. However, a countervailing institution, the right of recovery, balances this tendency, for it permits a greater degree of individual flexibility and decision, including that of endowing the non-heirs or cadets, the younger brothers and sisters. There were various legal refinements associated with definition of this right, including the period of time over which it might be exercised, by whom (the heir, and other members of the lineage), the terms of compensation, and means for the settlement of disputes. The right of recovery itself could be sold, or renounced and compensated, and restrictions placed upon the goods recovered.

The function of such rights was to protect property transmitted to cadets, so permitting them to marry. Each cadet might receive a portion or share in the form of money, livestock, or a mortgaged piece of land, to be redeemed by the heir. Again, the distinction between family property and acquired wealth must be kept in view: the share a cadet received returned to the family upon his or her death, unless he himself had produced offspring. Contrariwise, any property he had gained by his own efforts, or through inheritance of acquired property, he was entitled to leave by will.

VI

The corollary of this highly differentiated system of transmission is that there were two distinct matrimonial regimes. The first was between an heir of a property and a non-heir, or cadette, from another house; this regime involves unequal contributions from the two sides towards the household formed, the incomer's contribution being in the form of a dowry. The second kind was between two non-heirs, each bringing more or less equal contributions, and living under a regime of community.

The dowry regime was defined and constituted in the marriage contract. The agreement might be made between two adults, if the parents were dead, but more often, with younger persons, the two families committed themselves. The contract had two invariable clauses. First, the parents of the heir instituted him as such, although if he was the customary heir, this simply needed to be stated. Second, the parents of the cadette constituted a dowry for her.

The dowry itself had two aspects. The dowry proper was made up of movable property, and represented the cadette's portion; it discharged her claim to a share of the family patrimony. It was usually defined in terms of a sum of money, but paid in part or entirely in kind, for example, in livestock. In addition, the cadette brought with her a trousseau, consisting of clothes and bedding (and sometimes some furniture, such as a cupboard), which was itemized in the agreement. The interest of this paraphernalia is that it constituted a continuity of women's goods, passing from mother to daughter, and was a component in the transmission of the non-tangible status that the bride brought with her, a representation of the flow of symbolic honour that motivated the system – and which I think has been under-investigated.

In addition to these two components (of female goods, from the family; and of doubly female goods, from the mother), the bride's family might make a wedding gift to the groom's family, of money, or some valuable object, plus several female beasts and their young. The document defined the modality of each of these transfers, usually in portions, with the first part, the trousseau and the gift being delivered the day the wedding was blessed, and the others at set intervals, with penalties prescribed for non- or late payment. Each payment was recognized by a receipt, and when the transfers were complete, a notarized *carte de tornadot* was drawn up, detailing both the amounts delivered and a promise of restitution, which could be drawn upon according to circumstances by heirs of the beneficiaries.

There were variations upon these principles, with the aim of either offsetting or guaranteeing payments. The dowry might be set off against a debt, such as an earlier dowry whose return is owed. Land might be transferred as a mortgage, to be redeemed by the full payment of the dowry. The future son-in-law, in the case of a daughter being the heir, might be engaged as a worker, and part of his wages retained and set off against the dowry. And there was the structural ideal of a double marriage between two brothers and sisters, each heir marrying the other's sister, for example. In this case the dowries might compensate one for the other.[29]

If the marriage produced children who survived, the dowry remained in the house after the death of the incoming spouse. If her husband pre-deceased her, the incomer and her dowry remained; however, if she remarried subsequently, she had a right to retain only half her dowry. But if there were no children at the dissolution of the marriage, the dowry was in every case returned to the family of origin, either to the surviving spouse, or to the person who had constituted the dowry (normally her father), or to his heir. In case of repayment, matters of equivalence and fixed terms were specified, and penalties foreseen, and at the completion of repayment, the *carte de tornadot* was given up.

The dowry, therefore, was simultaneously a stimulus to the receiving house, in the shape of a promise of productivity embodied by a wife, beasts with offspring, and money; and a threat, for the promise at the same time constituted an obligation that might in some circumstances become a debt that undermined the house.[30] The *tornadot* constituted a charge upon all the goods of the masters of the house; in the case of non-restitution at the fixed term, the creditor had the right to take possession of the house and property, and to hold them in mortgage until repayment was made.

An indication of the nature of the dowry as a loan with retained rights is given by the recourse to law an incoming spouse might take to protect the dowry if she believed the value of the property as a whole was diminishing through mismanagement. Effectively, she could seek an act of assignation upon the dowry on her own behalf, to provide her with a living, to act as security, and to protect the dowry from creditors.

Houses therefore were linked as much by a network of potential and actual debt as they were by alliances. Because the property belonged to and defined the houses involved, the place of a widow was insecure, and was best protected by express provision in the husband's will. Her only right was, in the case of no children, to recover the dowry. In the case of offspring, she had a customary right to be maintained by the heir, but this needed to be reinforced by the husband's testament, and, at best, a legacy: he could leave her a share of any acquired wealth (up to half), although there was no community of acquired wealth under the dowry regime.

The other regime concerned the marriage of two non-heirs, where effectively family property was not involved, and was far simpler. Each party contributed such property as they could bring, both gifts and the product of their work. Such property as came under the heading of acquired goods was held in common; any property either gained through succession however remained individual property. Upon death, the common goods remained the property of any children, and the surviving spouse enjoyed the use of them. In the case of death without children, the common goods were divided, either the deceased spouse's half going to the family of origin, or being left by will. These were families on the margins of the intricacies of the transmission of family property: they exhibit community of property and equal division, or at least the freedom to achieve this. They look far more modern, reminiscent indeed of the 'unstable' family.

VII

Rather than there being an older, conservative autochthonous form of law, which becomes overlain by a newer, more modern and individualist one, coming in from the outside, the evidence points to a single complex simultaneity, capable of great flexibility. Effectively, there is a single 'economy', or distribution, in which two forms of law are articulated around two kinds of property, and which allows two poles – one of the differentiating and ranking of persons, the other of the equality of persons – to be expressed through two regimes of marriage.

In this case, it is clear that the conservative (prescriptive) core permits a modern-seeming (permissive) penumbra, or allows a place for it. And it is possible to surmise that the traditional may exist precisely in some such guise as giving shape to the reception of the new, being perpetuated in its own anticipated effacement. I call this 'economy' the 'co-inherence of contraries', although the 'contraries' are of different logical levels, and I suggest that this is the form of the continuity with which we are concerned.

Two comments follow from this. First, it is not useful to regard the conservative forms as an ethnic substrate. Le Play did so, but so do legal historians, including Poumarède. He sees the house society as a Franco-Cantabrigian substrate, linked to such features as the extent of the Basque language and certain blood groups, which is then acted upon by successive historical moments. He assumes a primitive state of absolute primogeniture, prior to any records, which is acted upon progressively by the principle of masculinity, from feudal law, penetrating from the plain to the mountains, subsequently supported by Roman law practices. Yet the only records we have contain a mixture of cases.

Second, then, can we offer any better account of origins? In considering comparable material, David Sabean[31] suggests that the 'house' society in Neckarhausen is the product of a particular historical, political and administrative conjuncture, and which endured for a specific period. He identifies three convergent contributing factors,[32] which are worth outlining. First, he points to the need of the state for viable tax units, and hence to the work of officials to revise and codify the inheritance laws and draw up cadasters, making the devolution of property a publicly scrutinized process. Second, he suggests that this process was helped by peasants defining themselves through the idiom of 'the house', in a context of population increase and social differentiation, in which there was a struggle by the wealthier to maintain their position through controlling the marriages of their children. In this respect, Sabean suggests, the state aided the extension of patriarchal control. And third, he claims these tendencies were served by a regenerated Lutheran clergy, who saw the causes of a crisis in social and political order in part in terms of a crisis in the family (echoes of Le Play here), and who sought paternalistic solutions to these ills by linking patriarchal authority, marriage courts, peasant elites, and the preservation of property and boundaries in an effort to create the conditions of stability.

In terms of Béarn, two centuries earlier, the third factor appears not to be a direct issue; there is little discussion of Church courts in the materials I have read. But there is a clear set of issues to do with the relations of the state administration to the developing population. We can point first to the licensing of notaries in 1256, which brought property transmission into public scrutiny. Then, there was a census of hearths in Béarn, ordered by Viscount Gaston Febus in 1385, for purposes of taxation (a census which is useful regarding the continuity of house names).[33] And third, as we have already noted, the production of the *Fors* in the early years of the fifteenth century bears witness on the one hand to the emergence of an elite – the Etats de Béarn, or Assembly of the Estates – which comes to some sort of settlement with the authority of the Viscount, while, on the other, offering evidence of the creation of an administration and awareness of law as a tool of social development. At the same time, the charters granted to new settlements testify to an increase in population, together with an increase in wealth and social differentiation.

In short, it might be claimed that the forms of inheritance with which we are concerned might be no older than the documents we have that bear witness to them, and even that the documents themselves are part of. the precipitation of those social forms.[34] And – a last comment – as an effect of their textual nature, the documents carry with them a deceptive shadow, implying a prior antiquity to the institutions described.

VIII

Let me add a codicil to this account. It is impossible, dealing with stretches of time as long as these, to be thorough in coverage. There is clearly a history to be written both of the life of the *Fors* and of the – loosely connected – forms of inheritance. The recasting of the *Fors* in 1551 (the New *For*) was a part of wider currents, of legal humanism on the one hand and of the codification of local law under the Ancien Régime on the other.[35] The New *For* emphasized the house as a unit of social governance, ordered by the same principles that were manifested by the political body and the wider social body: hierarchy, inequality, and guardianship.[36] Although some modern authors emphasize the degree to which the New *For* breaks with the mindset of the Old, it might be more accurate to say that it develops the principles contained in the *For de Morlàas*.[37] The New *For* also emphasizsed the liberties of the Béarnais, and the sovereignty of Béarn, standing as a charter of local identity until these ideals were consciously renounced by the Assembly as part of their adherence to the principles of the Revolution.[38] Similarly, learned commentaries upon the New *For* and its civil law provisions in the seventeenth and eighteenth centuries[39] reflected wider contemporary political debates, refracted through readings of the place of Roman Law and custom. 'The house' in this literature is simultaneously a political symbol and the subject of a civil law discourse, being prepared by fate as part of the local order that would be consigned to the past by the Revolution, and would be subsequently discovered by Le Play as a solution for its ills.

Detailed research on the notarial documents of the modern period does not, however, reveal a comparable evolution in practice on the ground. Anna Zink[40] prolongs Poumarède's historical legal geography up to the Revolution, and gives more detail upon, for example, the enduring rights of the lineage over the dowry, and the development of the rights of cadets to a share in the inheritance. Both these topics accompany the growth of the wealth of Béarnais farms, especially in the eighteenth century. But there is no evidence of the abandonment of the principles of primogeniture and the non-division of property. Zink locates the enduring force of these principles in the wider village community, looking to the role played by councils of neighbours and families that had the responsibility of witnessing marriage contracts and executing wills.[41] I have mentioned the role of debt and obligation; villages also had common rights in woods and pasturage, so that houses formed units making up the total local economy, and in many respects were also elemental political units. I shall touch upon the place of the modes of succession in local political life in the fourth chapter.

We have therefore good evidence of a continuity of these forms of social life that must come directly into conflict with Revolutionary laws prescribing compulsory egalitarian inheritance. What in fact happened?

Fortunately, there is a thesis published in 1942 that considers this exact question.[42] The author, Jean Saint-Macary, was the son of a Béarnais notary (and became one himself), and used his privileged access to the documents to examine changes in the agreements drawn up during the Revolution and up to 1940. The framework of analysis is not altogether satisfactory,[43] but the documents cited bear witness to an adaptation rather than any break in practice.[44]

The Civil Code is essentially individualist in its understanding, so that marriage becomes a contract between two persons with financial interests, and property is radically altered in meaning, becoming a personal possession. Nevertheless, the Code permits a variety of matrimonial regimes, including the possibility of both the separation of goods and the community of goods, and Béarnais documents employ these to their ends. The family and neighbours continue to be present, as witnesses; the option of the dowry regime is employed, in this case detailing the goods to be retained on each side, including the trousseau; and the various possibilities of agreeing conditions of return, delays in payment, receipt and reversion to the contributing parties, are all exploited.

But more than this, the aim of the pact, in the case of family property, is to avoid division. Saint-Macary concludes that Béarnais marriage contracts bend the law, and that notaries are the efficient cause of this adaptation. (This agency is no doubt assisted by passing on the notarial practice, which has a monopoly over local land transmissions, between generations of the same family in succession.) The pact institutes one member of a generation as heir, and concerns future successions, for the cadets are promised a portion in return for renouncing their rights. Similarly, a husband makes concessions, or gifts, to his wife, compensating in this way for the lack of protection the Code gives to her dowry. The pacts also recognize the reality of an heiress marrying an incoming husband, and nevertheless retaining her property rights. And lastly, the father-in-law, not the husband, receives the dowry, and partnership agreements are drawn up between the two generations associated in the exploitation of the farm.

Although the law undoubtedly has its effects upon the evolution of custom, particularly upon the right of recovery, which is attenuated, and does not apply to the heirs and successors of the parties who contributed property to the marriage, the evidence is that the form of life with which we have been concerned survives the introduction of the Civil Code with comparative ease. It is in no way frozen or archaic: there is some sort of continuity at work for over seven hundred years. I have tried to suggest the complex form in which it exists. In the next chapter, I shall look in more detail at the modalities of its expression at the present time.

Notes

1. Ourliac (1979 [1956]).
2. M.G.N. [Nogues] (1837[1760]); Mazure and Hatoulet (1841–1843).
3. Cf. Pottage and Mundy (2004).
4. See Bourdieu (1980c).
5. See Yver (1966).
6. Poumarède (1972).
7. Viazzo and Lynch (2002) present a contemporary version of this thesis.
8. See Ourliac's introduction to Poumarède (1972).
9. Ourliac and Gilles (1990: 6).
10. Following Poumarède (1972). See also Tucoo-Chala (1970); Laborde and Louber (1932); and Bidot-Germa, Grosclaude and Duchon (1986).
11. See, e.g., Poumarède (1972), and the work of Marca (2000[1640]).
12. See Tisset (1959).
13. Stein (1999).
14. Ibid.: 61.
15. Ibid.: 64.

16. Ourliac and Gilles (1990: 14); cf. Cadier (1979[1888]: 135–149), and Tucoo-Chala (1956).
17. Ourliac and Gilles (1990: 16).
18. Ibid.: 117.
19. With the partial exception of Rogé's work: see Rogé (1908); cf. the remarks of Poumarède (1972: 247, n.7).
20. Ourliac and Gilles (1990: 5).
21. *For* art.123 – see Cadier (1979[1888]: 59).
22. Ourliac and Gilles (1990: 120).
23. Ibid.: 126.
24. Ibid.: 7–8.
25. Luc (1943).
26. For a full list, see Poumarède (1972: 243). Luc (1943: 2, n.3) commends only Laborde (1909) on the dowry, Dupont (1914) on inheritance, and Cadier (1979[1888]).
27. See in particular Poumarède (1972) and Zink (1993); see also the recent work of Bidot-Germa (2008).
28. This distinction appeared in the *For de Morlàas* (arts 71, 80, 178).
29. I have not known any such case. For a discussion of well-documented historical examples in Gévaudan, see Lamaison (1979: 733ff).
30. We might note the potential complexities of return, given that the right of recovery may go back two generations, and the sustained separation of ownership, or non-amalgamation of property.
31. Sabean (1990).
32. Following Robisheaux (1989); cf. Sabean (1990: 93ff).
33. See Raymond (1873).
34. Cf. Riles (2006).
35. Cf. Stein (1999), and Desplat (1986).
36. Desplat (1986).
37. See Luc (1943).
38. See, on the assertion of sovereignty, Tucoo-Chala (1961), and on its relinquishing, Brun (1923: 11–58).
39. These commentaries, which remain in manuscript form in the local archives, have served as the basis for a good deal of local history, both institutional and legal: see note 26. See Labourt, *Les Fors et Coutumes de Béarn* (ms., Bibliothèque Municipale de Pau); de Maria, *Mémoire sur les dots de Béarn* (with an appendix: *Mémoires sur les coutumes et observances non écrites de Béarn*), and *Mémoires et éclaircissements sur le For et Coutume de Béarn* (both mss, Archives départementales des Pyrénées Atlantiques); Mourot, *Traité des dots suivant les principes du droit romain, conféré avec les coutumes de Béarn, de Navarre, de Soule et la jurisprudence du Parlement*, and *Traité des biens praphernaux, des augmens et des institutions contractuelles, avec celui de l'avitinage* (both mss. in private hands).
40. Zink (1993); cf. Zink (1997).
41. Zink (1993): 297.
42. Saint-Macary (1942).
43. It is marked by the Pyrenean feminism thesis.
44. For parallel testimony, see Assier-Andrieu 1986a and 1986b.

Chapter 3

THE CONTEMPORARY BÉARNAIS FARMING FAMILY

I

I want in this chapter to give a description of the key features of life in contemporary rural Béarn, paying attention (as always) to questions of continuity and transition.[1] I have worked in the west of Béarn, about fifty kilometres north of the Pyrenees, in the region known as *entre deux gaves* ('between the two rivers'), in villages on the river plain and on farms in the foothills, the fertile slopes rising to a height of 200 metres above sea-level. The peasants live on isolated farms that are scattered along country roads or gathered in hamlets around a church. As a rule, the farms lie outside the villages or the small market towns that serve as local centres for supplies and services. The properties are all small by English standards, being between 5 and 50 hectares (or 13 and 130 acres).

Taking continuity as a motif, it is of interest to cite Arthur Young, who described the local farms just before the Revolution. In his *Travels in France*, he wrote:

> Take the road to Monein (from Pau), and come presently to a scene that is so new to me in France, that I could hardly believe my own eyes. A succession of many well-built, tight and *comfortable* farming cottages, built of stone and covered with tiles; each having its little garden, enclosed by clipped thorn hedges, with plenty of peach and other fruit trees, some fine oaks scattered in the hedges, and young trees nursed up with so much care, that nothing but the fostering attention of the owner could affect anything

like it. To every house belongs a farm, perfectly well-enclosed, with grass borders mown and neatly kept around the corn-fields, with gates to pass from one enclosure to another... (T)his country...is all in the hands of little proprietors, without the farms being so small as to occasion a vicious and miserable population. An air of neatness, warmth and comfort breathes over the whole. It is visible in their newly built houses and stables; in their little gardens; in their hedges; in the courts before their doors; even in the coops for their poultry, and the sties for their hogs. A peasant does not think of rendering his pig comfortable, if his own happiness hangs by the thread of a nine years' lease. We are now in Béarn, within a few miles from the cradle of Henry IV.[2]

Young's observations were timely, for the oldest houses we have now date mostly from the end of the eighteenth and the beginning of the nineteenth century, built upon a basis of increasing wealth and population that owed[3] less to a revolution in techniques than to a gradual stabilization of agricultural cycles. More importantly, he has put his finger upon the critical point: the fact that the occupiers own the comfortable houses and the small properties. It is this feature that impressed Le Play.

The Béarnais peasant is a landowner, and his heir inherits the work he has invested in the property. The permanent association of a family with a property is a key to the understanding of Béarnais social organization; the basic unit of Béarnais social life is the entity made up of the property and the family that farms it, and this unit is focussed or symbolized by the house. The unit is termed, in Béarnais, *la casa* or *la maison* or *l'ostau*, and the house name, which is usually supposed to be the name of the first owner, serves to identify all the people who live there. Thus the answer to the question 'what is your name?' (*quin t'apèras?*) is the house name – for example, Jan de Morlaàn, or Jan Morlaàn. Third parties often do not know a person's surname (in French, *nom d'état civil*), so somebody who knows Jan Morlaàn will not necessarily know who is meant if he is referred to as Jan Capdeville, using his surname. (To ask for the surname, one asks 'how do you sign yourself?' – *quin te sinnas?* – and the surname is termed *lo nom de sinnar*.) The geographical locus, the house, defines the family by giving its members their name, and it is the house, rather than the family, that represents continuity in this society. Many house names are the same as that given in the Census of 1385, but continuities of descent, though they may be assumed by the occupants because they share that same name, are far less likely.[4] In the recent past, servants and farmhands also took on both the house name and the house's 'status': they too were defined in every sense by where they lived.

For, importantly, the house also gives its inhabitants a social and moral place in local society. There are, broadly speaking, two kinds of farmhouse, the small and the large. The houses are built from local materials: the walls of the smaller houses are built from pebbles and rocks taken from river deposits, bound by a cement made of sand and lime; the roof frame is made from hardwood, and the tiles from baked clay. In its original form, the typical small farmhouse has a central gable with the stable and grange under it, and a flat lean-to roof on either side, under one of which the family lives. The outer walls are double, with debris between; they stand on the soil, and there are neither foundations nor cellars. The roof is very tall to allow storage, the proportion of roof to wall being approximately one to one. In addition to its height, there are two features in the building of the roof which give the Béarnais house its characteristic profile. In the first place, there is a small rafter which prolongs the long roof rafter on its lower end outside the lateral wall, breaking the line of the roof. In the second, many buildings, in particular barns, incorporate a 'hip' roof, a triangle above the gable end. Older locally-made tiles usually have the lower, free edge rounded, giving a fish-scale effect. The house is oriented to protect it from the north and from the west wind; it therefore faces east or south-east.[5] Farm buildings are arranged around the house as the terrain allows; there does not appear to be any firm rule of orientation.

The larger, wealthier farmhouses are built from quarried limestone, and usually roofed with slate brought from the mountains; they are in general more solidly constructed, with lintels made of stone, not of wood, and they are two-storied, often with mansards above. They may have a gallery at the first-floor level. In such houses, the farmyard is often closed and entered by a portal; there may also be a dovecote. These architectural features of the larger house symbolize the social prestige and honour of the family.[6]

These physical features are of sociological significance, for the two sorts of house are linked to two broad categories of peasant: the *gros* and the *petit paysan*, the 'large' and the 'small farmer'. The most important criterion distinguishing the one from the other is certainly the size of the farm. Yet in Béarn the farmer's status is related to both economic and what we can call 'symbolic' worth.[7] All the properties are small, as has already been stated, most being between eight and forty hectares. It is not enough, however, to own one of the larger farms to be a large farmer. The large farmer is also distinguished by a big house, with two stories, a closed court and a portal, and perhaps a dovecote and, above all, by his moral qualities, by his honour, his generosity and hospitality. The worth of a family is always judged in terms that do not distinguish clearly economic from other features.

Obviously, the smaller a farm is, the harder it is to make ends meet. On a small farm, the land will not produce enough to service debts that have to be taken on to buy machinery or to cover the costs of fertilizer, feed and fuel. In these conditions, a peasant finds it difficult or impossible to maintain the farm and his family, and to ensure that his son marries well and can succeed him. There is thus a range of peasant success and failure linked, in the first instance, to economic factors, which also corresponds in an inverse fashion with a greater or lesser conformity to 'tradition'. The two poles, of economic success and hardship, correspond respectively to the large and the small farmer, and the families of the large farmers are better able to observe the traditional institutions – of marriage, endowment and inheritance, and of parental and conjugal authority – than are the families of small farmers. As a result, the former appear fixed and stable, while the latter are more fluid; they have to improvise solutions: they may sell up their land, or farm part-time and work in a local factory, or they may rent additional land and try to cross the threshold to become viable. The point to note is that what may from one angle be construed as a conservative social status or 'tradition' is associated with economic stability and, the other way about, economic success may involve the successful parties becoming more traditional in some respects.[8]

This seems to be an enduring situation, although the threshold of farm viability will alter over time. I have consulted the land registers, the census details and the civil registers for one village in the river plain over the period from just before the Revolution to the present. As one might expect, there are stable families and houses, which endure – in some cases, over the whole period – and there are families which are unstable, surviving for a generation or more, but disappearing and being replaced. Some in this latter category are artisans; many are tenants, rather than owners, or own only a fraction of the land they farm, and some are share-croppers (*métayer*). However, not all the families that disappear are poor, a point I will return to. But by and large the distinction is that between the large and the small farmer, and the turnover among the latter allow transfers of property, both accumulation by the large, and – sometimes – acquisition and growth by the small; the individuals use their talents and opportunities, they play their cards as best they can, and make their choices.

Moreover, the distinction is applied locally to individuals. Bernard Legeire is a large farmer (*un gros paysan*) principally because he has one of the larger properties and is rich, and also because he and his family show the qualities required, and because he lives in a particular farmhouse. The criteria invoked are in part economic, in part individual and moral, and in part inherited – through the house. To say of Jean Claverie that he is a small farmer (*un petit paysan*) is not to insult him or to condescend; people will apply this word to themselves and their family, or to their forebears. However, it is to suggest that Claverie is more peripheral to local life and its values, and more likely to come a cropper, either morally or economically, than is Legeire. As a consequence, the small farmer has in some respects had less invested in the system than the large farmer, and has always been less subject to some of the values of the local society. He has often had to give up farming, permanently or for a period, and learn a trade or emigrate.

The small farmer, therefore, is the point at which a certain kind of innovation or change happens in the society. In the twenty and more years that I have known the region, the non-agricultural population living in the villages have represented urban, metropolitan values. They are professionals by and large who commute to the town, together with artisans, idealists and militants, and holiday makers. Except for the latter, they are usually locally born. Their cosmopolitan values have been viewed sympathetically to an extent by the small farmers, and barely registered by the large farmer families. It therefore might look to the outsider as if the small farmers have modernity on their side, and that the large farmers are survivals or anachronisms, destined to die out. However, the present state of affairs is most likely simply a variation of the normal position: that the large farmer serves as a model, or core, and the small farmer lies in a penumbra, or on the periphery. It would be a mistake to imagine that the 'traditional' position, represented by the large farmer, is a position of weakness rather than of strength locally, for the large farmer is still the centre of local values, and not a remnant. And he is, as we shall see, the point at which agricultural innovation occurs, for it is only when he adopts new practices that they come to be widely shared.

In confirmation of this understanding, success or failure is interpreted locally entirely in terms of personal 'qualities', or stereotypes, which reflect these values. A man's material success is attributed to his qualities as a worker and as a man of honour, and the smooth running of his household to his wife's qualities as a good housewife, including her observance of his authority. Failure, on the other hand, is attributed to personal failings such as jealousy, greed and laziness, promiscuity and thriftlessness, in short, to moral shortcomings that show a disregard for traditional values. In such a world, an actor is always liable to attribute personal frustrations and failures to malice on the part of others, principally neighbours, and likewise to describe public situations by which he or she is affected in moral terms, as the result of corruption or conspiracy. Claverie is inventive, enterprising, argumentative and political; characteristically, he talks. He and his family attribute every event in life to hidden human intention. To explain any event that touches on the family, whether immediately or distantly, they invoke, according to circumstances, the concealed self-interest of politicians both local and national, of priests, of the rich, of the poor, of trades unions, of towns people, and – above all – of neighbours, both at a distance (the Basques or the Landais), and near at hand, in their immediate vicinity. This attitude provides a complete framework of moral explanation, for which the most general local term is *jalousie* ('self-interested envy').[9] In contrast, the more substantial farmer need have little recourse to these categories of blame and attribution, or indeed to any open expression of judgement; he can meet the vicissitudes of life with a certain calm, and in this silent way assert a public role both of example and leadership. Legeire is quiet, hardworking, apparently conservative in the sense of unpolitical, and mayor of the village; he said ironically of his neighbour Claverie, 'with his head and my shoulders, we could run a good farm'. The divide between the large and the small farmer is never absolute, they lie on the same spectrum, but the large farmer will always have a greater share of social prestige and honour than the small farmer, and he will (by the very definition of honour) have to live up to it. The values of local society therefore appear most clearly in the case of the large farmer; he embodies them, and in this sense, he serves as a model.

The term 'traditional' may then be used to denote the local values and practices that are central to a contemporary understanding of Béarnais social life, values and practices which are exemplified in the large farmer. The habitual usage, however, of the word 'tradition' implies that the peasant world is an isolated historical remnant, and the hypothesis of its isolation in turn suggests the destructive effect that 'modernity' will have, and is already having, upon it. But it is not the case that the peasant world is isolated, nor perhaps that it has ever been so, and in so far as the term implies the fragments of a formerly complete and functioning whole, it is misleading; and not only misleading, but inappropriate, for it applies an external perspective and valuation for which there is no local correspondent. It should be emphasized that the term 'traditional' here describes the active, ordering principle in local society, including how it meets an external gaze; and that its use is justified by the historical evidence of its longevity.[10] It is worth remarking the congruence between, on the one hand, the distinction opposing large and small farmers, presenting traditional and modern features respectively and, on the other, that opposing types of jurisdiction and patterns of marriage observed in the previous chapter. This argument concerning longevity is further refined in chapter five.

II

In the Pyrenean provinces, the traditional peasant family's vital interest is to ensure continuity of the farm. This is achieved, as we have seen, through the practices adopted of inheritance and marriage: continuity is achieved by instituting only one offspring out of each generation as the heir, usually on the occasion of his or her marriage.

This practice, which contrasts with the 'egalitarian' inheritance practised in many parts of France, has been long established and has persisted, despite the legal possibility of a division of the inheritance created by the Civil Code.

Continuity involves both succession between generations – the passing on of authority, ownership and responsibility – and the maintenance of the family's total wealth and property, which may be termed the patrimony. We might distinguish authority and patrimony to this extent: that in order to keep the former intact, one will disperse as much of the latter as is necessary. The effect of this is that in Béarn, one child – usually the first-born son – receives all the family's property without division, although the other children receive compensation, which is now often spoken of in terms of their legally entitled 'share' in their parents' property. Yet what is at stake is different to the individualist intentions of the Civil Code, and the fact that a woman might inherit the patrimony, despite the secondary role that women in general hold to men in matters of property and finance in Béarn, serves to underline the overriding importance of maintaining the patrimony whole, which is the keystone in the whole edifice of family law, and indeed of social and economic organization. Indeed, women inherit relatively frequently: many family histories involve an heiress in the four ascending generations (which is as far as memory recalls), and this pattern is confirmed by the records. There are instances of the adoption of heirs which also confirm this interpretation, that the aim is to retain the house intact.

As a result of this overriding aim, properties have been remarkably stable, both in size and in ownership. Any division of the land would threaten the family in two senses: economically, for the farm would become too small a unit to support a family; and symbolically, for the breaking up of the house would destroy the family's identity. It is important to emphasize the specificity of this solution, and the fact that it is not determined in the first instance by material constraints, for in certain other parts of France land is divided between heirs, and while one sibling may inherit the house in the sense of the building, farms are reconstituted in every generation, through marrying, purchasing and renting land.[11]

The house, although a humanly constituted category, has then an extraordinary power over the humans who constitute it. In practical terms, this power is expressed in the primacy the family has over its individual members, and in the way that each person plays their part. The head of the house and the heir are, in a real sense, designated by the family, and they carry the family's hopes. They exercise authority, in the house, at work and in financial matters, but only in so far as it is compatible with the interests of the family as a whole. This sense of 'election' appears particularly clearly in cases where the eldest offspring is considered to be unfit or incapable, for whatever reason, and has to renounce his rights of inheritance. These processes are normally negotiated, over time; I have known in detail cases where the second of six brothers has inherited, the third of three brothers, and a sister over her two elder siblings, a brother and a sister. In the first instance, the eldest became a Catholic priest. In the second, both of the elder brothers took university degrees and followed a profession, one becoming a teacher, the other a manager in a local agricultural business. In the third case, the brother had become proprietor of a local café, and the sister was married to a local farmer; an important further factor in the choice was the qualities of the man the sister who inherited was to marry: a hard worker of agricultural stock, who subsequently made a success of the farm (and bred a son). The historical records also bear the traces of comparable negotiations. The factors involved then concern aptitude, certainly, but also marriage, and, often, misfortune. A younger brother may replace an elder because he wishes to farm and the eldest does not; an heir may be replaced because he has not married, or has but remains childless; and a farmer may fall ill or die in an accident and be replaced from within his generation. Daughters renounce 'automatically', unless there is no suitable male heir.

III

Succession must be complemented by marriage, and this brings us to the heart of the complex of arrangements, agreements and adjustments. First of all, the family must have the heir marry to assure the continuation of the line. This involves the transmission of property between generations. But second, the family must also marry off the younger offspring or non-heirs, and each marriage involves the transfer of goods, sometimes effectively as a dowry, equivalent to the realization of the share of the inheritance owed to that person. At the same time, marriage of either kind not only involves financial exchange between families but also engages the family's symbolic status. The institution of marriage is central to the perpetuation or reiteration of the whole local social order; and it is, as Bourdieu has noted,[12] the occasion for the family to maintain or improve its standing in the local hierarchy.

There are three kinds of legal documents that need to be taken into account in this respect: two principal ones, the settlement of inheritance between siblings, or division, on the one hand, and the marriage contract on the other. The third is the will, which is of comparatively minor importance, for the first two acts carry out many of the functions that we associate with the last. I was instructed in these matters by a local notary of great experience, and have had access to contemporary (up to 1997) documents. This access is significant because the notarial documents available from public archives do not concern contemporary lives or touch upon them. The instruction I received confirms the picture drawn up from past documents, and demonstrates living practice.

If we take the marriage agreement first, this document details the property regime under which the marriage will be conducted. This is usually a mixed regime, with community of any goods resulting from the union, but separate ownership of goods brought into the marriage by each party. These goods are then detailed: they include whether one party has been named heir, and the goods, money and property he will inherit, and any property either party already owns, through inheritance or their own labours. In addition, the parents of each party often make a gift to their child, of furniture and money, sometimes together with livestock and land, and – in the case of the bride – there is a detailed inventory of a trousseau of clothes, bedclothes and linen brought to the new household. I have examined copies of recent documents, including ones made between persons of no great fortune, which exhibit such details, including the commitments of the parents to pass on the gifts promised.

To take a single example, the marriage agreement made between Pierre Hourcade (32) and Cathérine Mirande (24) involves their respective parents, who make a declaration from one side, and a gift from the other. The document first agrees to a mixed regime, with regard both to property and to debts; debts carried over are a separate responsibility, those incurred subsequent to the union are a joint responsibility. Then the property that each brings to the marriage is detailed. The few possessions belonging to each partner are given a nominal and equal valuation, before the gifts made to each by their parents are described. Pierre in fact receives no gift at this stage, simply the declaration on the part of his parents that he will receive the disposable part of their property at their death, subject only to the consideration of the surviving parent enjoying the use rights (usufruct) of the other's goods until death. He is permitted to marry by the act of being named as his parent's heir, to land which is not detailed in this document, but which will be in that document to come settling the division of property in his family. For her part, Cathérine is given a sum of 20,000 francs by her parents, together with a trousseau, which is listed – 1 mattress, 1 bolster, 2 pillows, 4 pillow cases, 2 blankets, 1 counterpane, 1 eiderdown, 24 sheets, 30 towels, 24 hand towels, 36 handkerchiefs, 3 tablecloths, and 36 serviettes – and for which an additional sum is estimated, making a total payment of 22,000 francs. The document concludes by defining the husband's powers with regard to common property, and the limits placed on those powers: he has to have the consent of his spouse with respect to the disposal of land or buildings, the granting of leases, and the use of profits. The document has to be signed by all parties.

We might notice certain interesting points about this kind of mixed regime. First, a husband never owns a wife's property and vice versa. In the case of a man marrying an heiress, this is particularly clear: he works the farm, but she is the owner. Their child becomes the heir and inherits, but the incomer is never the proprietor. One such farmer said to me, of his wife, 'she is the boss; I am the immigrant worker' (*elle est la patronne; moi, je suis le portugais*). This distinction of ownership comes into prominence in the case of early widowhood. Marie Castaigne was widowed at the age of thirty, with three daughters. She carried on her husband's farm, with the help of neighbours, one of whom she eventually married. Her second husband was a bachelor, about ten years older and with a small property of his own. Since remarriage, she has lived with her husband, with whom she has had a son; the son has been brought up with his half-sisters, and will inherit his father's farm. Marie has no rights over either farm; the first property belongs to her daughters, and she has farmed it on their behalf; the first and third daughters have now married away, and the second may take over the farm upon marriage; if not, the farm will be sold, and the resulting sum split between the three. In a second, comparable case, the parents of a dead farmer wished to dispossess the widow, who had a young son, and install instead one of their other, younger sons; the division had been made, but the debts not discharged, and in the parents' eyes, the widow had no rights. After prolonged negotiation, the widow persuaded the other parties to stick to the original agreement. She maintained the farm and paid off the debts, and her son has grown up to take over the farm.

Second, counterbalancing what would be the normal case, of the wife being the incoming party and therefore apparently without power, there are distinct lines of both male and female goods in every agreement. This is particularly clear in the case of the trousseau, and we might profitably ask: What is transmitted along with these items of cloth, passed from mother to daughter?

And third, in the separation of goods we glimpse the possibility of returning property to the contributing line, if the marriage ends without an heir. Absolute ownership is not transferred: the transition is provisional, and marked by obligation. A small-scale example of this: a farm worker married a woman, not an heiress but with a small dowry, who died in childbirth. Her family reclaimed everything and used the goods to endow a younger sister; the farm worker ended up sleeping on straw, while the blankets he used to sleep under went to a neighbour. In this case, he was taken in by a nephew, and a necklace which he had given his wife, which had been returned to him by his parents-in-law, was passed on in due course to his nephew's daughter.

If we turn to the settlement of inheritance, the *partage*, this clearly is connected with the commitments made at the marriage of the heir, and may be drawn up at that time, contemporary with the marriage agreement. Or it may be drawn up later, at the point where the parents pass over their power and retire. In these documents we see the effective renunciation by the non-heirs of their legal share or, at least, an adjustment of their rights that the continuity of the property demands.

This is how it works. The document makes an inventory of the parents' goods, held both separately and in common, as well as any gifts already made to each of the offspring, and – in the case of an heir already in charge of the farm – calculating the worth created by his labour and deducting it from the common stock. The legal position is that the parents may give one quarter of their property as they like, and the remainder is to be divided equally between the offspring. The simplest example is the case of a family with three children, where one – the heir – may receive a half, and the other two a quarter each of the property. The notary's task is to calculate the sums and then, with the agreement of all parties, to compose the shares. The heir will receive the farm, land, equipment and livestock. The others will receive financial compensation, and sometimes a piece of property, to complete their share.

At the same time, other considerations are brought into play. In particular, the business of maintaining and caring for the parents is defined in financial terms and, if undertaken by the heir, set against his debts to his siblings. Similarly, any earlier gifts the other siblings may have received are taken into account. And finally, a regime of payment for any outstanding sums is agreed, so that the farm is not unreasonably burdened. Again, we can note two things. First, a local notary aims to do the sums so that the farm is not burdened with debt, believing that in doing this he (or she) is fulfilling the spirit of the Civil Code, though he is simultaneously fulfilling the spirit of customary law. And second, one can see how the dowry (the share from the spouse's family) brought in by the heir's marriage can enable the house to pay its debts to the other siblings and, in some cases, enable them to marry. But in other cases, the siblings can afford to be generous to the house, in the sense of demanding very little of it. Certainly, it is the case that in many families, the non-inheriting siblings receive a longer education than the heir, and can earn their living independently, as teachers, engineers, agricultural advisers and so forth, and marry without recourse to the family patrimony.

Here again is a single example, the passing on in 1997 of a property in the river plain owned and farmed by Joseph Badiou (born 1932) and his wife Geneviève Haurie (born 1936). The couple have three adult sons, Jean, Michel and Louis, born in 1959, 1963 and 1965, each of whom is married; the two eldest live in local towns and have professions, being an electrician and a mechanic respectively, and the youngest lives and works on the parents' farm. Joseph and Geneviève married in 1958, without a marriage contract, the document notes; the property is owned under the mixed regime which we have already met. First, earlier gifts made by the parents to each of the elder sons are recorded: a sum of 250,000 francs to Jean in 1990, and property in the town where he carries out his trade made over to Michel in 1991, estimated at the same value. We can assume these gifts were recorded in marriage agreements, setting up each son in their own business. Then, the property to be passed on – buildings and land – is detailed, giving for each parcel the reference number on the cadastral plan, the locality, the nature of the land (meadow, field, coppice), and the area in hectares. The whole is estimated at a value of 1.25 million francs; together with the two earlier gifts, this comprises the property to be shared out, a sum of 1.75 million francs.

The origins of the property are detailed next. On the one hand, there are the fields held in common by Joseph and Geneviève, acquired since the marriage: two fields purchased from named individuals in 1966 and 1968, and a series of fields resulting from the consolidation of lands (*remembrement*, discussed below) in 1995, which were presumably exchanged for other lands bought since 1958. On the other hand, Joseph Badiou also owns property in his own name, the main farm buildings and lands, and further fields that he received in the consolidation of lands in exchange for inherited land. Joseph received this property by will from his adoptive father, Bernard Badiou, who was born outside the commune in 1897, and died in 1972. We might note a number of issues of interest which cannot, however, be resolved from the document to hand. These relate to how Bernard became proprietor; to Joseph's antecedents; to Joseph's marriage to which neither party brought any property, since there was no marriage agreement; and to his and his wife's remarkable achievement in accumulating land and making a success of the business. We may guess that Bernard married an heiress who died without issue or surviving family, and that he adopted (at his death) a farmhand, Joseph, who had shown his qualities in working on the property that he subsequently inherited and developed. It is appropriate enough that a farmhand, if he marries at all, marries a woman of no property. We have no indication as to whether Joseph had any blood relation to Bernard (or his wife), such as nephew. All the details of the various transfers, including the adoption and the will, are recorded in dated notarial deeds referred to in the document.

The distribution is made as follows. As we would expect, the youngest, as the designated heir, receives the quarter of the property that is at his parents' disposal, and a further quarter as one of the three recipients among whom the division is made. The two elder brothers as co-recipients receive one quarter each. Two conditions are agreed to by all parties: the division is to take place immediately, under the father's guidance, and the three recipients undertake to pay the costs of maintaining their parents, including food, transport and medical care (but excluding the costs of surgery and of hospitalization). Furthermore, before the division is calculated, two further sums are taken into consideration. First, Louis is owed for two years hitherto unremunerated labour on the family farm as a youth, in 1985 and 1986, paid at the rate of the minimum wage. And second, a sum is deducted from the value of the properties belonging solely to Joseph, being 20 per cent of that value taken in usufruct to provide the retired couple with an income; a particular field is designated to this end later in the document, subject to restrictions as to disposal or the erection of buildings.

With this second sum deducted, the total to be divided comes to 1,560,000 francs, of which Louis is due 780,000, and Jean and Michel 390,000 each. With the consent of all parties, Louis receives the farm and all the land (with the restriction on that part of his father's property that will endure until the death of both parents), which is worth, when the wages owed him is taken into account, some 300,000 francs more than his share. Each elder brother receives his share in three parts: the gift already received, and 100,000 francs as a payment from their father; the remaining 40,000 francs owed each is discharged in return for Louis undertaking in their place the obligation to care for the parents (or surviving parent) in old age. There is provision made in the agreement for the case of Louis being unable to support his parents, in that they can demand to convert this condition into a life annuity, set at 13,000 francs a year, and in the case of Louis's death, his heirs continue to have responsibility for their care or for the annuity.

In brief, the farm is handed on intact to the heir; the other brothers are paid in part out of accumulated capital that belongs not to the father as an individual but to the father and heir together as the co-owners of the business; and the parents are protected for the rest of their lives, the burden of this falling upon the heir. The document represents a finely-tuned balancing of interests and sacrifices, opportunities and obligations, to which the various parties consent willingly because it makes good sense to them to do so. The document thereby offers a shadow picture of some ordinary but nevertheless remarkable life stories, which are specific in some important respects to the region and to the way of life it contains.

It is worth remarking how often brothers and sisters of the heir who are well established renounce any claim to a share of the division.

This is particularly the case in farming families with a modest property, where any distribution would impair the viability of the farm; it is also true, for the same reason, in the case of big farms where there are many siblings. The Labrit family exemplify the first instance, where three sisters renounced their share in favour of their brother, two being married to farmers and one to an electrician; they would however have received a part of that legal share upon marriage. The Bomprat family offer an example of the second case; Jean-Michel, the second of seven siblings, inherited the farm upon marriage after working with his father for eight years, and his siblings, each of whom has a profession or a trade, have settled for a modest sum, to be paid when they marry. Three of his brothers who work locally are unmarried and live as bachelors in the farmhouse, together with the married farmer and his parents. Jean-Michel and his wife are building a new house for themselves across the yard.[13]

For the sake of completeness, the will should be mentioned. In two mirroring documents, the husband and wife leave one another the enjoyment of the other's property for the remainder of their life, so that an incomer in particular cannot be dispossessed in his or her widowhood by the eventual owner. The right of ownership and enjoyment of use are strictly separated in the document, which consists therefore of two significant paragraphs: the one leaving the use of all the testator's goods and property to his or her spouse for life, the other confirming that the ownership of that part of the property over which the testator has right of disposal passes to the named heir upon the testator's death, but may only be enjoyed after the death of the other parent. Citing an example would add no more detail, although it is worth adding that some wills can contain more, as in the case of Bernard Badiou's will cited above, and some less, as when an incoming spouse is not offered protection and is left dependent upon the heir's generosity. In the latter case, the widowed party may be left vulnerable when young, as in the cases cited above where the heirs were still children; more commonly, they are at risk in their old age. Claudette Pedezert married in and was treated with suspicion by her parents-in-law; in her turn, she treated in like fashion her son-in-law who married in. In her old age, she fears being sent to an old people's home, for she has no security from her deceased husband's will, nor any insurance, nor has she built up for herself a fund of good will. It is unlikely, nevertheless, that she will be put out. In another instance, however, in a nearby village, a widow had her house sold by her children in order to keep the fields while paying off the farm's debts; it was sold to urban outsiders seeking a country home.

IV

There is therefore a range of constraint and freedom in local marriage, depending upon whether one is an heir or not, upon the status of the family, upon one's rank in the family, and upon one's gender. It is considered more important to marry off daughters than sons, and the later-born children have a lesser chance of receiving a dowry of any substance. But the most important factor constraining marriage chances is the social rank and wealth of the family, both economic and symbolic, for it is this complex value of the property which controls the amount of the dowry/share, which in turn controls the ambitions of its holder. Conversely, a non-heir from a poorer house is more likely to marry completely outside the system, for lesser families appear to subscribe more readily to modern mores; that – as we know – is a function of the distribution of values within the whole.

To concentrate upon the core houses, the amount of incoming wealth or dowry a family will require at the heir's marriage is related to its own wealth, and so the dowry functions as a mechanism controlling marriage exchanges, and demanding marriages between families of more or less equivalent rank.[14] Although one is told that, as elsewhere, young people marry for love, in practice there is a calculus concerning the importance of farms that allows one to predict which of the young women in the vicinity are potential partners for the heir of a particular property. Marriages, however, are not simply determined by the amount of the dowry, but also by equivalence in social status. A large farmer family will not wish to contract an alliance with the family of a small farmer simply on the grounds that the dowry offered is large enough.

The ideal of a 'good marriage' has most force among the more traditional peasants and, like them, to an outside view, it appears to have an anachronistic flavour. When land is at stake, however, the rules hold good: one party owns land, or is about to inherit land, and the other brings a dowry, of property, livestock, money and a trousseau. Some non-heirs make 'good' marriages because they come from families of worth, and the family's reputation takes the place of a large dowry. In these cases, the incomer's contribution will be detailed in the marriage contract in the usual way, although its economic worth is slight.

It is not only the case, then, that some families appear to observe the 'traditional' rules more closely than do others, but also, within families too, certain of the offspring will appear to be more bound by these rules than others. The eldest son of a family that owns a large farm appears particularly 'traditional' in these respects, even while his younger siblings appear when adult to have assimilated more modern, urban values. As in the contrast between the large and the small farmer, it is the local social values that determine who is more and who is less bound by the rules.

There is a contrast, too, between what is expected of men and of women, which serves as a 'fine tuning' device backing up the economic and symbolic discriminations and tends to ensure marriages between families of roughly equal status. Bourdieu is particularly acute on this topic. The principles of male supremacy and masculine honour demand the safeguarding of the family's prestige and the patrimony. If the heir marries 'above' himself and receives a dowry that is disproportionate to his family's wealth, he faces two threats. First, if the dowry forms too large a proportion of the farm's wealth and has to be returned – as in the case of the marriage proving infertile, or in the case of a later contested division within the incoming spouse's family of origin – this can ruin the farm. Second, and more important in the day-to-day, the wife's relative authority increases with the size of her contribution and the status of her natal family, and this may threaten both her husband's domestic authority and the authority of his parents. She may also bring dishonour upon the family: a wife's adultery, for instance, is seen as being a result of the husband's lack of authority.

If, on the other hand, the heir marries 'beneath' himself, first, he and his family are dishonoured by the misalliance, and second, he will be unable to endow his younger siblings, both failing in his duty and opening himself and the farm to destructive claims in due course.

A younger brother must not marry too high, for he will lack domestic authority, nor too low, for he himself will not be able to bring enough wealth to the marriage to escape poverty. And if he should marry a younger sister (a *cadette*), the couple will have neither land nor house and, upon marriage, they lose their right of residence in their houses of origin. They will have no option but to depart, although they may still live locally, building, buying or inheriting a house without land attached. In any case, they will have to make their own way and earn their own living.

In short, although economic reasons tend to suggest a man should marry up rather than down, for the sake of his honour and his authority (and for that of his family) he should marry down rather than up. The case of the woman is less ambiguous: both economic and social rules suggest that she should marry up. He tends to remain in his sphere, while she is socially adaptable and flexible. Jean Lavignotte, heir to the largest farm in the village, married Marie Brun, the daughter of small farmers. He was the eldest of four brothers, the other three with established professions, and came from a distinguished family that counted other farmers and owners of businesses among their collateral relations, and Catholic priests, including a bishop, army officers and politicians among their ascendants. Jean had taken over the job of village mayor from his father. His wife had two brothers, one of whom had taken over the small parental farm, the other of whom was a policeman, which is not a prestigious job. The contrast between the fathers of the couple was that remarked earlier between Legeire and Claverie, the one slow to speak, judicious, detached and hospitable, the other talkative, always joking, complaining, and offering accounts in moral terms. The contrast between the mothers was equally marked in terms of their demeanour and speech, the one considered, self-effacing and maintaining social distance, concerned to support and serve the male members of the family; the other outspoken, opinionated, argumentative and, on occasion in mixed company, salacious in her choice of topics. On the face of it, the marriage could have been considered a misalliance. The wife brought little property and no land. However, she brought both beauty and character: she was strong-minded, enterprising and hard working, and also charitable. She learnt to imitate some of her mother-in-law's ways. Apart from running the household, she contributed to the income of the farm by producing various luxury goods, notably *foie gras*, sold through a network of local outlets and distributers. Jean remains one of the leading farmers of the area, displaying the characteristic virtues of his father; Marie demonstrates very clearly the ability to adapt to different social milieux, adopting new habits and establishing new contacts and social relations.

We can see that forms of authority (so much of interest to Le Play) – parental authority over the children, the authority of the eldest offspring over the younger ones, and the authority of the husband over his wife – are all functions of the status and wealth of the house, in a more or less circular fashion. In the families of the large farmers, these forms of authority are more or less unquestioned, while rebellion has well-defined forms. Problems in authority arise essentially only on farms that are threatened or going under, usually where the farm is small and poor and prestige is low.

We can see, too, that to an outside gaze, the local landscape is a complicated one, peopled by many subtly differentiated personae who are difficult for that outsider to evaluate in detail and who are easily misconstrued. Certainly, people representing cosmopolitan, urban values are numerous and easily met, and therefore populate the foreground, yet the perhaps fewer, more traditional figures, who are less easily met, nevertheless hold a disproportionate symbolic importance for local residents that is not easily articulated and expressed by any of the parties concerned. This distribution of personae is moreover a product of the categories of interpretation at work, and cannot be subject to straightforward enumeration; one cannot take a census of who is traditional and who modern. An important aspect of how to read this local society – and a ready area for misunderstanding – is how to construe failure.

V

This brings us to the question of change and decline. Practically without exception, the descriptions that we have focus upon the imminent demise of the local society we have been describing. Just as the family as a sociological topic was discovered as being in a state of crisis in debates around the legalisation of divorce during the French Revolution, so Le Play discovered the Pyrenean family as the emblem of a traditional way of life which had evolved a system of inheritance permitting a balanced and sustainable form of authority and property relations, but which was also under terminal threat from the disordering consequences of national legislation upon family law. Social historians tend to echo this judgement unconsciously, either by ceasing their investigations of the Pyrenean family at the end of the Ancien Régime, or by assuming a parallel but later decay, as the effect Eugen Weber described as 'peasants into Frenchmen'[15] comes into play.

Among the ethnographers, Bourdieu[16], writing a hundred years after Le Play, similarly portrays a local society in the last stages of crisis, but places the break with the past in the period around the First World War, evoking broadly the same reasons: inflation in land values inciting the recalculation of divisions and imperilling the dowry, together with various cultural changes that undermine parental authority founded in the power to disinherit. Augustins's work in the Hautes Pyrénées is also based upon historical materials.[17] A more recent demographic study places the transition around 1960, as peasant families become the minority and the local economy takes on new forms relating to tourism, skiing and secondary residences.[18] And I myself, a hundred and forty years after Le Play, have known an important local family for over twenty years which, during this time and in the transition between generations, has abandoned the land and adopted modern, urban ways of living. I will return to this case below.

So one way of posing the question is to ask: What is the nature of this long-lived structure that appears to persist in part through offering these signs of decay to the outside gaze? We already have elements of an answer, in that the local values persist through their generating both what we might call anachronistic figures and citizens for modernity. It is indeed a good question to ask (and one already asked by Le Play): Where do the citizens for modernity come from? In this case, they are permitted by the core, yet flexible, values that perpetuate and are embodied in certain farming families, certain houses. These values constrain considerably at their maximum intensity, while permitting considerable degrees of freedom at the penumbra, a freedom that is paid for by a lack of influence or local significance. The houses are the apparently immobile centres that organize desire and obligation, possibility and permission, for more people than simply their members.

This immobility can of course be seen as the product of a certain passive contingency: the effect of geographical isolation and cultural inertia. For example, one could claim that the land is sufficiently broken up not to attract big capital and, moreover, that this countryside is hundreds of kilometres distant from the nearest large urban centres, Toulouse and Bordeaux. Outsiders who move in, to live or to farm, do not then start afresh but have to deal with local families, suppliers, notaries and others who are in large part unaware of the extent to which they embody a particular way of life. All these factors of passive resistance imply that the predictions of the incursion of modernity, though much delayed, will be fulfilled – and that in speaking of a local society we are simply dealing in a survival, a living fossil.

But this is not an adequate account, for two kinds of reason. The first concerns the complex network of ties and relations, even on a passive model, between the farm and the non-farming families. Pitt-Rivers makes the point that there is a community of interest between farming neighbours in the hamlets and suggests this is in opposition to the non-farming interests of the larger villages and towns (*bourgs*).[19] Yet in the region, through the complexities of marriage and settlement, there are also solidarities that link farming and non-farming households; these are often expressed politically at a communal level (see the next chapter). Moreover, families may be seen as spread out over time and space, linking a variety of trades and professions and including households engaged in business or commerce in the local towns, with a flow of spouses, capital and labour between their various components. The emphasis upon the importance of the house is only a starting point; it must be complemented by a perspective that traces family connections and trades, linking together households over time, crossing between isolated farms, hamlets and local towns, and which qualifies any simple opposition between farming and non-farming populations. To begin to map out a single network, the Portariu family are wealthy farmers from a village in the plain. The family used to pasture flocks in summer in the Vallée d'Ossau, to the south, until the end of the 1960s; they now concentrate upon dairy cattle, maize and tobacco production in the plain. The present farmer, Pierre, has an aunt, his father's sister, who married the owner of an inn at the entry to the valley; that family subsequently moved to a hotel in the regional capital, Pau, and then bought a farm and vineyard south of Pau; of Pierre's cousins, one is a hotelier, while two run farms and one a commercial winepress. One of Pierre's brothers runs a café in the local market town; of his other siblings, two – one the wife of a retired teacher, the other a teacher elsewhere in France – have bought properties in the Vallée d'Ossau, in Laruns; these last two might have the appearance of incomers to a casual eye, but in practice they are related to a series of both rural and urban local families and businesses. Pierre has other cousins who farm, as does his brother-in-law, and a son with a well-paid skilled profession in Pau. The opposition of town to country, or of farming to non-farming family, has limited purchase, though a strong ideological persuasiveness.

Second, the farming society is not itself passive and immobile, but rather active, contemporary and, we might say, generative: it actively makes sense of its situation. It has coped quite successfully with two enormous recent changes, the revolution in agricultural technology since the Second World War, and the process of consolidation of land holdings. We should consider briefly both of these transformations.

VI

The first change is detailed in Henri Mendras's classic *La fin des paysans*,[20] at the heart of which is a case study concerning the introduction of hybrid maize into Béarn.[21] The book as a whole is an account, by an admirer of Le Play, of a thesis we can recognize: that a thousand-year-old peasant civilization is coming to an end, and that the industrial agricultural producer engaged in the market is replacing the self-sufficient peasant farmer. Mendras is most acute on the inapplicability of historical models of industrialization to the peasant world and on the potential or otherwise of French agriculture for forming new relations of production and consumption. He sees the peasant world as irreducible to economic and instrumental criteria and hence argues that both modern Marxist and liberal theories are inapplicable. This is close to a reformulation of Le Play's central interest (a third way). But he is also sure that this world has ended: that agriculture, through joining in with the second wave of industrialization – the internal combustion engine and the application of chemicals – has become agricultural business. Here, I think, the evidence is ambiguous. Let us consider his case study.

Mendras claims that the decision to adopt hybrid maize demonstrated a conflict between two logical systems of life and behaviour: between rational economic reasoning and a local world-view. In Béarn, the absence of any abstract, quantitative view of time and space, combined with the absence of differentiation of roles and with participation in village society, created an incomprehensible situation from the point of view of the discipline of economics, and left the farmer with a choice which he could make either in terms of individual morality or by yielding to fashion, but never by economic reasoning.[22]

Hybrid maize was introduced from the American Midwest during the 1950s and 1960s, following the pattern of the introduction of maize from the Americas in the eighteenth century. In contrast to previous practice, the new type of maize demanded annual seed purchase (for hybrids are sterile), large quantities of fertilizers, and – being more sensitive or vulnerable than native strains – weedkiller and mould treatment. Because its initial growth is slower, it demanded well-ploughed fields, and hence encouraged the buying of tractors, hastening the replacement of oxen. Hybrid maize does not need its leaves stripped or its tops chopped, so it demanded less labour, but resulted in less fodder. Properly handled, its yield was double that of the strains it replaced.

From this description, it can be seen that the introduction of hybrid maize engaged the farmer in the cash economy and credit, making him dependent upon the regular purchase of seed, chemicals and equipment. It turned him away from using livestock to plough, from self-sufficiency, from dependence upon neighbours for co-operation and expertise, and from an ecologically sustainable polyculture, towards a dependence upon machinery, cash and agricultural experts, which together supported a monoculture.

Mendras explores the hesitations of local farmers to adopt the new techniques and to modify the old, both in positive terms of habits that resist, and negatively, in terms of 'de-skilling', conceived both as the abandonment of old techniques and as the loss of autonomy to experts from the city. He also traces the importance of the lead given by the large farmers:[23] they weighed the pros and cons, discussed among themselves, and oriented towards the market. The middle-sized farms – defined as those who listened to those who did the talking – followed suit. The smaller farms were threatened with destruction, having as a class neither a broad outlook nor the financial means to adapt. They were indeed caught by a shifting upwards of the financial threshold to viability.

Such an enormous upheaval, Mendras notes, was accompanied by all sorts of fears, myths and attributed causalities or blame, and even law suits. The change in agricultural technique became politicized: it was opposed by the Left, as coming from America, but supported by the Catholic farming unions. And that opposition gave rise to suspicion and conflict over who was getting subsidies, advice and aid. Hybrid maize caused changes in the distribution of political power in villages. These changes as a whole, Mendras claims, are part of the shift from peasant autonomy to dependence, from subsistence to production, from the values of land to those of trade.

I do not wish to deny Mendras's analysis, but to note that, rather than doing away with the peasant society we have described, it reproduces many of its lasting features. The opposition of large to small farmers, with the smallest always threatened with falling out of the system, the interpenetration of all aspects of life, and the opposition of (conservative) rural land practices to (radical) urban trade practices have been present, not for fifty or a hundred years, but since the twelfth century. There is a longstanding 'economy', for want of a better word, in which apparently incompatible practices co-exist by lending certain aspects of themselves for the other to grasp on to, and hiding other aspects. Certainly, from my period of work, just as polyculture – balancing the four basic elements of livestock, grain, vine and timber – continues to co-exist with hybrid maize, preoccupations to do with inheritance continue to occupy the minds of farmers that are otherwise given over to the concerns of money and the rules of the market.[24]

The other innovation I will mention briefly is the phenomenon of consolidation of land (*remembrement*).[25] This is more recent. Under the guidance of outside advisers, local farmers agree to exchange pieces of land assessed in terms of equivalent value, in order to bring together fewer and larger fields – once again, a characteristic process of rationalization in Weberian terms. There are parallels with the account of the introduction of hybrid corn: the projects have taken off slowly, and have incited distrust and disturbance; the lead of the large farmers has been vital; and the advantages are clear, in terms of permitting the financial viability of introducing new techniques – irrigation, for example, and larger tractors – and consequently new crops, aimed at specific markets (tobacco is a case in point).

Consolidation works best in the fertile plains. There is little benefit to be gained in the foothills or in the mountain valleys, and so it serves the larger farms better. The interest of the process from my point of view is that it emphasizes the ideal nature of the house or *casa*. The larger farmer does not fetishize the land as such: he is not overwhelmingly attached to the particular hectares that his father farmed before him.

And the same is true even of the building in which he lives. We began the chapter with consideration of the sociological significance of the physical farmhouse; the evolution of the building over time in certain respects can express the life of the family and changes in its status and purpose. Some farming families move from one house to another in the village as their lot changes; others rebuild, or build anew, so that the present barn is the former farmhouse, facing the newer house across the yard. Some couples build a new house upon marriage, and even re-convert barns, leaving behind their parents in the original 'new' house, even though they continue to share the farm work. These processes may be seen in the life of one farmhouse, named 'Bailacq', situated in a hamlet in the foothills. The original small house and surrounding land was purchased in the 1830s for a married niece by an émigré who had gained his wealth in Buenos Aires. The property passed to a daughter, who purchased more land and who had the large house built in the late nineteenth century, on the opposite side of the courtyard, with extensive gardens and a dovecote on the far side of the house. The original house became a barn, and the court between enclosed, being entered by a portal on the south side, with a series of buildings closing the yard on the north; these were farm buildings, and included the original eighteenth-century barn. The property has passed through three further generations, in the male line of succession, becoming the largest farm in the village, and with various developments and additions to the buildings. The house has been further improved; there is a gallery that runs around two sides of the internal courtyard at the first floor level, joining the old farmhouse via the portal to a balcony from which a series of bedrooms are entered on the first floor of the big house, and from which also a staircase descends to the hall and kitchen. There have been alterations to the barns, associated with developments in farming techniques; for example, the building of a milking parlour, stabling for calves, and the conversion of part of the complex into offices, to control the paperwork. The old farmhouse has also undergone a series of transformations; it has been used for storage, and neglected; it has served as a residence for a widowed mother and, at a later time, for a farmhand (*domestique*); and recently it has undergone a metamorphosis through restoration into a thoroughly modern rural house, full of antiques and paintings, to accommodate an unmarried adult son of the farmer, who has a well-paid professional job in the regional capital.

These mutations in ownership, structure and use are well-established practices, so we may conclude that the house is a moral identity manifested in a changing constellation not only of persons and beasts over time, but also of buildings and fields: it may mutate in every aspect. The house is a good deal more mobile than one might think, and perhaps therefore for this reason a good and efficient principle of continuity.

VII

But this extreme fluidity over time has its own potential for loss. I want lastly to consider cases of the disappearance from the system of individual large farmers. As we have seen, outside accounts have always described the local way of life both as being constructed around the transmission of land and as being about to disappear – for whatever cause. I suspect this perception of imminent loss is less due to the erosion of the small farms – which will have been a constant feature of the region, though at a variable rate – and owes more to the perceived threat to the way of life of the large farmers: hence, indeed, the themes of the erosion of authority, the loss of continuity and history, and the breaking-in of modernity.

I made a historical profile from the 1780s to the present of one village in the river plain, a settlement around two foci, one old and one more recent, totalling about sixty houses. In this sample, discontinuities, either through non-marriage and non-replacement, or through moving away, in fact occurred at both ends of the spectrum, both the poor and the wealthy. With poor families, effectively without land, the problems are self-evident, and in the second half of the nineteenth century at least were frequently met by emigration, to Argentina or California. With some wealthy families, a period of accumulation of land and consolidation was followed by the introduction of tenants, often sharecroppers, and the move of the owners to the local market town. In such cases, the children often married into local urban commercial or industrial families. The land holding in the village was then shared out between siblings at one or subsequent divisions, and first let to local farmers, and then eventually sold, allowing other families to begin the process of accumulation. Such a wealthy family has perhaps ceased to hold a local interest; without a radical break, they have moved from a local rural focus to a local urban focus, doubtless still with landholdings, but without that defining their identity.

I might add, however, that this work is incomplete, for in order to map fully the families 'in the middle', the ones that continue uninterrupted over the whole period studied, one would have to trace the land holdings, civil registers and censuses for the adjacent communes also, for these families have a strong tendency to marry locally. And a perspective that maps out related households and steps outside a simple focus on families that farm might also discover the continuing local involvement of those wealthy families that appear to have left the area; this is supported by the connections of the Portariu family, mentioned above. But these networks are not my present concern.

I mentioned that, almost a hundred-and-fifty years after Le Play, I too have known a family whose trajectory resembles that of the Mélougas. Although reconstructions are always tentative, I have observed the following features that might contribute to an understanding of this phenomenon, of the loss of these key large farming families that so strongly impresses outside observers, not least with a certain sense of tragedy and loss.

It is not of course experienced precisely as loss in indigenous terms, although it has its sadness and other emotions: these I have had to learn to comprehend in their context. The meaning of a son not following you in your profession is, I would suggest, different – sadder, perhaps, and certainly more acute – for a Béarnais farmer than it is for a middle-class urban professional. But the features that seem to contribute to certain families 'falling out of the top' of the system play not upon disaster but principally upon the characteristic virtues of the large farmer and his wife. For the farmer, a self-sufficient local sphere of agriculture and male neighbours, together with the embodied qualities of hard work, domestic authority and hospitality, combine to create an enclosed and seemingly changeless world, despite the farmer's involvement in contemporary markets and technical innovations. The wife's virtues concern, by contrast, upward mobility and a consequent receptivity to incoming social signals. Her qualities both make her ambitious for her children, and hence sensitive to more urban values, such as using French in preference to the patois, and also far more mobile in fact: she supplements the farm income by dealing in luxury items, whether it is local produce, antiques, or holiday accommodation, trading not with co-operatives or dealers, like her husband, but with urban suppliers.

Essentially, the opposition we have been considering at different levels may become embodied within a single family: the large farming families are the focus of maximal definitional intensity of the local values.

Under these circumstances, it is easy for virtues to become vehicles expressing flaws. The children, as modern, urban citizens, can be turned against their father, with his limits, his force and virility. Similarly, the parents may become estranged from one another, one with the values of land, co-operation and labour, the other with values of trade, bargains and profit. But note there is no possibility of divorce when land is at stake (only violent death). This is to return to a Balzacian theme evoked earlier. So there are three possibilities. First, the wife can support her husband's values, and bring up the children to admire and follow him, and work to supplement the farm's income. Under these conditions, with good fortune, the farm flourishes. Second, the husband can learn to adopt the wife's values, and to move gradually away from the values of the land and into the values of trade. These are still not economic values, strictly speaking; indeed, they are closely related to the local land economy, but they express the values of the other pole. This could be the case with the families I outlined above, who slip away, over a generation or two, from the village's life. And third, the family can live in partial disintegration, and function poorly. Here we can observe such behaviour as mistrust, jealousy, violence, alcoholism, adultery and various forms of sexual deviancy: not that such options are absent in other families, but here each can take on a prominent role expressing dysfunction. These possibilities can work in combination.

I have two observations to make. First, such destructive behaviour is generally permitted, and to a degree contained, by being associated with the town, or the local capital. It is there that sexual liaisons are carried out, and different life styles adopted, for example, so that the town has non-conservative ways of life projected on to it. The town carries the symbolic burden of dysfunction (and secrecy) that allows rural life to continue to appear conservative. This is a pattern with a considerable time depth.

The second observation is this. If we take seriously the claim that the range of behaviours described is in a sense a function of the virtues manifested in large farming families, then the values of the house control every aspect of life. Not simply the 'normal' transmissions of land, persons and labour, but the various fates and potentials of each individual in detail, concerning emigration or remaining, employment, marriage partners, and sexuality. These values simultaneously control the transmission of land, provide citizens for the modern world, and generate behaviour that will lead to closure, when matters can go no further. All options are covered. Every actor is free, in the sense of being free to play the cards dealt to the best of his or her ability or bent, but there are clear patterns that emerge from the exercise of this freedom.

I close this chapter by returning to this single point: that the citizens for modernity have to come from somewhere, and that they are generated – whether in total or in part I cannot presently tell – from particular forms of local life such as the one I have been describing, which are curiously durable. At the very least, in order to understand contemporary social life, you may have to look closely, not broadly, for details explain the life forms of generalities. In the next two chapters, I shall explore this claim from different angles by examining some of the forms of local political life, where wider frames impinge on local life, but in forms that have the property of lending themselves to the reproduction of indigenous categories.

Notes

1. In addition to studies of the region mentioned already (see chapter 1, note 7), there is a strong tradition of ethnographic studies of rural France to be noted. Leaving aside a few early monographs (e.g., Hertz 1983[1913]; Dumont 1951; Bernot and Blancard 1953), this form of writing developed in the 1970s and 1980s. In a contemporary article (from a lecture delivered in 1979), Zonabend (1985) suggests that the ethnographic monograph was defined against two other kinds of studies: the statistical monographs of the Le Play school on the one hand, and the regional or national surveys of 'beliefs, customs, material culture and oral literature' produced by French folklore studies on the other. In a valuable recent survey, Rogers (2001; cf. Rogers 1995, Jones 2003) notes that this anthropological engagement with rural France came from two institutional centres, the Musée des Arts et Traditions Populaires (with the journal *Ethnologie française*), and the Laboratoire d'anthropologie sociale at the Collège de France. A series of monographs concerning traditional rural communities, using oral materials and archives, were produced, focusing upon 'earlier lifeways in one or another rural

French setting'. (Examples of works of this kind from this period include: Favret-Saada 1980[1977], Verdier 1979, Zonabend 1984[1980], Assier-Andrieu 1981, Claverie and Lamaison 1982, and Segalen 1985. Rogers was involved in this period: see Lamarche, Karnoouh and Rogers 1980, as well as Rogers 1991). Rogers comments of this body of work that it dealt with 'the stuff of folklore', essentially the remains or records of a peasant of way of life, and that it concerned itself with archaic isolates, relatively simple societies within France. It did so by deploying the conventional tools of ethnographic analysis, 'kinship, ritual, sorcery, collective and private property, concepts of time and space, processes of social cohesion' (Rogers 2001: 490). She relates this work to the Annales school's concern with the social history of ordinary life, especially with rural society in pre-Revolutionary France – of particular interest is Alain Collomp's study of the stem family in Ancien Régime Provence (Collomp 1983) – and she distinguishes it from the perspective of contemporary rural sociology, which was concerned with the changes the countryside was undergoing (e.g., Mendras 1976[1961] – discussed below).

By the end of the 1980s, this style of approach, with its engagement with the past, the employment of a series of standard anthropological topics, a separation of anthropology and sociology, and a sense of recovery of what was being lost, was replaced by another set of concerns. Rogers relates this shift to the establishment in 1980 of the Mission de Patrimoine Ethnologique within the French Ministry of Culture (with its associated journal, *Terrain*), though clearly the refocusing of intellectual interests relates to wider changes in the humanities. The shift is to an engagement with the 'ethnology of the present', concentrating upon 'the social processes ... by which social difference, cohesion, and complex forms of integration are produced, expressed, and maintained' (Rogers 2001: 492), identifying the self-construction of particular groups, and with an emphasis upon the creation of meaning rather than anomie in contemporary society. For two examples, see: Vialles (1994[1987]) and Le Wita (1994[1988]). The change in focus involves turning away from some earlier concerns, with rural society as such, with historical materials and their continuities, and with some of the repertoire of anthropological topics, in particular, questions of kinship and property. There have been few attempts to do as this essay does, to integrate the ethnography of a small part of France within a wider framework, though the work of Marc Abélès is an exception: it offers a model of how the local may contribute at the national level, through an account of the category of 'electability' (Abélès 1991[1989]; see the brief discussion in chapter 4). This essay, then, takes the techniques and concerns of the earlier French monographs, and attempts to put them to work in the spirit of the more recent work.

For the sake of completeness, mention should be made, beyond the work of Rogers (1991), to two other monographs in English: Wylie (1964[1957]) and Layton (2000). Wylie's work in particular has been influential.

2. Young (1929[1792]: 53–54).
3. If we follow the thesis of Emmanuel Le Roy Ladurie (1975: 383).
4. Cf. Luc (1943: 7); for the census, see Raymond (1873). See also Bonnain (1986: 179–200).
5. The points of the compass in Béarnais are determined by two factors, the mountain-plain axis and the orientation of the house: north is *devath* (below, under) or *capvath* (towards the valley); south is *dessus* (above, over) or *capsus* (towards the mountain); east is *davant* (in front) or *l'endavant* or *cap abans* or *cap davant* (the face or front of the house – *cap* meaning 'heading' or 'toward'); west is *darrèr* (behind) or *lo darrèr* or *caparrèr* or *cap darrèr* (the back of the house). Alternative terms for east and west are *só lhevant* or *au lhevant* (sun rise) and *só coc* or *au só darrèr* (sun set) respectively.

6. The study of vernacular architecture would start with Cazaurang and Loubergé: see Cazaurang (1968, 2: 21–55), Cazaurang et al. (1978), and Loubergé (1958, 1986). For a more general introduction and bibliography, see Bonnin (1992).

7. After Bourdieu (1962a, 1972a).

8. These findings suggest at first sight that the Béarnais materials would not readily lend themselves to analysis in terms of the concept of 'limited good': the idea that, in peasant societies, all desirable things – including land and wealth, but also less tangible things such as honour, friendship and status – exist in finite quantity and are competed over in a zero-sum game, so that one person's gain is necessarily another's loss (see Foster 1965). This is despite the fact that Ladurie invokes Foster's notion towards the end of his broad discussion of marriage, inheritance and folklore in Ancien Regime Occitania; his argument is not necessarily convincing (Le Roy Ladurie 1982: 511). Nor would related models of moral community, as in the notion of 'amoral familialism' (Banfield 1958), be applicable. The obvious difference between the societies where these accounts were developed and the case with which we are concerned is that Béarn escaped the radical changes of land ownership in the nineteenth century that underlie much twentieth-century Mediterranean anthropology: see the discussion of Banfield in Gilmore (1982).

9. See Bailey (1971) and, in particular, Blaxter (1971).

10. Cf. the account of Susan Carol Rogers of a comparable situation in the Aveyron: Rogers (1991).

11. See Augustins's comparative survey (Augustins 1989).

12. Bourdieu (1962a, 1972a).

13. This small detail raises an important issue: that the domestic group is of greater significance than household size; see the work initiated by Goody et al., in Goody (1971). Statistics can then rarely capture the underlying categories; Segalen rightly argues that it is not the size but the structure of the domestic group that is significant, for 'it reveals a certain form of organization governing the transmission of practices and cultural values, and linking family and work, family and power, and family and possessions' (Segalen 1986[1981]: 22). She, however, then goes on to cite Laslett's work classifying household types by size, which appears to obscure the point; see note 18, below.

14. Compare the discussion in Goody (1973).

15. See Weber (1977).

16. See chapter 6.

17. Augustins and Bonnain (1981, 1986). See also Fauve-Chamoix (1984).

18. Etchelecou (1991). Although we might worry that recourse to statistical methods, and their correlation with social structures, contains many uncertainties; this concern in many ways recapitulates Berkner's debate with Laslett over the stem family; see Laslett (1965) and Berkner (1975); for a summary, see Verdon (1979).

19. Pitt-Rivers (1960). This opposition is also developed by Bourdieu (1962a). Concerning neighbours, see Sandra Ott's discussion of this institution in the French Basque Country (Ott 1993[1981]).

20. Mendras (1976[1961]).

21. Mendras's study has curious contemporary echoes in the introduction of genetically modified crops.

22. Ibid.: 97.

23. Ibid.: 116.

24. This question of continuity or crisis connects to broader issues in the 'peasant studies' literature concerning how appropriate an analytic category the concept of 'the peasant' is, either in the present or in the past. There are two linked issues at the heart of these debates, one focusing upon independence from the market and market forces, the other upon the size and nature of the domestic group serving as

a self-sufficient, independent unit of economic production. Initial claims for both the independence and the importance of the extended household have been subjected to doubt, and the significance of the individual in the long-term, the near universality of the nuclear family, and the implication of all forms of domestic group in trade, have been advocated. Relevant early studies include Arensberg and Kimball (2001[1940]), Redfield (1960), Geertz (1961), Wolf (1966), Shanin (1971) and Goode (1970[1963]). Later critiques include Macfarlane (1984), Scott (1976) and Shanin (1990). The work of Georges Augustins, discussed in chapter 4, which distinguishes cases where the integrity of the property is favoured at the expense of the kin group, may contribute to resolving some of these debates, or at least help clarify the terms. See also the mention of discussions of domestic group and household size in notes 13 and 18, above.

25.   See also Amann (1990).

LOCAL POLITICS AND LAND USE

I

My aim in the previous two chapters has been to establish in the first place the longevity and in the second place the present form of what has been loosely called 'the Pyrenean family', or, more precisely, 'the house'. I have suggested its form serves as a mechanism that both generates and accommodates change, and so persists, at the same time casting an interesting light upon the claims of modernity. And in the conclusion to the last chapter I attempted to indicate how, and in what respects, this complex identity or value survives any particular material instantiation, and how it determines in fine detail the personal options of the individuals who, at any given moment, make it up.

In this chapter I am going to expand the frame, for we have been rather narrowly focused, and expand our concerns in two directions, returning to some of the ideas introduced in the opening chapter. The first direction is to consider a pair of anthropological topics that may cast light upon the phenomenon with which we have been concerned, and to which, reciprocally, it may pose questions. And the second is to look at the matter of local politics: to ask whether these domestic values impinge upon a wider scale, and if so, how, and to what extent, and to consider what would count as evidence of their appearance in a public sphere. This direction concerns the thoroughly anthropological question of the contribution of property to civil society, in this case, how the transmission of goods affects wider relationships of legitimacy, authority and power. These matters are offered as sketches, rather than fully fleshed out, though some of the topics introduced here will be given more substance in the following chapters. First, matters of theory and comparison.

II

There are two contemporary anthropological ideas that may help make sense of the continuity that has been outlined. Neither will surprise the anthropologist. The first is Annette Weiner's concept of an inalienable possession.[1] An inalienable possession is that which the possessor will try to keep at (almost) any cost, including giving away what else he or she has. The possession confers identity and status, and organizes the distribution of rights and duties, gifts and services, as well as the flow of goods and persons, labour and wealth. It is transmitted between generations in a strictly ordered way: an immobile point that shapes the flux of everyday life. The authority vested in inalienable possessions constitutes the motivation to keep them; this is expressed in reciprocity, which is a strategic attempt to avoid relinquishing status. However, 'inalienable' is a statement of value rather than of fact, for in Weiner's account, there are circumstances in which the goods can be lost.[2] It is a way of naming what, in philosophical terms, we might call the priority of difference over equivalence,[3] or the basis of obligation in the Oceanic societies she is considering.

This account is a development of Mauss's insight into the nature of the gift, which he claims may be logically (rather than historically) prior to the more readily recognizable orderings of the unitary polity (with its repressed violence), and the reciprocities of the economy.[4] Groups of humans may retain their sovereignty, and yet relate to one another, not through the ascendencies and subordinations of power, nor through the calculations of trade, but through the gift. Equivalence and violence are both secondary to and built upon the possibilities of generosity. Mauss is invoking an ambiguous force, for it contains the dual aspect of the assertion of worth and the negotiated recognition of that worth. These are in an implicit tension, and he points to the always-present possibility of violence, even of war, as a consequence of the failure of the gift. But the notion has the merit of recalling attention to the fundamental anthropological topic of rank, or that human facts are evaluative.

Weiner's contribution is to concentrate upon the locuses or sites that organize these evaluations in particular case studies and in a particular ethnographic area: she identifies the transmissible objects in which these definitional intensities are at their maximum. These, as we have already suggested, are things that move people, and which therefore create persons and groups, and organize society. Because inalienable possessions endure, their transmission constitutes the group's autonomy, identity, status and authority.[5] And, Weiner adds as a central theme, because women control these objects, or participate in their control, this participation forms a counter to men's economic presence.[6]

Although Weiner's work is based upon societies in Oceania, the broad concept she identifies is useful in talking of the transmission of the farm in Béarn. As we have seen, in Béarn, the property – land, house and livestock – is at once that which confers identity, reputation and personality, and that which one would sacrifice more or less anything to preserve. The farm orders not only the honour, status or rank of the members of the household, but also all their life possibilities, for example, the alternatives of residence and emigration, the degree of authority enjoyed, including local political office, possible marriage partners, and flows of money and labour. The house and its land are the focal point around which local life is ordered. In its orderly transmission, one can see clearly the business of what must be given away – the dowry, and various compensations, the strategies of mortgage and recovery – in order for the inalienable possession to be passed on intact.

Some of the detailed questions Weiner raises are most instructive, too. For example, it would be useful to look at the importance of the sibling relationship (between the heir and his sister, married in to another house) compared to that of husband and wife, or the role of female productive work and property compared with that of men. In the fine detail of the marriage agreements one can glimpse analogies to the flows of female and male goods: in the forms of ancestral goods and disposable chattels, in the separation of goods coming from the husband's and the wife's side, and in the distinction within the dowry between the trousseau and other property.

In sum, the (complex) object of transmission is the single feature that touches everything, including the local landscape, and every aspect of local life: who goes and who stays; who rules and who obeys; who counts for much and who counts for little. Moreover, in this influence, it is the key not only to the family and the neighbourhood, but also to local economics and politics.

Weiner has been criticized for imposing Western categories – of persons and groups, property and ownership, persons and things, and agency – upon Melanesian ethnography.[7] Mark Mosko's view is that Weiner is essentially rethinking Western concepts of commodity and community.[8] Whether this is true of the Melanesian material or not, it is clear that the Pyrenean material has come to prominence in precisely such debates; it lends itself to questioning the self-evidence of Western ideas of equivalence and exchange, and to self-doubt concerning a loss of polity. 'Inalienable possessions' may be a productive concept in the refinement of a Western European self-understanding, even as a formative absence at the heart of our troubled identity.

III

This Western context or an element of reflexivity is also clearly present in the second anthropological idea, that of 'house societies'. Using European noble families as a starting point, Lévi-Strauss took 'the house' to be an intermediate form between simple and complex kinship systems, one in which the language of kinship is put to work to pursue political and economic interests. In medieval noble families, 'the house' combined material and intangible qualities: it comprised the possession and transmission of dignity, origins, kinship names and symbols, position, power and wealth. From this beginning, Lévi-Strauss turned to North American materials and, following Boas, claimed that here the house is likewise a moral person, possessing a domain that comprises both material and immaterial goods. The house in these ethnographic materials is perpetuated by the transmission of its name, its fortune and its titles through a real or fictitious line, and its legitimacy and continuity are defined in terms of the language of kinship, or alliance, or, more often, both together.[9]

Although Lévi-Strauss was concerned with non-European societies, this account would also serve to delineate the Pyrenean house. It is worth asking why it might do so. Lévi-Strauss's perspective is to divide societies into two broad categories. On the one hand, there are societies organized by elementary forms of kinship, unilinear or bilinear. On the other, there are cognatic systems, where the individual finds his position in the social structure and the elements of his status from sources other than the paternal or maternal line. In this framework, the house society draws upon a mixture of forces that were held to be incompatible in the classic ethnographic categories, so that instead of opposing as mutually exclusive patrilineal and matrilineal descent, or residence and descent, or marrying up and marrying down – or marrying in and marrying out – or hereditary right and election, these terms become alternative possibilities, to be selected and employed according to a strategy dictated by pursuing the interests and continuity of the house. Lévi-Strauss was determined to see this condition as an intermediate form between elementary and complex societies.

In their broad significance, Lévi-Strauss's categories of elementary, complex and house societies fit with Le Play's classification of patriarchal, unstable and stem families. The anthropologist had an evolutionary, and quasi-Marxist, perspective, so that the intermediate form is a transitional stage. The sociologist's interest, however, was to find a third way between the subjection of the individual to society on the one hand, and the reduction of society to the sum of individual actions on the other. For Le Play, as we know, the significance of the stem family was that it was an intermediate form lying between the reactionary (and primitive) patriarchal family and the modern (and progressive) unstable family, uniting the qualities both of tradition and of adaptability.

I noted earlier what a powerful ideological 'operator' Le Play created. One could identify the two poles between which one was steering – paternalism and anarchy – as the Ancien Régime and the Revolution, or as state power and capitalism, according to taste. The interest of the operator, I think, is this. However coarse the distinction is between the Leviathan of the State and the State of Nature, for instance, or between state power and the market, the preoccupation to find the bases for civil society, and to defend it against such threats as unbounded political authority, and self-interest and greed, is an enduring one – one that fits better with contemporary interests than the notion that civil society is a transitional state, between supposed primitive and advanced societies. Le Play's concern with the enduring importance of civil society is a good deal more liberal than Lévi-Strauss's perspective; it is also, interestingly, truer to Mauss's preoccupations, which haunt both discussions of inalienable possessions and those of house societies.

To reiterate a conclusion from the earlier chapter, then, the significance of the stem family, or the house, is that it stands as a trope for civil society. And in its ambiguities, it raises the question as to whether the forms of civil society do not in some sense shape the forms of both political and economic life and, indeed, create the possibility of their existence, being then of a different logical order, not altogether different from 'the gift'.

IV

These concerns are, of course, primarily European in focus, and may best be pursued by looking at ethnographic cases. With that in mind, let me draw attention to a remarkable survey of forms of transmission in peasant Europe by Georges Augustins, and to his account of the house.[10] His book would merit translation; it is of particular interest both because it privileges French materials and because Augustins's original fieldwork was in the Hautes Pyrénées, so he has detailed insight into what has been called the Pyrenean family. Augustins identifies the house as one polar type of the perpetuation of forms of human life and order through property. As he points out – and as we know – the house as a form of transmission privileges the integrity of the property at the expense of the kin group, by uniting in a single heir the transmission both of authority and of all goods, movable and immovable.

It is worth examining Augustins's account in a little detail, starting from this apparent opposition between the integrity of the property and the interests of the broader kin group. This opposition appears in many forms, as for example between household and family, and Augustins is following Jean Yver's pioneering work on Northern France,[11] which showed that transmission of wealth is caught in a tension between residential and kin principles. Augustins's refinement, or redefinition, of the terms of the problem is twofold. First, he suggests that, in principle, there are two ends that confront any society: that of perpetuating a social entity, and that of shaping individual destinies. In this way, he places the question of (in our terms) civil society at the centre of sociological enquiry. And from his survey of materials, he distinguishes different ways of reconciling these two ends. In his account, two broad classes of solution exist. But here he introduces his second point, and real innovation. He distinguishes the transmission of authority – of role and status – from the transmission of property; the one he terms succession (to office), the other inheritance (of goods). In this way, he avoids giving priority either to the family or to the household, for the solution depends rather upon whether succession (to office) or inheritance (of goods) is privileged.

The house is of the first kind; it is residential in form, and the key is a single successor (who need not, at the limit, be kindred). In the north of France, on the other hand, inheritance is the lynchpin, and the destiny of the kin group through division is privileged. Here, the key actor is not the house, but the kin group – either made up of brothers and sisters, or of brothers only – and the principle of kinship holds over that of residence.

This analysis redefines the tension between residential and kin principles, and Augustins's further distinction between succession and inheritance allows him to discriminate between three types – house, lineage and parentela[12] – and to identify both what he terms mixed and hinge types. The interest of this approach is that, rather than identifying the household, or the family, or relations of authority (egalitarian or inegalitarian), as the primary unit, it focuses on the combination of the social forces that simultaneously organize the distributions and relations of power and kinship, wealth and destiny. It is concerned not with a single generative essence, but with the elementary forms of not only kinship, but also political, legal, economic and cultural life.

V

This approach is of interest in one further, particular refinement for the light it throws upon the notion of 'strategy'. This has enjoyed a certain prestige in recent sociological theory, and it is a concept to which the Pyrenean region has made a direct contribution. We have seen that the overwhelming importance accorded to the project of perpetuating the house is expressed simultaneously in the flexibility of the system – with respect to such topics as masculinity, primogeniture, adoption and dowry – and its stability. If the 'stem family' had better be redefined as 'the house', nevertheless Le Play had identified a principle of considerable sociological interest, one that can plausibly be recast in terms of the analogy of strategic thinking. We might say that because we are concerned with what I have called an elementary form of social life – and not the expression of some timeless concept or essence, such as family or household or authority – the processes in question will readily resemble those of a mind at work.

I can point to two direct lines of descent from Le Play to strategy theory. First, there is Tilly and Scott's analysis of the role of women in the domestic economy of pre-industrial times, based upon Le Play's monographs;[13] and second, there are Bourdieu's important articles concerning the Béarnais family (which show considerable theoretical awareness of both Le Play's approach and the Lavedan monograph).[14] The concept of 'family strategies' is a product of the region.

While it is possible to criticize the notion's lack of clarity as a theoretical concept, both because the analogy with mind is taken to establish the reality of strategic thinking, and because it has become generalized and applied to a wide variety of social contexts, there is little doubt that it has a certain ethnographic 'fit' in the region. And it needs to be born in mind that the solutions that it offers concerning questions of authority and transmission lend themselves to a broad political discourse concerning projects of social reform, and that this has supported its wide sociological relevance. As an intermediate or third form, the Pyrenean stem family, and the associated notion of strategy, has made a contribution to social history as well as to family sociology and social anthropology.[15]

Ethnography is not, of course, the sole source for the theory of strategy. In sociology and economics, rational choice theory plays a large role in discussions of strategy, as does Barth's transactionalism in a strand of anthropological thought.[16] Rational choice theory is predicated upon the maximizing individual, and the summation of the effects of such behaviour, giving rise to problems concerning the scale of social action and the scope of social actors' choices. This is less a problem for Bourdieu, his theory emerging as it does from empirical examples rather than abstract concepts. It allows the linking together of questions of individual choice and social structure. Criticisms nevertheless concentrate upon the problems of, firstly, with whose strategies we are concerned – those of the actors or those of the historians – and, secondly, whether their strategies are long- or short-term, unreflective or meditated upon, aggressive or conservative, and so forth. These ambiguities largely result from the concretizing of the metaphor of mind.

I draw attention to the concept of strategies, then, less as a supposed resolution to certain problems, and more as a regional product. It lends itself to certain interpretations, and draws together – as has been suggested – a number of terms that are generally kept apart: the domestic and the political, the familial and the economic. Indeed, it draws us on to the second broad area I wish to consider, that of local politics. The concept of strategy, even if only as a metaphor, draws attention to the role played by the community of houses. Succession to the role of head of a house not only involves the task of managing the wealth of the house, not least through marriage and inheritance, but also involves possessing rights to common land and pasturage, and to local political office. Once the principles of transmission have been grasped, we can understand how the ethos is less familial than communal, and it is therefore possible to see how it is that all local forms – whether of household, family, farm or politics – may evolve and change without continuity being broken. 'Strategy' is indeed a good metaphor to apply to local politics, as it mixes the two poles of conscious human decision and rational action, on the one hand, with involuntary solidarities and the constraints of custom, on the other.

VI

So let us turn to the subject of local politics. In this part, my focus is upon the authority transmitted with the house, and its wider public effects. I want to consider three topics – eligibility (for election to office), land sales, and European law – as they impinge upon local society. As the scale of effect we are considering expands, questions of causality and of what counts as evidence become more acute. Nevertheless, the business of expanding the horizon is important for clarifying the present – and future – impact of the anthropological categories with which we are concerned, and to see the context to which they contribute. The first and the last topics identify areas to be studied further; the second reports on research conducted by the Geography Department of the local University of Pau.

The first, then, is election to office. Abélès has made clear that, in northern France, eligibility for local political office will be linked to the network of kin and clients that one can mobilize.[17] He notes, further, that different systems of land inheritance will produce different forms of eligibility, and points to the related questions of kin and prestige, social position and local forms of authority. He also raises the question of the role of the *notable*, a category designating persons of local prominence and social authority, as a crucial intermediary between the state and local society.

In Béarn, the following factors have to be taken into account. There is technically a democracy of houses; for example, in decisions pertaining to the common land, woods and pasture of the commune, each head of house has an equal vote. Nevertheless, as we have seen with respect to agricultural questions, there are leaders and followers. In each commune there is a hierarchy of houses, defined by such matters as wealth and prestige, and linked by descent and alliance (and debt). In rural communes, the mayor and the deputy mayors come from the leading families, and the other counsellors from among families that embody local values. All will be heads of houses.

Within a small commune, consensus is always the desired option, but will be contested at intervals. When it is, the mayor is frequently from the biggest farm, and if there is a leader of the opposition, he may represent the main rivals to that family. The oppositions mobilized in such a context are shaped by the dominant moments of the French national political imagination: the Revolution, the Church/State conflict of the 1880s, and the German Occupation and its aftermath.[18] These are translated into such enduring oppositions as Right and Left, Catholic and secular, Collaboration and Resistance. These values are expressed through local persons, and the histories they represent, and the legitimacy they have both inherited and built up. Local politics at this level is both expressed through and prolongs the significance of the house, although, clearly, the one cannot be reduced to the other.

This continues to be true as local government evolves after the decentralization of 1982. The effects of this reform are still emerging, as is its significance.[19] The mayor continues to be an intermediary, negotiating indispensable grants from government bodies, but he needs more technical expertise, for example, concerning employment, tourism, and protection of the environment.[20] Here, questions of scale are important. Decentralization has meant very different things to small communes and to towns: it gives more power to the latter than the former; it is perceived by the former that the state hands over more costs than money to the countryside. It also gives more power to unelected figures – to administrative intermediaries – and to new territorial initiatives that do not map on to electoral constituencies: the *syndicats des communes*, districts, and *pays*, which lie in terms of scale between the commune and the canton, and relate to the centre.

In these new games, however, local leaders have not been diminished; they are the 'strong men' representing civil society to the state, and playing upon its resources.[21] Eligibility continues to be transmitted through kinship links and matrimonial alliances, playing through local political networks. And with multiplicity of office (now under attack), we can glimpse how, within a 'Jacobin' state, the local may have a determinative influence even at national level.

It would be premature, then, to assume that our topic concerns only the smallest scale of communes, although even in the countryside we need to pay attention at the local level to conflicts for political power between incomers and the farmers, for farming is no longer the undisputed, predominant interest. But in local politics, questions of land use still play an important part, and as the peasants keep hold of the land they tend to make their strategies prevail.

VII

This brings us onto our second broad topic. It concerns the place of land sales and economic development in the commune, which forms a large part of the business of local government. We have to ask whether there are local factors at work in these processes. Here we are fortunate to have a series of studies organized by Guy Di Méo, an economic geographer from the University of Pau. One of these studies, for example, contrasts two towns in the region, one of which has developed while the other has stagnated; the one seemingly integrating the new, the other apparently being destroyed by it.[22] Di Méo looks at such factors as the ownership of land, the ideology of sale or retention, the control of local government, and the response to central government initiatives. These are all factors that dovetail with the issue raised in the previous chapter concerning families that leave the village and move to the town on account of their wealth rather than their poverty. I have not the space here to examine the whole question of the relation of villages to the local towns, though it is an important topic; instead, I want to look at another study, concerned with the question of land sales.[23]

The focus of this work is the expansion, in the post-war period, of residential housing in villages within the orbit of the regional capital. Di Méo is concerned to give some precision to the concept of suburban spread, or *péri-urbanisation*. A number of questions need to be posed. First, where does the land come from that is built upon? By studying the mortgage register (a summary of notarial documents), it can be shown that very little agricultural land is given up to this purpose, and that such as there is, is in small plots and so of little agricultural use. We do not see the disbanding of farms, but rather, farmers looking for capital funds to promote the farm.[24] This is related to the fact that local agriculture gives a good living, in both the dominant local forms: of maize, beasts and crops relating to animal husbandry in combination, and of market gardening. There has been little diminution in farm numbers (since 1945), in marked contrast to other regions of France. This surely relates in a loose fashion to the local forms of inheritance.[25]

Second, two thirds of the area of land transferred between persons involves successions, although successions constitute only one third of the number of transfers effected. However, division affects only one sixth of this area; it effectively concerns only small plots: the sharing out of non-viable holdings, one may hazard, among non-farming heirs.

So, with respect to the land that is sold out of agricultural use, the third question is: To what extent does ownership by city dwellers precede its functional change? I have hinted at the abandonment of the land as wealthy farmers become *rentiers* and city dwellers: a falling-out from the top end of the system. Is their next move to sell their property for development? Di Méo's conclusion – in these communes around Pau – is that over the twenty years between the 1960s and the 1980s, twice as much land came on to the building market from non-agricultural owners than from farmers.[26]

Even so, this needs clarification. The selling up by city dwellers who were formerly farmers must be a transitional stage: the disappearance from any important role in the countryside of the dominant classes, a high bourgeoisie who live in the city but have rural interests and family connections. Around Pau, in any case, these members of the upper classes were never very powerful in the countryside compared with small- and medium-sized resident owners and the effects of collective (communal) ownership. Moreover, the agricultural revolution of the 1950s – the introduction of hybrid maize, the suppression of hedges, the increase of field size and the clearing of marginal land to bring it into agricultural use – effectively eliminated this group's tenuous hold.[27]

Indeed, land transfers have been largely local. In the 1950s and 1960s, the local dominant classes, who were not notable for their dynamism, sold up land that was not bringing in much through rent or sharecropping, and it was bought by younger farmers. They invested in farm property and equipment, looked to education and training, and built up the co-operative movement. Modernization saw the consolidation of farms.

Most of the land sold by families who have moved out of agriculture therefore remains in agricultural use. Indeed, analysis of land transfers indicates that only about one fifth has been for the purposes of new building.[28] Of those building, most are older, wealthier couples, professionals or retired people. However, more than half those building already live in the commune, or in an adjacent commune; this includes a proportion of cases where building is to enable the generations on the farm to live separately. Di Méo believes that we are not dealing principally with a centrifugal force distributing families out from the city, Pau, but rather with a local Brownian motion, micro-migrations associated with social improvement and the search for a better environment. In fact, in a zone where speculation has raised land prices, the opportunity to build is usually a function of inheritance, or a gift from parents: a city-based family building in the village is usually connected to an agricultural family. The notion of incomers, then, has to be strongly nuanced: although incomers will have urban ideologies, attitudes and incomes, they will not, by and large, be indifferent to the agricultural interests in the villages.

Nevertheless, the partial suburbanization of the area around the city is evident, so a fourth question arises as to whether development is controlled, and if controlled, by whom? Here Di Méo's study contrasts the successful control of land use by the farmers to the north of Pau, where larger acreages and maize cultivation predominate, with the fate of the smaller market-gardening farms to the south. The crucial factor is not farm viability, for both types of exploitation are profitable, but the construction by the farming sector of a counter-strategy to the suburban fragmentation of the land.

In one northern commune, the larger and medium-sized farmers have kept political power. They have a leader drawn from their ranks. They have formed a small, homogeneous, modernizing group which has taken over the leadership and moral ownership of various key institutions: the Crédit agricole, the Chambre d'agriculture, the Mutualité social agricole, and the Co-operative movement. And, at the same time, by integrating certain of the incoming professionals in their networks, they have maintained a presence on the Municipal Council. The results are striking. In the 1970s and 1980s, over 1,000 houses were built in the commune, and the population increased from 749 in 1968 to 2,126 in 1986, and a large industrial zone was developed upon communal territory. Yet, at the same time, the area devoted to agriculture increased slightly, and the farmers, benefiting from the improved infrastructure, extended their activities to other communes, sometimes at a distance (the Landes), in this way reinforcing their economic status and their prominent share of local power.[29]

They could achieve this because municipal authority gives its holders the power to control the use of space, through the adoption of certain official development statuses, and the use of powers of economic intervention. The commune in question very early adopted a planning policy for local land use (*plan d'occupation des sols*), with the clear aims of protecting the agricultural use of land, and of defending agricultural land from building and from being broken up. Diffuse development ruins land for agricultural use (just as consolidation improves it). Planning powers were used to locate areas for working class and wealthier housing – the best houses are on the hillsides, the more modest housing along the roads – and for industrial development. They were used, too, to equip the commune with roads, drainage and other utilities, including the agricultural sector in these benefits.

The local politics pursued by the farmers through land development made the two tendencies, of agricultural modernization and the spread of suburbanization, complementary rather than antagonistic. The key factor has been the presence of larger farmers, who have common interests, are used to leadership, and are outward looking. On this basis, a modern, mixed population has been developed, and industry attracted. By these means, too, a tertiary base has been created that pays sufficient taxes to support a large budget, allowing the Municipality to provide good services, and so strengthening the profitability of local agriculture. A virtuous circle is formed, one that shows a considerable continuity with past forms. Or, older forms give a framework to newer forms.

In the contrasting communes, to the south, where there are smaller farms, the farmers have lost political power, even in places where they are numerically more significant,[30] for small farms do not readily produce leaders. In one such community, although all the small farms have heirs and are profitable, there is little farming participation in politics and in power. The commune was late to become involved in planning procedures, and has no zoning with respect to the allocation of land use; its authorities are not alert to farmers' needs. There has been considerable loss of land from agricultural use, and many of the landowners are not resident in the commune, a factor that threatens to continue the process.

We may conclude, first, that planning restrictions are needed in order to support transmission; second, that patterns of political power reflect the distinctions we have noted between the large and the small farmer; and third, that patterns of settlement and land holding continue to transmit some long-lived categories. In short, 'house' society is neither confined to the domestic sphere, nor is it an anachronism: it can be seen at work in the distributions of suburban sprawl and new industries, and more generally in the local politics of contemporary Béarn.

VIII

The third and final aspect of the effects of the Pyrenean house on local political life to which I wish to draw attention is the role played by the representation of local life (of which it is the keystone) in the dialectic of local and national politics. I have in mind two distinct histories, which impinge upon the resources at the disposal of local politicians, and the stakes for which they are playing. Although this is to speak of the Pyrenean house at an ideal or mental level, I believe the effects to be quite as material as in the cases of election to office and land sales and use. And this is despite the double difficulty of tracking ideas and their transformations, and of attributing any specific causality to them. Both themes return to matters raised in the first chapter.

The first history concerns the rise of regionalist politics as a theme in French political life. A major component of this move is a meditation upon French identity after the Revolution, and the place of civil society between the (caricatured) extremes of individualism and state power, epitomized in the couplet, 'we are all anarchists' and 'we follow strong leaders'. The north/south divide has been mobilized in these meditations, associated with such oppositions as German culture to Latin civilization, customary to Roman law, and *langue d'oïl* to *langue d'oc*. Within this broad – and, for the most part, unsatisfactory – set of binary opposites, the regionalist movement has claimed the merits of local particularity and practical wisdom, a democracy of differences and dialectal variations, in contrast to the vices of uniformity, abstraction, Jacobin centralism and the suppression of difference. In this ideology, the Pyrenean family has played a role.

The regionalist movement – thoroughly and appropriately subdivided – has played its part in twentieth-century French politics, taking on conservative, radical and socialist colourings as appropriate, having both Catholic and anti-clerical expressions, and finding its way into both Collaboration and Resistance. Although we cannot follow it now, this is a history worth tracing, not least in its Béarnais form: the local movement in Béarn has been active since 1890, and has intriguingly shown a distinctive form. Unlike the movement elsewhere in the south, where the oppositions between extremes – of Right and Left, for example – have been lived out, the Béarnais movement, true to its Le Playsian calling, has embodied a series of rather un-French compromises.[31]

But the reason I draw attention to this broad history is that the regionalist agenda had its moment, and real effect, in the already mentioned Socialist reform of 1982, which decentralized political power, transferring considerable authority from the Prefect to local politicians. If, as Abélès suggests, the three key dates for understanding local politics in France are 1789, 1880 and 1945, there must be a question as to whether 1982 will in due course have to be added as a fourth. The effects on the ground of this (partial) triumph of the regionalist idea are multiple, still to be studied in detail, and still developing. But one effect is clear: with the new levers of power available, local identity has become an issue that is no longer confined to militants and enthusiasts but is a tool to gain economic aid and political power. The business of representing what is local as a part of local politics has been transformed. For example, one finds local politicians – who have long signalled their eligibility by a capacity to speak the patois – discovering their local roots and starting to defend the particularity of local life. This represents a complete volte-face: previously, they would have regarded any reference to specifically local culture as retrogressive and anti-political.

One might claim, therefore, that the forms of transmission of forms of transmission are multiple – and that the disappearance of local forms is by no means a foregone conclusion: modernity positively reinforces them in certain respects. One unexpected side effect has been that, because regional identity has become of vital interest to tough local politicians, the regionalist movement is in disarray. Certainly, the present generation is very different to their militant parents, born out of 1968: 1982 paradoxically marks the defeat of all the older generation's (impracticable) dreams.[32]

The Pyrenean family plays an honourable but minor part in this first history: it is the epitome of what is at stake in these debates which are essentially about the scale and localization of civil society, though an acquaintance with the local political and cultural literature since 1890 convinces me that, with rare exceptions, it plays there the role of 'the world we have lost'. However, in the second history it plays a more positive role, though one far less tied to the territory.

This second history concerns the importance of Le Play's notions of social reform, in which the Pyrenean family (as we know) formed the keystone. Just as Le Play has had a remarkable progeny in local studies and in broader sociological and historical theories, he has also had a lasting influence on French political thought.

Here again I can only indicate the path we would have to follow to establish this claim. The importance of Le Play, and of the sociological strand – emerging from Bonald – that he represents, lies less in his (debatable) conservatism, and rather – as I have suggested – in his linking the project of social reform to the question of the forms of flourishing of civil society. He rejects both solutions based upon the state or classes and those based upon the individual, looking instead to the 'middle distance', or the intermediate scale, that of family, property relations, work groups, neighbourhoods, churches and other voluntary organizations. This way of thinking is constructed, as we have seen, around a meditation upon what appears to be lost to modern society, or to be repressed as its unconscious: an order structured by separation, hierarchy and interdependence. It therefore gives rise to an approach that emphasizes differences, authority relations, and groups and corporations, in contrast to one based upon identity, equality and the organization of the individual by the benign state or by the class struggle.

In the late nineteenth and early twentieth century, Le Play's influence can be traced in two directions. On the one hand, it appears in the French social Catholicism of Albert Mun, and the strand of radical Catholicism deriving from Lammenais. On the other hand, it is present in the thinking of Action Française, particularly through La Tour du Pin and Charles Maurras.[33] In these writings, the relations of property and authority have been transformed, but they always serve as an emblem of a third way between the alternatives of the individualism of the market and the single power of the – usually socialist – state. In the interwar period, these ideas fed into both Christian Democracy and the 'personalism' of the *Esprit*[34] movement,[35] and led too into the non-fascist ideology of Vichy France.[36] And they may be traced after 1945, through a combination of persons, ideas and movements, notably to the École Normale d'Administration (ENA), founded in 1945, and the European Coal and Steel Community. And these two institutions have in some respects defined the French contribution to the European Community (later the European Union), which is of course a social project that attempts to harness both the liberal market economy and the various states' powers, without being overwhelmed by either.[37]

So the final recension of the representation of transmissions of property in the Pyrenean house to be considered could well be found in European Union social policy, including the recognition of local identities that is a sub-theme of the struggle between the EU and national governments. It has effects on the ground, for it emerges in legislation and, more importantly, offers both financial resources and forms of legitimacy to be exploited by local political actors. It creates the phenomenon, for example, whereby a new generation of regionalist militants (so far, few in number), do not – unlike their parents' generation – make demands primarily of the French state, but rather seek to form alliances with local politicians in order to argue for resources to develop the local economic and cultural identity. In this interplay of interacting representations, the Pyrenean house, by distributing itself between apparently old and immobile forms on the one hand, and new and innovative forms on the other, prolongs itself, transmission transmitted, in much the way that it has done for at least the last seven hundred years.

In short, the effects of the Pyrenean house go a good deal further than the transmission of domestic goods. It lives in political questions of authority, legitimacy, pragmatism and resources at the local and higher levels, which in turn create a context for its domestic prolongation. At the same time, those of us who distrust the Roman law tendencies and the abstract intellectualism of certain European politicians, should perhaps be grateful for the practical understanding it embodies. It is an important component in the advocacy of a human scale and dignity within the European project, which appears to be our future, for good or ill.

IX

I have looked, then, at the discovery of the Pyrenean family, the evidence for its longevity, its current expression, and its potential for future existence. To draw it together in a sentence, my conclusion is that the life of property is curiously multiple, complex and enduring. Or to put it in a slightly less condensed form: in the first place, the delineation of the life of property is multiple. For it is not possible to distinguish transferable property completely from property that cannot be alienated, and to explain the mechanisms of contract, debt and the alienation of goods quite independently from those that allow for a variety of rights – by transmission, lending or mortgage – in the same property. Indeed, to attempt to do so, and to take one term of the opposition and to turn it into a sufficient principle of intelligibility of the social order, is to participate in one of the myths we live by. Then, the delineation of the life of property is complex, in that many levels of 'memory' have to be taken into account. Beyond the forms of family law, they exist in persons' behaviour, and political actions, as well as in the conformations of the land, and economic transactions – and in many other things. And finally, the delineation of the life of property is enduring: we have seen plenty of evidence on this score. I would express it in this way: the form of the life of property is an instance of the conformations of time.

There are also certain wider anthropological issues that may be drawn into the picture. Considered in a broad perspective, the thesis presented here represents both the challenge and the opportunity of ethnography in Western Europe, with its historical depth of materials, density of local variation, and long influence of national institutions. These features are focused in the issue of interpreting the interactions of local and more cosmopolitan forces over time, both in terms of the initiatives each party can take and the marks left or changes effected by the one in the other. In most non-European ethnographic studies it is possible to claim some kind of real separation between the history of the local categories being investigated and the history of the categories of the investigating community. Something of this kind underlies the original project of anthropology, although even in these cases it appears there are complex histories which permit certain anthropological and sociological agendas to find privileged territories which present them with materials appropriate to think through their specific problems.[38]

In Western Europe, however, there can be no pretence of separating the two histories: the metropolitan society, which generates sociological investigators, is in a long-term and close relationship with the local 'provinces', so that its terms and theirs are mutually defining, in a hierarchy of official and unofficial discourses.

Moreover, just as it has become increasingly clear that the more distant 'objects' of anthropological study are not passive, awaiting discovery, but rather negotiate the encounters in which they are met with and perceived, it has also become apparent that these objects have more power to shape the terms in which they are apprehended than was initially acknowledged, so that metropolitan or Western categories bear within them the marks of previous, historical encounters with their 'others'. Within a European country, this process becomes of major importance. Michael Herzfeld is the first to have explored these interactions thoroughly in the case of Greek society.[39] The practices and representations by which a population live have their own history, and have to be drawn from somewhere; likewise, despite an ideology of being from nowhere, the metropolitan population has to gain its ideas from somewhere in particular. The forms of legitimacy and self-obviousness to which it subscribes will have emerged in these long-term processes of negotiation between local and metropolitan ways of life, in which aspects of local categories and institutions will have been taken up and used by the wider population under particular circumstances in its thinking, and applied back to the territories of their original conception, curiously altered. That is why political ideas concerning governance and reform, for example, will only have legitimacy in the eyes of the population if they fulfill certain criteria of common sense, which will relate to popular conceptions of obligation and choice, modelled in part in the experience of what in broad terms we call kinship and alliance. You do not choose your kin, but you can choose whom to marry, within important limits: these experiences of local practices offer basic models or frames for a whole range of social functions, divided into prescription and permission, of what you must do and what you may do, setting unconscious limits to the kinds of activity considered to be legitimate or illegitimate or, at the limit, to what we might call rational and irrational behaviour. These are in practice not universal categories, despite their cosmopolitan provenance, but will differ in form and content according to place and history: they will show a certain particularity, responding to the particularity of local categories.

Local, small-scale, anthropological activities of mapping out relations – between humans, between human and non-human life, between institutions, between places, and between other forms – will therefore be experienced at 'higher' levels, in wider activities and broader categories, in such matters as national politics, economics, culture, and religion. This is not a simple matter, however, for it is not just a matter of reflection between levels, so that local categories appear untransformed in other places. Rather, there are specific histories of local matters being taken up and incorporated into wider stories, and then returning to be applied, instantiated on the ground; and, from the other perspective, there are local histories of self-definition and self-defence, of revealing certain aspects of local life to an outside gaze and, by so doing, of concealing other aspects, that together constitute the continuities of that local life. The preceding chapters have been concerned with the description of one such case.

X

From this account, two broad conclusions follow. First, although the local scale and broader perspectives – local history and national history, ethnography and politics, local culture and high culture – cannot be fully identified one with the other, nor can they be treated as wholly separate. They are mutually implicated, in ways that cannot be anticipated but have to be explored and narrated, and the marks of their mutual implication over time – their mutual effects – have to be identified. Second, different institutions – familial, agro-economic, political, legal, and cultural – are also engaged one with another, and one cannot readily be separated out and analysed in isolation from the others. We are dealing, in short, with what Mauss terms 'total' social phenomena; it is worth remarking, against the conventional expectation, that such complex social facts appear in European ethnography and history, and play a central and continuing role in the complexities of modern culture.[40]

These considerations give rise to the form and limits of this account which, although it represents a great deal of research, analysis and synthesis, only sketches out the topics and perspectives that need to be embraced in offering a description of one such total phenomenon and attempting to portray its various interrelations over time. An anthropological rather than a historical description, it focuses upon the most important issues and points to the places where other matters fit in; I believe that the form adopted allows these quite difficult issues to be presented with a certain clarity and brevity.

In the following two chapters, I propose to develop and illustrate the thesis proposed here through two case studies: the first an analysis of a novel by Simin Palay, written in Béarnais; the second a discussion of the Béarnais ethnography of Pierre Bourdieu and its place in his work and thought. The former focuses in fine detail upon the local reception and indeed generation of 'the new', the latter upon the contribution the local may make to wider debates and the mechanisms by which it does so. In each case the materials discussed are taken simultaneously as contributing to the understanding of the life of property in Béarn and as exemplifying that life in the texts.

Notes

1. See Weiner (1992).
2. Ibid.: 37.
3. Ibid.: 40.
4. See Mauss (1950a[1924]).
5. Weiner (1992: 23–43).
6. Ibid.: 3.
7. See Mosko (2000: 385).
8. Ibid.: 392.
9. See Lévi-Strauss (1991: 435).
10. Augustins (1989). For an appreciation, see Déchaux (1991).
11. Yver (1966).
12. A group defined by cognatic kinship (Augustins 1989: 172).
13. Tilly and Scott (1987[1978]).
14. These articles are collected in Bourdieu (2002a).
15. Although it should not be isolated in this respect from a cluster of related concepts, including the notions of developmental cycles and the domestic group. Cf. Viazzo and Lynch (2002).
16. For a recent discussion of these trends, see James (2003: 33ff).
17. Abélès (1991[1989]).
18. Cf. Abélès (1986:14).
19. The effects of the legislation, of course, are not precisely as was intended. For an initial survey, see Levy (1999). The movement for reform owed something at least to regional movements for minority languages post-1968; we shall touch on the effects of this achievement below.
20. See Abélès (1984: 327).
21. Cf. Abélès (1986:12–13).
22. Di Méo (1987).
23. Di Méo and Guerrero (1985).
24. Ibid.: 34.
25. For earlier confirmation of this hypothesis, see Saint-Macary (1939).
26. Di Méo and Guerrero (1985: 37).
27. See ibid.: 39; cf. Lerat (1963).
28. Di Méo and Guerrero (1985: 40).
29. Ibid.: 45.
30. Ibid.: 45.
31. Hence talk of an east/west opposition being as or more important than a north/south divide: Dinguirard, personal communication. See also Sarpoulet (2005), Barraqué and Thibon (2004).
32. See, e.g., Jeanjean (1992).
33. See Silver (1982: 303, note 28).
34. A left-wing, Catholic journal founded in 1932 by Edouard Mounier, and re-founded after 1945.
35. Personalism was an anti-liberal, anti-individualist, anti-political creed, with left-wing, Catholic-ecumenical, pro-European and federalist tendencies; it influenced Jacques Delors, and Vatican II (see Laughland 1997: 62 ff).

36. The three bases of the national revolution were the anti-democratic nationalism of Action Française; the Personalism of young Catholics; and corporatist economics: intermediate bodies standing against state power. See Laughland (1997) for continuities of political and economic thinking, and Hellman (1993) for persons, ideas and institutions. Cf. Aron (1954: 196–217).
37. Present critics of the EU like to emphasize the National Socialist vision of a Europe united against the twin threats of Marxism and gold (e.g., Laughland (1997: 61) on anti-capitalist and corporatist thinking). A more nuanced view would encompass the wider concerns of those seeking a lasting European peace, which set in a new framework various prewar concerns, including the alienation of youth, the destruction of the social fabric by the Depression and inflation, and the rise of nationalisms. 'Collaboration' between Germany and France, upon new bases, still has to be the key to a European renaissance, according to these thinkers.
38. See, e.g., Fardon (1990).
39. See Herzfeld (1987) for a programmatic statement, and subsequent works, esp. Herzfeld (1992).
40. Cf. the conclusion from an earlier, English, study: Jenkins (1999: 219).

Chapter 5

MARRIAGE, INHERITANCE AND SOCIAL CHANGE IN A GASCON NOVEL: SIMIN PALAY'S *LOS TRES GOJATS DE BÒRDAVIELHA*

I

Simin Palay's novel *Los tres gojats de Bòrdavielha* ('The three young men of the Old Farm') was published in 1934.[1] The account is written in Béarnais Gascon throughout,[2] and is the first novel to be written in the language. Its writing belongs to a period of intensive effort on the part of Palay (1874–1965) and the poet Miquèu Camelat (1871–1962)[3] to produce means to serve the revival of the local language. In 1909, Palay and Camelat distanced themselves from the journal *Reclams* ('Echoes'), produced by the regionalist Félibrige organization L'Escole Gastoû Febus (EGF), on the grounds of the amount of French it employed, and founded a popularly aimed newspaper, *La bouts de la tèrre* ('The voice of the land'), published entirely in Béarnais. In the same year they began the project (in conjunction with the EGF) of a Gascon–French dictionary, which appeared in 1932. The novel forms a third strand in this work: Palay states in the foreword that he wrote it around 1914, although it was only published twenty years later.

In the 1934 foreword, Palay claims that he had wished to portray Béarnais life at a period when the region, having recovered from the upheavals that followed the Revolution, had regained its rhythm. He had wanted to show the concerns of that small world in the middle third of the nineteenth century and, having published some articles under the rubric *petita vita* ('everyday life') in the magazine *Reclams*, had begun a book on the same theme. However, the Great War and other matters, he writes, changed the course of life of these people, and *Los tres gojats* is the only part that he completed.[4] It is effectively only a fragment, and was set aside, being published at a later time in a different context.

At first sight, the book adopts a familiar literary form, offering a retrospection and a memorial; it is indeed subtitled 'a Béarnais family of the last century', and its subject is the end of a Béarnais family, 'the Fall of the House of Bòrdavielha'. This literary form lends itself to a conservative political and social discourse on the family and the countryside.[5] Moreover, the condition of the peasant family – portrayed as being about to disappear – gives a clue as to why it might have served as a suitable vehicle to express the condition of the minority language: the state of the language is replicated in the condition of its speakers.

Nevertheless, these observations do not exhaust the interest of the book, for it is a complex ethnographic document.[6] Rather than focusing on the language movement and the language – save, in the latter case, with respect to certain ethnographic details and citations – I am interested in a reading of the novel that takes seriously its local perspective. This may be construed at two levels.

In the first place, Palay was born into an artisanal Béarnais family, with a father who composed and recited both in French and in the dialect,[7] and the novel offers detailed materials concerning the habits, values and practices of the local society, for the narrative turns upon issues of marriage, property and inheritance within a Béarnais farming family. As we know, there are available to us detailed ethnographic and sociological accounts of Béarnais peasant society.[8] The interest of Palay's account with respect to these writings is twofold. First, as an informed local source it serves to introduce in quite a complete way the various elements concerned in the life of property in Béarn, without, however, offering a sociologist's comprehensive synthesis. We can note where his local account gives detail, and where it occludes or ignores matters. Second, Palay offers an unusually detailed account of the psychological investments the various actors have in aspects of local life, expressed in emotions and motivations, and so of the way in which the interactions of everyday family life, based in the relations between the sexes, generations and households, are bound up with and play in and out of local issues of transmission and marriage. Following Bourdieu, we can call these schemes of perception and appreciation 'dispositions'.[9] Moreover, the detailed account of motivation allows Palay to relate the plot's successive crises to current events in law and politics, in an interplay between local and national levels. This invocation of the wider frame is sometimes absent or underplayed in ethnographies, and left to social historians.[10]

Palay does not wholly succeed. From a literary point of view, the book is imperfect: the overall narrative lacks any sense of necessary connection, and each crisis is first contrived and then inconsequential. Nevertheless, minor literature of this kind serves ethnographic interests better than a well-drawn narrative that inexorably draws us into its own concerns and mechanisms. Another, in this case French, account of the disappearance of a Béarnais family, Charles de Bordeu's *Le dernier maître* (1889),[11] is better written, but the setting is incidental to the motivations of the characters described and local categories are effectively absent from the plot. Palay's less sophisticated novel is both more accurate and more accessible as a social document.[12]

In the second place, Palay's novel would only be of limited interest if it simply pertained to the past. But it does something rather different, for it also offers an account of change. It succeeds in integrating local and more cosmopolitan perspectives, and contains a detailed description of the factors involved in the evolution of relations concerning property and personality. Moreover, it offers some sort of theory as to how the elements articulate and interact with legal and political events. In short, the novel contains an account of how a local society, rather than simply suffering change passively, both generates and projects change: modernity is at least in part a locally generated phenomenon. The novel offers us an indigenous perspective on history, one that may be of wide interest, for it suggests that local actors play a more significant historical role than is often supposed, a claim that gives rise to a number of issues.

First of all, Palay's account of how the local world actively participates in history may be related to the regionalist politics being developed by Camelat and himself, a politics that both offers a critique of local society and a way forward. The politics on offer is far from being a simple celebration of a world that is being lost, and in this respect it both contrasts with the melancholic and nostalgic atmosphere of Bordeu's book and is somewhat concealed by the conventional form of his narrative.

This viewpoint draws, moreover, on contemporary local resources. Although cast in a past idiom, describing life in the mid-nineteenth century, Palay's novel also concerns a contemporary world that has come out of this past and the possibilities it contains. It offers an account of how the local world generates both 'traditional' and 'modern' events, and how these are expressed in encounters with wider forces. In doing so, it simultaneously offers a description of how this world presents and conceals itself and its activity, offering itself to an outside gaze in the form of 'being about to disappear'. The novel not only offers an account of the world it describes and emerges from, but embodies, in part unconsciously, the ways that world works and interacts with our – the observer's – world. It makes our understanding of the local society more complicated, in part because it reveals the power that society operates over how we understand it.

Last, because it pushes us in this direction, the novel offers a partial corrective to the perspective adopted by many ethnographies, social histories and other writings on the region which are cast in a past idiom, uncritically accepting the face that local society offers to the outside world.

These are strong claims for a book published in small numbers, written in a minority language, and which has not attracted much attention. To establish them, I shall first consider Palay's portrayal of the successive crises that confronted the members of a prominent Béarnais family over the division of property and the possibilities of marriage in the aftermath of the introduction of the Civil Code. (A good deal of quotation is justified by the book's obscure status.) I shall then look in turn at such ethnographic topics as the house, authority, character, property and its transmission, and marriage, in order to describe the motivations contained within local categories and social order, and their complex relation to modernity. Then I will sketch a sociological interpretation of the material, explaining and refining certain of its features, before considering the book's climax in the politics of 1848, to demonstrate the interpenetrating of local social forms with political events. I conclude with a summary of the account of history and social change contained in the narrative.

II

The novel's subject is the fall of a house – a house in the sense explained in the previous chapters, as when we speak of a noble family – simultaneously incorporating persons, land, buildings, wealth, descent and reputation.[13] In a short and economical introduction, Palay begins with the building, describing its appearance of worth, its size, solidity, the height of its roof, and the great chimneys, these features all serving to indicate the antiquity and honour of the family. He then turns to the family: they are both members of the minor nobility and of farming stock, with a wide local reputation – honoured in the local capital, Pau, and in Bayonne, but not as far as Paris. This reputation is embodied in the master, the head of the house, who is known to the dignitaries of both circles: respected by the cattle traders in the local market towns (Orthez, Morlàas), and received by the elite in Pau. An ancestor had sat in the local parliament, the Estates of Béarn, and some younger brothers of the house had served (as lawyers) on the supreme court (*Cor maja*) of the (feudal) viscounty.

The people of Bòrdavielha – the house name – are, in short, a good family. Indeed, the book as a whole is concerned with good families, with the elite, in carefully graded ranks. The ordinary people, farm workers and others, scarcely appear beyond the occasional mention of their presence at meals, at festivals, and at ceremonies such as a wedding or a funeral. The servants are, however, integrated into the house. In an organic image,[14] the author describes the unity of masters and servants as that of a single body – the masters the head and the servants the arms – with a single soul. He also refers to their social integration.[15]

There is, therefore, a distinction to be made between the physical properties of the building and the value of the house: the one serves to symbolize the other. The house has a name, and a certain reputation locally, and that is shared by all who live there: the house includes members by descent, marriage or simply residence. And each house has a distinct reputation, forming a detailed local order.

This careful attention to local detail and its use in pointing up these distinctions is repeated through the book. Bòrdavielha is accurately located between Denguin and Lescar, which lie in the flat, fertile plain of the valley of the Gave de Pau. The local geography is meticulously portrayed throughout. Likewise, the house has the physical appearance of a fortified country house; it is different to the surrounding farmhouses, and is known locally as 'the castle' (*lo castèth*).[16] The terms employed locally for the master and his wife are also differentiated: they are known as *lo mossur* and *la madama* (which are French forms), and not by the more common Béarnais terms *lo mèstre* and *la dauna*; likewise, their sons are *Mossur Jan, Loïs* and so forth. The local world is constructed out of the significance given these physical and linguistic discriminations; in such a household, the author remarks, masters and servants eat together in the same room without effacing distance or respect.[17]

III

Having established the continuities of the house, Palay immediately introduces the other protagonist in the story, the law. Or, to be more precise, new laws and, with them, new ideas. 'A good family, certainly. But at the time with which we are concerned, in 1840, the new laws and the stir from Paris had somewhat disturbed it'.[18]

Perhaps more profoundly than being the story of a house, the book is concerned with an alteration in the nature of authority. The new legal possibilities both reflect and facilitate this alteration, and the book is a meditation upon the interplay, at a given moment, between two notions of authority, one portrayed as being in essence local and traditional, and the other as being more cosmopolitan and newer. At the same time, the notions compete and interact within a single family, and within each member of that family. The study portrays the evolution of authority through the choices that each person consciously makes in turn; the grounds of their decisions, their values, even if contradictory and divisive, are already within them. The story therefore is concerned not with an outside imposition, or a moment of imperialism, but with an inward change of bearings under particular circumstances. It is an attempt to describe a local psychology, an identity.

The laws of inheritance pinpoint the issue, evoking an old opposition between written law and custom. Local practice, following custom, is that the eldest son inherits without division.[19] This is the system of primogeniture, ensuring the continuities that together compose Bòrdavielha: the continuities of property, blood and reputation, which the name symbolizes. Revolutionary law, however, had universalized the practice of dividing an inheritance between all the legitimate offspring of a union, and the compulsory division of the property this entails inevitably threatens the continuity of the house. As Palay writes, 'As long as the eldest, following custom, had by right been the heir, the position at Bòrdavielha had not changed ... but once eldest sons were obliged to acknowledge the legitimate claims of their younger brothers and sisters, the houses of Béarn were greatly shaken and the day-to-day life of the region a good deal altered'.[20]

The story begins when the master of Bòrdavielha dies (in 1839) at the age of fifty-three, leaving a widow and three adult sons in their twenties, Jan, Loïs and Andrèu, bringing the issue of inheritance to the fore for the first time since the changes in the law of succession.

> The father, having no faith in the new laws, had left all the property by his will to the eldest, together with the usual charges. Although he knew the will could be contested, certain in his mind and conscience that the old custom was best, he left the responsibility to his first-born of protecting the mother-house intact, to perpetuate the hearth of the race and to preserve the family's shelter. He had not wanted to go against himself by a division according to the civil law of Paris; Béarnais custom was tried and tested; it was best to hold to it.[21]

The opposition is clearly laid out, between an undivided and a divided inheritance, between Béarnais custom and new Parisian (or French) civil law. Equally clearly, so is what is at stake: along with the old custom goes the integrity of the house, the perpetuation of the line, and the continuation of a certain way of life, defined by hierarchy and obligation – command for some, shelter for others. In brief, a certain model of authority is at issue.

The father embodied this authority. The future crisis is anticipated in a brief encounter between him and Andrèu, the youngest son, who is training to be a lawyer, and through whom, appropriately enough, modern ideas are first introduced into the house. The apprentice lawyer raises the question in terms of the equality of the brothers, in nature and before God: 'You would admit, the young man said, that we are all your sons, the younger ones as well as the eldest! Weren't we all born the same, naked but of the same blood and filled with the same life? Aren't we equal before God?'[22]

The father invokes a wholly sociological set of reasons, with a theological sheet anchor, to meet these individualist and natural law claims, and to defend the principles of difference and hierarchy, of the division of labour and the distribution of rights and responsibilities.

> In order best to guarantee the good running of things, to maintain the land in the ordered state that serves everybody's peace, we need those who command and those who obey. For a family to be what it ought, it needs a head. The master takes the major responsibilities and it is right that he has the major part of the house's goods. His father should give him authority over everything he is able to, because it is he who must look after those who come after. The true family, following the will of God, is the one that endures and that endures always united and linked to the land of the ancestors, as flesh is to bone.[23]

He concludes this defence of local values by declaring that a man is something, a family more, a region (*pays*) still more.

In this account, the conservative nature of the father's sociological explanation, concerned with the differentiation of roles and opportunities, and their ranking and interdependence, contrasts with the radical nature of the son's natural law account, with its emphasis upon identity, equality and independence. They contain very different accounts of obligation, liberty and human flourishing; they also contain very different accounts of time. And we might remark that, while reflection upon social relations is not tied to a conservative position, in French thinking it begins there.[24]

On the other hand, although its subject matter is authority, the father's account bears no authority of itself. His dogmatic statement simply overwhelms the son's interrogation for the moment. Palay suggests the contrast is between the latter's intelligence and education and the father's experience – *la vita-vitanta*, 'life lived', is Palay's expression, which plays an important role in his journalism. We might gloss this opposition as one between theoretical and practical reason. The contrast contains within itself an account of the period, as the balance shifts from one to the other, from local to cosmopolitan, from experience to the ideal, from time to the abstract outside time. This shift is triggered, in strictly local terms, by the father's death.

IV

Although the story that follows will conclude with the disappearance of a house, we should note at the outset that it does not include an explanation of that disappearance, which is due to contingent, unrelated causes. For the threat of division is contained. A further story – behind the narrative of an alteration in the nature of authority, and behind the telling of the fall of a house – is the entry of theoretical reason into a practical world, and the factors in that world that favour its penetration. It is through the legal possibility of equal inheritance between the brothers that it gains entry.

This metropolitan possibility only gains access, though, through local conditions: in this case, the awareness on the part of the young heir, Jan, that times have changed. This awareness is itself a function of the heterogeneity of local time, for the new master, simply through lack of experience, cannot exert the same authority as his father. The point of transmission of authority is necessarily a point of vulnerability, for authority here is a compound of tradition and reputation, and the realization of that tradition in terms of a personal apprenticeship over time. This is local time expressed in terms of a practical memory of the past, and re-enacted through experience; in both forms being consented to and acknowledged by the people around. The initial point of weakness, of openness to change, is contained within the local texture of persons formed over time. Moreover, there is evidence from legal documents that the moment of transmission of authority in a house has always been one of vulnerability and anxiety. This is borne out in the novel by the fact that the extinction of the house results from the death of Jan's son in 1870.

We are dealing therefore with a case of the local reception of the new. In 1840, a year after their father's death, Jan is twenty-eight, Loïs twenty-five and Andrèu twenty-four. The three are good friends. Jan is a man of strength and good sense, the image of his father, with whom he worked in harness as heir presumptive. Loïs is something of a cipher, devoted like his elder brother to the land, and also to his family, respecting his elder brother, and admiring the younger's skill with words. Andrèu, as we know, is training to be a lawyer, in Toulouse.[25]

Given the vulnerability of the eldest son, a good deal hangs upon Andrèu's character and choice of career, for he is the catalyst for change. Of the three, he is their mother's favourite. This is important, for through her a certain hereditary disposition is introduced. She came from the castle of Pèira-clara, near Lembeye in Vic-Bilh (the north-east part of Béarn), and from a comparable, or even more distinguished, family, but one that in some respects is the reverse of that of Bòrdavielha. The men of her family used to be received at court in Paris. It is from this strain that there enters an interest in politics and a taste for luxury, and also the self-interest required to achieve them. Her mother ran things inside and outside the house, while her father was impractical; he enjoyed hunting, books and writing, and his head was full of follies.[26] Moreover, they produced no son to inherit. This household is, then, an inversion of all the qualities represented by Bòrdavielha. So a certain abstract, cosmopolitan, idle and bookish strand, coupled with a social infertility, forms a flaw or fault line running through the latter household. If it is associated with the female line – and, as we have seen, female goods are transmitted independently of male property – it also manifests itself in the feminine intelligence, expressed in sensitivity to ideas and enthusiasms, shown by the male members of that line.

This fault line which runs through the group also emerges within each individual. It represents a potentiality for modernity that anticipates the alteration of the countryside, a form of indigenous heterogeneity that should cause us to wonder to what extent modernity is a product of the local society, rather than an externally imposed change. Change is a potential within the local disposition; modernity is a local fatality rather than a historical destiny.

The use of the term fault line or flaw is not to impute any failure of character to the brothers' mother who, as wife and widow, ran the household effectively and was charitable. But she was sympathetic to Andrèu's ideas and aspirations, and perhaps indulgent to his weaknesses. Andrèu was educated – at the Collège de Pau and the Faculty of Law at Toulouse – and had a taste for novelty and stimulation; he was drawn to the town; he rose late and dressed carefully. This is of a piece with his ability at conversation, and with his interest in politics, which he had gained in Toulouse. There is indeed an opposition between Pau and Toulouse: the family had anticipated that Andrèu would rise in the service of the courts in Pau, whereas he chooses to stay in the courts in Toulouse.[27] And Toulouse serves both to represent cosmopolitan as opposed to local values, and as a relay for ideas from Paris, which thereby descend to Pau and the surrounding countryside. There is a charged symbolic geography that facilitates the commerce of ideas.

The fault line in Andrèu is expressed less, then, in the choice of the law as a profession than by the attraction of Toulouse. Apart from a taste for luxury and stimulation, the experiences of Toulouse and of the law there hint at more serious moral flaws. Andrèu is essentially ambitious, and tends to take a sophistic stance. For example, he has a poor fellow student writing his Latin thesis on his behalf, and he defines a lawyer, to his brother's disgust, as someone who takes on the mind, conscience and appetites of his client. But at the same time, he has inherited sufficient moral qualities from his parents to prevent his contesting the division of the property, and to guard him against the banal excesses (alcohol, women) of his fellow students: he has the threefold protection of his family's rectitude, his father's advice, and his desire to succeed.[28]

Early in the story, the desire to succeed is balanced by a certain idleness: he considers the possibility of living off the income from his inheritance, living locally and marrying advantageously. But his love of novelty, movement and luxury leads Andrèu to an interest in politics, and this awakens ambition in him. Here Palay's conservative narrative predominates. The desire for novelty, power and wealth are all connected, and associated in this account with radical politics; as a set, they contrast with the conservative politics of wealth represented by Jan and the countryside. This radical politics is an expression of the universal disturbance of minds that follows periods of political intensity – the Revolution, in this case – as we are told at the beginning of the novel. Palay summarizes the radical spirit as a restless desire for novelty, combined with a lack of experience, perhaps better expressed as a desire to prove oneself against those in authority. Politics, in this view, comes down to the ability to excite the desires of the electors so as to gain power, in order to introduce novelty. Progress is a form of restlessness designed to replace those in power.[29]

This combination of novelty, power and wealth emerges in the sequence, at the beginning of the third section, which deals with Andrèu's fate, after the defence of his thesis, once he is launched as a lawyer. He begins to gain notice at the bar in criminal cases and to attract aristocratic clients in civil ones, and so has the prospect of wealth. He mixes with lawyers and politicians, and hears himself being spoken of as a future deputy. To further his political ambitions he needs a wife, for the sake of her money and connections, and his mind turns to the daughter of the Professor of Civil Law, recently nominated a Senator.[30] Andrèu's ambition is therefore the motor of the two connected sub-plots that run through the book, concerning the division of property on the one hand, and marriage on the other.

V

Andrèu originally favours division of the inheritance on grounds of natural equity; later, he wants means to pursue his political ends: his motivations and needs change as his ambitions develop. A year after his father's death, he raises the question of the will, and of his inheritance. Jan surprisingly agrees to the division of the property; moreover, he states that he has decided not to accept the will, and that he refuses, too, either to be the master or to marry. In short, he renounces his position as heir. Loïs is appalled at the prospect, but Jan offers to sell him his share after a valuation, and to remain as an unmarried co-worker. Andrèu agrees likewise to sell his share, for he intends to pursue his career and to make a good marriage.[31]

Two comments may be made. First, we know that Béarnais local society adapted so as to conform to the new law of equal division whilst maintaining the local custom of single inheritance,[32] and the narrative offers us an example. So once Jan had decided to accept the legitimate claims of his brothers, the normal solution would have been the one proposed: for the heir to contract debts to buy out the shares of his brothers. These debts would be spread over time, in order to maintain the farm intact while at the same time not ruining it with an impossible financial burden. The substitution of Loïs for Jan is therefore the only surprise, and it is a poor one, for the master has to marry in order to provide an heir. And while Jan has doubts as to his adequacy to be a master, and his fitness to marry, Loïs, we learn later, has no inclination for women,[33] and therefore could not readily be the master. Moreover, in the course of the story, Jan becomes the master, marries and has an heir. The renunciation is a detour without any practical outcome, possibly to serve as a vehicle for his initial acceptance of the new law.

Second, there is the question of the widowed mother's personal (moveable) property, which (we presume) she brought as a dowry. This property is, as we have seen, always kept separate from that of the farm, in the mother's interest; indeed, one of its purposes is sustaining her after the death of her husband. When the eldest son elects to divide the property (including money) into three equal portions, the mother's property is excluded: it is at her disposal, though, if she wishes, the sons will include it in their management. The subject reappears when Jan elaborates the reasons for his renunciation to his mother: his duty as master is to stand in for his father, and therefore to establish his brothers as if they were his sons, and to protect the integrity both of the property of Bòrdavielha and that of his mother. It is mentioned again in the listing of the property, and recognized in the legal document that is drawn up and which she has to sign.[34]

However it is handled, the decision poses the task of first valuing and then dividing the property, before selling back the devolved portions to the heir. Jan undertakes to value the property, while Loïs takes on the running of the farm.[35] There is a brief listing of the different parts making up the farm, and a longer description of the ideology of the land: 'Outside the two rented farms at the foot of the slopes there were two paddocks of equal worth. The one around the castle was worth more, not because of the land but because of the buildings'.[36] The last, it is agreed, should go to the eldest. It is also agreed that the younger brothers should have the right to reside in the mother-house, as custom dictated (but the new law did not). Their mother's portion is readily protected, since there is a large wood beyond the fields, the yield of which showed it was more than equivalent to her legal entitlement. The money, of which there is not a great deal, is divided likewise. The brothers invoke the local notary, M. de Labatut from Lescar, to draw up a formal agreement.[37]

In the course of this description there is a contrast made between the sensibilities and feelings of the actors. On the one hand, there is the appeal of the land to those who farm it. This account sounds a strongly ideological note. Palay delineates a solidarity between farmers, the land and its products, which he likens first to a common blood, and then to the mother–child relationship: *la tèrra mairana*. The land has a soul, open only to the native born. Each piece of land has a name, and is measured, not in metres and centimetres but in the old units of feet, perches and canes. On the other hand, there is Andrèu's sense that he has received very little cash to fund his ambitions.[38]

This contrast between the local and new conditions is accentuated as these ambitions accelerate. Once he has realized the importance of appearing rich in order both to attract and secure wealth and, in particular, the daughter of the Senator, Andrèu's conscience weakens and he raises his demands by asking his brothers, through their mother, to buy his portion outright for cash.[39] It is this demand that creates the second crisis of the narrative.

Andrèu approaches his mother over his need for the money and his anticipated marriage. She – who sees nothing wrong in his behaviour either with respect to his strategic view of marriage or his political ambition – conveys the message to Jan, who subsequently discusses it with Loïs. What new idiocy, Jan asks, has seized Andrèu, that he wants all his capital, and so quickly?[40] For peasants, Palay adds, most money is invested for income (*rentes*); they do not have cash in hand, and Andrèu's demand for all his capital represents a potential disaster.

There are other, more intimate dimensions to the issue that we shall come to below, and which affect the small-scale life possibilities and freedom of movement of the members of the family at Bòrdavielha. But the demand that the law be enacted in detail, without consideration for local conditions – the need to retain the family business intact for the sake of all its members – could provide a climax to the tale, for it brings the protagonists, a way of life and the new law, into collision. However, just as the renunciation turns out to be a damp squib, so, it turns out, is this crisis over the division of the inheritance.

Palay does not handle this confrontation with dramatic skill, for the crisis over the inheritance is resolved in a series of small-scale settlements and compromises. The bleak state of affairs is represented in the book by the harsh winter of 1841, which at least has the merit of postponing settlement of Andrèu's claim. Then, Andrèu's mother promises to make him heir to her property, and it appears that the father of his fiancée in Toulouse is content with this disposition.

Moreover, Loïs proves able to buy part of Andrèu's land. So Andrèu is content to leave things as they are, and to pursue his ends with the means at his disposal. Then, six months later, in an interview with the notary, Jan makes clear that, despite Andrèu's ambitions and the necessity of matching the size of the dowry his bride will bring, the land will not have to be sold in part. For – with the payments made and promised (including an inheritance from Andrèu's maternal grandmother) taken into consideration – he has saved enough to pay the outstanding difference, or is within sight of being able to do so. Finally, in a discussion with his mother and brother, his mother reveals that she has gained enough return on her dowry since entering the house as daughter-in-law to be able to fill the gap.[41]

Therefore, although the division of property, or the influence of the new laws of inheritance, appears to be the topic of the book, it fades away: that dog does not bite. However, the account of division is also a vehicle for exploring the second sub-plot, a narrative of marriage, for there has to be a legitimate heir to whom to transmit the property, as well as the means to marry off non-heirs.

VI

The book points to the complexities and ambiguities of marriage. Just as the moment of transition between generations is one of vulnerability for the house, so is the business of importing a wife a risk. As we have seen in the case of the parents at Bòrdavielha, there are financial implications, for the dowry has to be protected so that the widow is provided for. Under unfavourable circumstances too large a dowry can threaten the integrity of the recipient farm. The sum will have to be repaid to the family of origin if the wife dies without producing an heir. There are also moral implications, indicated in the story both by the status of the incoming bride's family (a 'good' family) and by the invisible heredity that she brings.

The dilemmas around the heir's marrying are therefore great, and it is these that lie behind Jan not having married. In ideal circumstances, he would have married during his father's lifetime, the devolution of the property being settled through a marriage contract, where the rights and obligations of all parties would have been defined. It is indeed unusual in this area (and was so in the period in question) to settle these matters through a will. But, we are told, Jan had thought of marrying, having met, at a hunting party at a chateau at Denguin, the daughter of a former captain in Napoleon's army who lived close by at Arbus. He had raised the question with his father, who had discouraged his passion: 'It is good to marry as young as you can, provided you are capable of being a father of a family and a head of house according to the law of God and of men'.[42] His father pointed out the need for experience, the knowledge that comes from running a property and a house, in order to be able to judge one's own capacities. Jan, respecting his father's authority, did not pursue the matter, and the young woman married elsewhere and left the region.[43]

There is a clear hint in this account of the other side of the hierarchical order of country life, implying that the power of parents over children has harmful effects as well as good ones. This restricting atmosphere is indicated in more general terms in the care that country people have to take to avoid gossip, in the difficulty of courting someone, the need to return an invitation, and the secrecy surrounding Jan's meeting with Sorina.[44] Here again we glimpse what we might call the indigenous roots of modernity, a local critique of the regime of authority at issue.[45] The destructive effects of parental authority left Jan without sufficient resources when confronted with his responsibilities and the question of division and, being an intelligent person, he knew this. As Palay says, at the opening of the book, 'The eldest was too sensible not to have grasped immediately that, without his father, whose strength and ability dominated everybody, Bòrdavielha could not go on as before'.[46]

At the point of his renunciation, Jan refers to his earlier decision not to marry in discussion with his brothers. Loïs says that marriage is a matter of feeling or chance, and each person must suit himself. Jan replies, yes and no: a father is responsible for his family for the future and before God. To assume such a responsibility demands both a force of personality and virtues that he lacks. In discussion with his mother later, he sets the risks of marriage against the duty, which we have already encountered, of keeping intact both her property and that of the house. He then elaborates upon the reasons he has given his brothers, which again we have met: 'upon my father's death I became master, in other words, his replacement, with the obligation to look after my brothers as long as they are not established, as if they were my sons'. Jan has already suggested that, proverbially, one woman is sufficient in a household, so one might deduce – the unspoken thought – that his father's wife stands in the place of his potential wife. One practical issue is that the widowed mother, as an incomer, has no rights, and might withdraw, or be forced to do so, upon the entry of a new bride, and would then have to demand the return of her dowry to provide her with a living. This may be the sense of the threat posed to the house by the heir's marrying. Whatever is the case, this decision to remain unmarried is a sacrifice to the authority of the father, even if a transitory one.[47]

Loïs's lack of interest in women has been remarked, though it is not elaborated in the text. Although Jan announces that he has a vocation to be an 'uncle', that is, a bachelor brother helping in the running of the farm – elsewhere there is praise in general for these unmarried non-heirs, and their contribution to the farms[48] – it is clearly Loïs who embodies this calling.

It is Andrèu's marriage, as we have already glimpsed, that provides the motor for the middle part of the narrative. But his emotional affairs are in fact more complicated. Andrèu's taste for novelty and the town are mentioned early on, as is his desire to make marriage a means for developing his fortune, although, as we know, money is needed to find money. His mother, with knowledge born of her high connections, expected him to marry a daughter from a rich bourgeois family.[49] However, his affections first turn elsewhere.

M. de Labatut, the local notary from Lescar who has the job of drawing up the division of the property, is impressed with the growth of the wealth of Bòrdavielha (which one presumes he previously appraised when drawing up the marriage agreement of the now-defunct father), and conceives the idea of marrying one of his daughters to the house. He has a pious wife and five daughters, two of whom have entered an Ursuline convent. Of the three that remain marriageable, Nineta, Maria and Sorina, the parents decide that the youngest should be introduced to Andrèu.[50]

In revisiting the question of the limits inherent in the exercise of paternal authority, Palay discusses the role of parents in the past in arranging marriages for their offspring, and the substitution of material motives then by those of affection now. He also hints at the responsibility parents incurred in marrying a daughter without consulting her inclinations and tying her for life to a man about whom they knew little enough, though he balances this criticism against the impossibility of persons of marriageable age knowing the capacities and virtues that will be demanded of either their spouse or themselves for the marriage to work well.[51]

Sharing the same profession, the notary is well placed to cultivate the law student. Nevertheless, they make an interesting contrast. M. de Labatut is a member of the circles around the court at Pau and is recognized in that local society. It was in this society and court that the family at Bòrdavielha had hoped that Andrèu would distinguish himself. They had desired an urban distinction for him, but in a local version; he however rejected this, being drawn into the metropolitan world of the Toulouse court and society. M. de Labatut, in contrast, is distinctly provincial; though shrewd and decent, he lacks both the moral force and insight of the former master of Bòrdavielha, and the sophistication of the more urban courts and society. In this last respect, his gluttony is mentioned.[52]

Andrèu and Sorina are brought together in a coach journey from Pau to Morlàas, they begin a correspondence, and contact is renewed during festivities celebrating the visit of the Bishop to Lescar. On this occasion, the Labatut family are able to receive the family from Bòrdavielha, and the young persons have the opportunity – silently – to make clear their feelings for one another, a moment observed by Loïs. Loïs tells Jan, forcibly reminding him of his own past love for the army captain's daughter, equally undeclared. Jan suggests to his mother that she return the invitation, which in turn leads to the brothers visiting the notary's household upon the feast day of Saint Julian. The difficulties of meeting under such conditions are mentioned, as are the pleasures and, indeed, the intense emotions that are aroused. In the course of these visits, not only is Andrèu's affection for Sorina fuelled, and hers for him, but also Jan's interest develops in the older sister, Maria. However, no declarations or proposals are made, either by the parties or within their families. Andrèu has no desire to marry at present, and keeps his intentions to himself. Jan, aware of the situation, believes Andrèu would not have revealed his affection to Sorina had he not been satisfied with the portion with which M. de Labatut could endow his daughter.[53]

Under these conditions, Andrèu's increasingly successful career in Toulouse both raises the complacent expectations of the two families and leads to their betrayal. His awakening ambition forces him both to ask for his money, as we have seen, and to decide to drop Sorina, who has no formal claim upon him, in order to woo the wealthier and better-connected Mlle. de Pèirasac.[54]

Although Andrèu's demand for money precipitates the crisis, it is the dishonour Jan perceives his brother's action to have brought upon the house that really strikes at the heart of the moral sensibilities of local society, bringing the two codes into an intimate confrontation. Ambition has led to a weakening of conscience and a lack of honesty and, because of the solidarity of its members, to a diminishing of the house through shame, which in turn affects Jan's own life and tempo. He would not, for example, be able to visit the Labatut house again. The text, we might note, echoing a trope that goes back to Bonald, attributes this effect simultaneously to a failure of moral character and to the influence of Voltaire and Rousseau, who have enabled many to say 'each for himself'.[55] The two incompatible moral systems impinge closely upon one another in this episode, which honour demands cannot be declared or recognized in language, in order that Sorina's reputation remain untouched. The same consideration compels the notary to repress any recognition of his own lack of judgement in promoting the prospective match. Shame, again an indigenous category, enables the new forms to interact with and alter the local ways of behaving and thinking, and even of not thinking.

Sorina is aware of Andrèu's growing coolness, and in the terrible winter falls ill, and dies after hearing the news of his engagement.[56] But before she dies, she contrives to see Jan, and extracts a promise from him that he will treat her sister Maria better than his brother has treated her.[57] Jan tells his mother of Andrèu's betrayal; although she has approved, as we know, of both his political ambitions and his plans for a marriage in Toulouse, she perceives the dishonour to the house, and agrees to the necessity of Andrèu's wedding being delayed, both out of respect for the dead and a sense of shame at his being the indirect cause of Sorina's untimely death. Neither reason, however, can be mentioned publicly. Jan writes to his brother, and their maternal grandmother's death offers a timely excuse to delay his marriage. His fiancée's family accept the postponement, as she in particular wants a grand wedding, and he, whilst claiming to attend his grandmother's funeral, in fact goes to Bordeaux to make contact with some Liberal leaders there in exile from Paris in order to promote his own political career. Sorina's death, Palay comments, more or less suits our man's purposes.[58]

By the time Andrèu marries, Jan has married Maria. In the course of his negotiations concerning the marriage agreement we learn he has paid off the debts on the farm; Jan then can propose because he is prepared to marry Maria without a dowry. The two weddings, one in Lescar and the other in Toulouse, are contrasted, as is their local importance: Andrèu's counts for little in the neighbourhood, because he is not expected to return to the region. Characteristically, he and his bride pass through on their honeymoon, on their way to a series of luxurious resorts. Maria proves a good wife (unlike Sorina, she has no taste for the social life of Pau), and gives birth first to a son, and then a daughter.[59] By the penultimate page of the book, Jan is the master of Bòrdavielha, with an heir, and the property is secure.

VII

Some of the broader sociological questions associated with the mutation in regime with which we are concerned are worth considering at this point, to introduce a comparative framework. From one angle, from what we can call an ideological perspective, the change seems of great significance, for it concerns the replacement of one system of authority and legitimacy by another. One system is marked by the authority of the family, expressed in the legitimate power of the parents to decide the fate of the children. The other is characterized by the authority of the individual, expressed in the principle that each follows his or her bent, whether for ambition (the longer-term view) or pleasure (the shorter). One might imagine very different personalities developing under each regime with its demands of duty or pleasure, self-denial or self-expression, and so forth. The contrast is represented by Jan and Andrèu, and what is held to be at stake is the future of the house: of the family, the property, the business, the name and the reputation. We are offered an account of two models of authority, two regimes of inheritance, two kinds of personality, and even two notions of time, the one emphasizing the continuity between past and future, the other focused upon the present moment.

From another angle, however, the significance of the change is less clear cut. In a broader sociological perspective both inheritance regimes bear strong similarities to each other. They are both variants of what Goody terms 'diverging devolution',[60] whereby property goes to children of both sexes. Goody identifies this as a characteristic of European (and Asian) systems of inheritance, in contrast to 'homogeneous inheritance', whereby a person's property is transmitted only to members of their clan or lineage of the same sex, which Goody sees as characteristic of African societies. The significance of this broad distinction for our purposes lies in its focusing attention upon the fact that in Europe women are the recipients of parental property. Whether this property is received by inheritance or dowry, it establishes some sort of conjugal fund, which in due course provides the woman with support in widowhood, and eventually goes to provide for her children.[61] This is true broadly speaking both under the traditional Béarnais system and under that promoted by the Civil Code.

The primary issue here, then, is that property devolves to all offspring, irrespective of sex, and the distribution of property within that devolution is of secondary importance. Clearly it matters whether there is equal division between all heirs, or simply between male heirs, or whether the bulk of the property passes to a single heir, but what is significant is that the non-heirs also receive property, usually as dowries, sometimes also as gift. There are contrasting regimes, but the contrast is a matter of degree, not of kind: they share a number of features in common.

These shared features extend beyond the institution of inheritance. Goody suggests that 'there will be certain "adhesions" (to use E.B.Tylor's term) between the modes of transmitting property and other social institutions'.[62] In particular, he links the forms of inheritance to the forms of marriage, of authority within the family, and of kinship terminology. The first two of these features emerge in the society we have been describing.

To take the first, it is clear that if family property is transmitted to the offspring, the nature of the marriages they make will be affected by this fact. Three broad features will follow. First, marriage will be a significant social event, being the occasion for the transmission of property. The event will be particularly marked when the basic means of production – land in an agricultural society – is included in the inheritance.[63] Second, monogamy will be the rule, and divorce will both be rare and be regarded as a major, and potentially disastrous, disruption. We might say that divorce is the negation of this system, an ever present threat, felt even in its absence. Third, late marriage and non-marriage will be relatively common, both because the distribution of family wealth is at stake, and because of associated demographic factors.

Each of these features is a function of the internal relations of authority within the family, and is an expression of the control exerted by the family over its individual members. This control also has a number of aspects. First, there is the question of a 'suitable' marriage partner, and – its other face – misalliance. As Goody observes, 'if women are receivers of "male" property ... then the nature of the marriages they make will be influenced by this fact'.[64] This will be particularly true in the case of an heiress. Under such circumstances, women will tend to marry within the local order and with men of equal or higher status, status being a compound of wealth and reputation. The position of an heir is effectively the same; he will seek a wife of an appropriate status. The control of marriage partners will tend to encourage alliance within rank and kind, and to give rise therefore to social castes. Then, connected with the control of marriage partners, such a society will try to control courtship and restrain choice; the chastity of women will be an issue, as will the brokerage of marriages. Third, it follows that parental and, in particular, paternal authority will be critical, as will be the sanctions at the parents' disposal, including the power to exclude from inheritance, and the related matter of the acceptance of this power by the children's generation.

There are other linked issues. To mention two, residence upon marriage relates to property rather than gender: the couple reside where there is property to be inherited. If a daughter is the heiress, residence is uxorilical; if a son is heir, residence is virilocal. And the production of an heir is of great significance, and so issues of legitimacy, infertility, child mortality and adoption are all prominent.

With respect to kinship terms, Goody suggests that when children inherit from parents and siblings are cut off from one another at marriage, siblings will be differentiated terminologically from cousins. The isolation of the nuclear family is a function of direct inheritance, and the accumulation of property and its inheritance by individuals are crucial factors in the development of descriptive (individualized) nomenclatures for kin rather than classificatory ones.[65] This aspect – unlike the others – is not explored in Palay's account.

In sum, there is a complex of connected issues which links together economic, domestic and personal facts. Social control is exerted over the most detailed aspects of the lives of men and women, and that control – and its possible failures – will affect the personalities and characters of all those involved. This is the sociological frame within which the novel's action takes place.

Two further points should be made. First, viewing the community as a whole, this control and these rules apply with greatest force to the most important families. Control of marriage will increase with the value of the property at stake, and the matching of status and wealth will be more of an issue among the biggest land-owning families. This is indeed why some features of the behaviour of a Béarnais house may resemble that of a European aristocratic or even royal house. The interest of the family at Bordavièlha is that they are in local terms exceptional in their wealth and reputation: at the extremes of wealth and reputation, a marriage will be the focus of ambition and the opportunity to negotiate new status. This observation echoes Bourdieu's discussion of parallel cousin marriage and especially matrimonial strategies.[66] Male kin will be decisively involved when a marriage is between powerful families, the marriage may be made over a greater geographical distance, and wealth, reputation and political power will be decisive features in the choice of a spouse. 'Lesser' marriages may be made locally, and through the contacts between female kin – through the wife's family, for example. Issues of wealth and power will be of less significance than a good name. The freedom to improvise according to necessity will also vary with the status of the property to be transmitted; where the property is significant, and family honour great, women rather than collateral males will inherit in the absence of male heirs.

At the other extreme, there will be poor families for whom property is of small practical concern, and whose members behave in a manner that resembles 'modern individuals'. The offspring, once grown up, will seek their fortunes elsewhere, leaving the parents to fend for themselves in old age. Under these conditions, there will be little collective authority or responsibility, continuity of property, trade or possessions. And in any locality there will be a scale of families in between to which these considerations will apply in differing degrees.

Second, from the individual's point of view, the degree of control or freedom to act will relate not only to the status of the family into which one is born, but also according to circumstances including one's sex and order of birth. Different options exist according to whether one is a son or a daughter, first-born or later-born, including the likelihood of marriage, the age of marriage, the number of offspring borne, the possibility of gaining wealth and power, and even good health and length of life. Not only is there a scale of families in any locality, with outlooks running between the traditional and the modern, but also within these individuals will contain different potentialities, some who embody tradition while others embrace the modern.

With all these variations, it follows that 'modern' individuals and behaviour may be generated both at the periphery of the system, in the cases of poor families with no property to transmit, and at its heart, in the matrimonial and inheritance calculations of the younger offspring of the wealthiest families. There is a curious coincidence between the behaviour of the extremes that is, despite appearances, a function not of their intrinsic freedom as individuals but of their particular place in a matrix of inheritance and evaluation.

We might therefore argue that, instead of taking up an external perspective in which a traditional way of life is confronted by a modern one coming from the outside, we should adopt a local perspective in which both are held in play by a single schema. While the property is passed on intact to the heir, non-heirs are generated who may according to circumstances get caught up in either a 'modern' or a 'traditional' way of life, each with its own opportunities and limitations, and potential for interaction with the other. These circumstances will include new legislation concerning inheritance, but the laws are not, in the local instance, primary; they are, rather, secondary features that come into play in the expression of the life of property.

VIII

It is worth dwelling briefly upon the psychological potentialities and limitations imputed to the story's characters by these property regimes, and wondering whether these are significant. To take each regime's most prominent feature, we have noted the power of the parents on the one hand, and the principle of each following his or her own bent – whether for ambition or pleasure – on the other.

It may be no more than a literary characteristic of the period that, in Palay's writing, the women in both regimes are by and large ciphers. They are without much initiative, vulnerable either to the demands of constancy or to the desire for pleasure, and in large part created to be the vehicles for the transmission of property between fathers and husbands, just as they are vehicles also for the transmission of heredity.[67] Women's natural powers of transmission are congruent with their social role of transmission; indeed, the two forms of inheritance are not fully distinguished. Their character can either add to or detract from the value of the goods passed, but cannot be determinative in its own right in either system. The inalienable property of wives in the Béarnais system, for example, gives them a residual individuality and a certain power of initiative, but it is limited. Women, one might say, are essentially socially determined.

But their crucial characteristic is that they appear to lack (on the evidence of the novel) a capacity for experience such as seen in the difference between the young Jan and his father, and which Jan, in time, overcomes. So, despite her qualities, their mother's affection for her youngest blinds her to Andrèu's faults until the last episode of Sorina's death – and then she recognizes that Jan has acquired his father's authority.[68] Sorina simply serves the interests of the plot: despite her goodness and intelligence, she uncomplainingly accepts Andrèu's perfidy and acts as the catalyst to Jan's marriage.

However, the men, as we have seen, are not free operators either; their fate is also a function of the spirit of property. Jan temporarily believes himself to have a vocation to celibacy, in large part because of his obligations to his mother. Loïs has no time for women. Andrèu effectively jilts the woman he loves and then calculatingly denies the claims of affection for the sake of ambition. He, too, we are told is not given to womanizing. Is there a discernable reason for these refusals to relate to women? In practice, they each represent a position within the sociological frame described.

Without pretending to give a complete answer, there are two factors that need to be taken into account. First, in an economy where wealth is transmitted through women, both in terms of dowry and in terms of the production of heirs, relations with women are bound to be highly controlled. With respect to the children, the mother will be highly valued (although always a guest), and this value is a function of her having served the purposes of the house. The Oedipal aspect of this is well represented by Jan's declaration to his mother, though her preference has always been for her youngest son. A new wife, correspondingly, is a potential threat until she produces an heir, for if the marriage ends without issue – either through death or divorce – the dowry has, as we have seen, to be returned. And marrying out – with a dowry – is only an option under certain circumstances, and assumes the appearance of a crisis in Andrèu's case. In brief, outgoing and incoming wealth associated with marriage may both threaten the patrimony.

In his rebuttal of the youngest son's claim to an equal share, the father suggests, after his defence of single inheritance, that a younger son can marry an heiress and become a master of a house in his turn.[69] In addition to the options of celibacy or marrying out, a younger sibling may marry into another house. This too demands a dowry; in local marriages, less for a man than a woman marrying in. In Andrèu's case, we have seen that the amount needed comes from the efforts of both parents and brothers. But it may be an important point that the further away one marries, the greater the threat to the house – and the higher the status or honour of the family, the greater the likelihood of such a marriage. Status raises the possibility of a distant marriage, and also the cost of achieving such a match: one should not imagine that honour is equivalent to wealth, even though the two may go together. We have here indications of a possible limiting line: the highest status families are most vulnerable to these dangerous marriages, and hence to dissolution. What seems to be the heart of the system has an inherent weakness.

The other (and consequential) factor is that there is a male–female relationship not portrayed in the book, that of brother and sister. If a brother is the heir to the house, his marriage may bring in sufficient wealth to allow the subsequent marriage of a sister. If she marries the heir to another, local house, not only are the fates of the brother and sister closely linked, but through them also the fates of the two houses. There may be substantial flows of co-operation, gifts and wealth between these houses, organized through the brother–sister relationship. In addition to the strong and ambiguous relation of mother to son, then, there is also a potential strong and positive relation of brother and sister, established over time, but in this case strengthened through marriage. Within this regime of property, the relations within the family may have different effects upon the potential for and expression of alliances.

In short, there is a calculus with several active dimensions at work. Whilst we have talked of 'good' families, Bòrdavielha in fact represents an extreme on this spectrum. The 'best' families, where prestige is highest, are the most vulnerable through the marriage of their non-heirs far away, where family solidarities in practice count for little. The heir and the home farm are correspondingly weakened by these demands. This is the case for Bòrdavielha, and explains why the most prominent houses appear always on the point of extinction. In contrast, good families marry their non-heirs locally, where practical ties and links of honour consolidate the status of the home farm and family. These less visible forms of continuity are part of the unexamined background to Palay's account of repeated crisis.[70]

IX

While the book begins with the local effects of national legislative change concerning inheritance, it concludes by considering certain manifestations of national politics at the local level. If the first crisis concerns Jan's renunciation and the division of the property, and the second Andrèu's marriage and share of the inheritance, the third concerns Andrèu's political career. As we saw, Andrèu's ambition emerges from his education and his taste for luxury and ideas. It is first given shape by his success in defending his thesis and his early professional successes, combined with his reception in Toulouse society. But it is hearing himself spoken of as a potential Liberal Deputy[71] that sets him in a new orbit: 'The devil of politics had entered his head through that overheard prediction'.[72] Once married, Andrèu settles to the serious business of developing a career in politics. Once again, this crisis has an inconsequential structure.

It is worth recalling the historical framework of Palay's narrative (and remembering too that he wrote around 1914, and published in the 1930s). Under the July Monarchy (1830–1848), the franchise was restricted to those who paid above a particular threshold in direct taxation. Given that the form of taxable wealth was principally land, this qualification constituted a land-owners' franchise, and the politics of the period were those of an oligarchy of land-owners. When the qualification (*cens*) was lowered in 1846 to 200 francs paid in tax in a year, the electoral constituency (*pays legal*) comprised an estimated 241,000 electors, 90 per cent of whom qualified through taxes on property. It was of course only open to individuals drawn from high status families to engage in politics. This narrowly based electorate was organized at a local level into electoral colleges, which were often small and could be managed by the national government's administration.[73]

The political ideas of the opposition in this period concentrated upon the self-interest and the lack of social responsibility of the governing classes, and upon reforming social relations, looking to issues of property ownership and suffrage as keys to creating political, economic, social and domestic harmony. Its proposals often took the form of utopian schemes of ownership and authority, which is characteristic of oppositional political discourse at a distance from the discipline of the practical exercise of power; in this, they echoed the Revolution itself. The earlier reformers – Fourier, Proudhon – were more radical; the later ones, after 1848 – including Le Play – were more conservative. In practice, the narrow context of agitation for reform was the struggle for power between factions of the governing classes. The issues of parliamentary and electoral reform were taken up in 1845 in pursuit of an agenda of political advantage, in the first instance, to unseat Guizot from office; and in doing so, the politicians succeeded in mobilizing wider interests than simply those of the electorate. The government was subject to attacks by radical newspapers and at public meetings concerning scandals (sexual and financial) and corruption (including the manipulation of elections). These attacks led to agitation for the extension of the suffrage that spread far beyond the property-owning classes.

Palay's novel has material on the elections of the period, including mention of the writings of the poet Navarròt, the employment of outside agitators, and the use of drink. There is also discussion on the political role of newspapers. The *Memorial* was on the side of the government; the *Observateur des Pyrénées* on that of the opposition. The latter was a propaganda sheet edited by lawyers which had taken the place of the *Montagnard des Pyrénées*, suppressed after agitating for universal suffrage in 1841. Palay reflects that as a candidate was asking for a 'place', seeking pleasures, honour and profit, it was quite natural both that he would offer something in return, and also that the electors would seek their own advantage. Under such conditions, extending the voting qualification spread the rot.[74]

The power of the capital in formenting political agitation extended through a series of links deep into the countryside. Andrèu's first foray into politics was at the beginning of 1847, following discussion in the Chamber of Deputies in Paris of the Duvergier de Hauranne proposition to lower the voting qualification. This had evoked widespread interest locally among small businessmen, and excited a good deal of Republican (*Rouge*) activity in the local towns. Countervailing measures were taken by an alliance of nobles and bourgeoises, including the closing of a newspaper in Oloron. Andrèu made a pact agreeing not to stand against a local aristocrat, Monsieur d'Arista, who was standing as Conseilleur général for the canton of Lescar, and who represented a moderate Republicanism, against the extreme forms that attacked nobles and priests, invoking Revolutionary ideas. Palay suggests that in Béarn, with its values of family and land, order and religion were bound to prevail. In any case, the electoral college consisted only of some fifty electors. Andrèu's candidate won, and a temporary calm returned.[75]

As we have seen, Palay represents Radical politics as restlessness raised to being an end in itself, a perpetual dissatisfaction expressing a wish to rule disguised as a desire for social progress. As ambition develops, conscience weakens, leading to a 'chemical' change in the house, a loss of honour. This unsettling of the house does not stop here, however, but takes hold of Loïs. Loïs has always admired Andrèu's skill with words, and has accepted his account of the justice of the new laws; he now develops an enthusiasm for Andrèu's political ideas and tries to serve his cause. Andrèu sends him Radical journals, whose views he spreads among local labourers who, despite their doubts, accept his authority, lucidity and assurance. His hearers expect to gain the vote, although not to pay taxes.[76] In this way, the ideas that unsettle the house penetrate ever deeper into the countryside.

Andrèu's second foray takes place during the 1848 Revolution. The government fell on 25 February 1848. Pau followed Paris, but quietly: the change of government was achieved in a quiet and orderly fashion. Loïs is excited by the news, and travels around the district disseminating Radical ideas. He is aided by it being the season of pig butchering (*pèlha-pòrc*), which gathers men into clans, and the local butcher is one of his followers.[77]

Andrèu is caught up in the second election of the year (6 March), and – alerted by his brother – returns home from Toulouse to pursue the campaign and his own interests; he again attaches himself to a noble patron. Andrèu distinguishes himself in public meetings in Pau, among the agitators, drunks and politicians. His patron designates him as the candidate for Deputy,[78] and his candidature is successful. But at the moment of his victory he is assassinated by an agitator whom he had encountered and humiliated on the hustings, a forger who had been saved from the galleys by his eloquence in the Toulouse courts.

This is a clear instance of putting words to work and their having unintended consequences: an encapsulation of the modern spirit. The restlessness of modernity consumes its own, in Palay's account, quite as much as it corrodes the embodiments of tradition. Both the radical lawyer and the criminal agitator end up dead from the disturbance, for Loïs kills his brother's assassin. Andrèu's dying words reflect upon the emptiness and uselessness of his activity: 'To have done so much to no end'.[79]

As with the others, this third and final crisis comes to nothing; there is no outcome, other than Andrèu's belated realization of the emptiness of his ambitions, and his brother's infatuation, a germ incubating future restlessness. One might understand the book as a meditation upon the nature of history as repetition: the agitation of 1789, represented by the new laws on inheritance, has its outcome in the lesser emptiness of 1848. Or, to cite Marx's contemporary comment: 'Hegel remarks somewhere that all facts and personages of great importance in world history occur, as it were, twice. He forgot to add: the first time as tragedy, the second as farce'.[80] We might understand it, too, as a reflection on the political threat to order that Palay experienced while writing it, and which was to be acutely relevant at the time of publication.

X

If the book is a meditation upon the various threats to the integrity of the house of Bòrdavielha, none of the three crises, as we have seen, in fact touch it. Yet on the last page, Palay announces that Bòrdavielha's time is over. Jan's son, we are told, died as a soldier in 1870 and Jan dies soon after, leaving a widow and daughter. When the daughter marries, Loïs dies too, not wishing to see the property auctioned. The widow, Maria, goes with her daughter to the Landes, where her son-in-law has property. Now only a few local people remember the name of the house, which has passed into the hands of outsiders.[81]

In this perspective, the story ends because of a chance tragedy: this is a view of history as a simple chronicle of events without any internal relations. Yet the text is of interest to an ethnographer precisely because it reflects in a different way upon the internal mechanisms of continuity and change, or the nature of time, which is also an essential feature of the life of property. There is, effectively, a struggle in the text between two stories. On the one hand there is the sense – which is widely shared – that a way of life, represented in its highest form in the family with which we have been concerned, is coming or has come to an end, destroyed by the invading spirit of modernity. On the other, we have quite a different narrative, of how various disparate threats to local forms of life are transformed, or overcome, or turn out to destroy themselves, in the course of time. One is a simple account of history as the replacement of one form of life by another; the other is a more subtle and multiple account, which does not invert the first but offers a different view of time. The text overall favours the first account, but it does so at a price: the ending, as indeed much of the action of the book, is contingent. The two accounts of time, and how they are related to one another, form part of the ethnographic interest of the book.

I have commented upon the depiction of local capacities both to generate change and to respond to it. Although there is a distinction made between the local and the cosmopolitan, that concerns both powers and forms, the book's focus is an account of the flaw that runs through local life and which generates both kinds of response. It is a hereditary flaw that contains within itself both features of modernity – the love of novelty, ideas and power, summed up as restlessness – and the forms of traditional authority, many of whose forms of expression are ill-adapted or even counter-productive to its own preservation and transmission. This double inheritance is lived out in various combinations and expressed differently by each of the three brothers.

It allows for two possible readings. One might view the different places – Paris, Toulouse, Pau, Lescar, and the small villages and isolated farms – as a chain along which contagion passes, bringing ideas and disturbance from the capital to the countryside. Or one might regard the different places with their different values as projections of the struggle between the two principles in this inheritance, as the effects of a local distribution of difference. It is not that one account is true and the other false, that the countryside is either passive and controlled or else active and determining. Rather, both accounts relate to a single 'economy'; reality here contains, and is in part made up of, the interactions of two incompatible interpretations. We have here the hint of a theory of history as the generation of symbolic geographies and the events (psychic, familial, demographic, political and others) they contain, produced by the interactions of two distinct, incompatible but inseparable, principles. We have termed this a 'co-inherence of contraries':[82] an obscure principle under which two series of events interact, influence one another and share a common fate, a sequence of captures and escapes such as the book portrays, an engine to create and absorb change. This is history at an intermediate scale.

This obscure principle has a structure that reveals the priority between the series. If one series is concerned with hierarchy, order, embodied time, local particularity and practical reason, the other is characterized by equality, restlessness, abstract time, generality, and theoretical reason. But the two cannot be equivalent. To suppose equivalence would be to give priority to the latter series and imply that it makes intelligible the former. It also would produce the paradox that the principle of equality or equivalence had priority over that of hierarchy or difference, in other words, that it was evaluated differently and not equivalently. The two series are not equal, but the series we might label 'tradition' contains the possibility of the other, 'modern' series, which simultaneously appears to be destroying its ground. While the first implies the second, it is only expressed, by and large, in its own denial and loss.

We might put the lesson the book teaches in these broad terms: it is not that anthropology comes first, in the form of a timeless culture, and history second, replacing the static, ethnographic status quo with the restless temporal movement of modernity. Rather, the novel concerns the role of what is 'always about to be lost' in the progress of civilization, the broad nature of the continuities – or the transmission of possibilities and constraints – in the social order. The book offers us such an account in its description of a flawed heredity, a continuity without determinate content that both generates and copes with change, and that exists and is transmitted through its own seeming denial. Palay gives us a local perspective on the truth of history: it takes the form of the transmission of property and personality, focused in the always-present possibility of its disappearance, and he expresses it in the key idea of the fall of a house.

XI

This little-known novel illustrates the complex form described in the previous chapters while adding to our understanding. It lays out in detail the seemingly contradictory resources contained in an indigenous way of life, which appeared in the earliest materials as a play between two jurisdictions (loosely attributed to town and country respectively), and which emerge in the novel in two contrasting systems – not only of law and inheritance, but also of personality, solidarity and ethics – embodied in the life-possibilities of the various characters. These contrasts are taken up in the interactions between that way of life and an outside, metropolitan gaze, which employs them not as complementary but as opposed terms, in order to tell a quite different story – of the replacement of one way of life by another. These interpretations – which, of course, have their effects but do not offer a 'true' account – and the interactions of which they are a part are, in turn, exploited in the local context by the various actors, who play upon the different elements in the mix to pursue their ends. In doing so, they transmit the complex form of life in new guises, through a series of events. This is, to repeat, a rich ethnographic source.

The claim that the novel reflects specifically local forms, despite its engagement with a powerful external mode of registration, is borne out by returning for a moment to the contrast drawn earlier with the novel by Charles de Bordeu, *Le dernier maître*.[83] Although Bordeu's novel is also set in rural Béarn in the second half of the nineteenth century, and despite offering a number of seeming parallels – it is concerned with the fate and eventual disappearance of a house, and with the themes of marriage and dowry, of non-marriage, and of inheritance, simultaneously of character and reputation as well as of wealth and debts – it is nevertheless without any trace of the local forms of life with which we have been concerned. It is in fact an exemplary narrative of the fate of the French rentier class during the nineteenth century, and none of the issues with which it is concerned step beyond the conventional provisions and opportunities contained in the Civil Code. The financial crisis that eventually engulfs the house is indeed precipitated by the requirement to return a portion of the wife's dowry, the sum being unavailable because the money has been spent on her spendthrift father-in-law's debts (which mark him, according to the book's notions, as a 'traditional' figure). But the motive behind the return of the dowry is a division according to equal inheritance within her family of origin subsequent to her marriage; she by this time is the mother of two legitimate children. This is quite alien to the concerns and practices we have been discussing. The sister of the heir remains unmarried, but her dilemma is essentially romantic: she is wooed by an inconstant lover; there are no issues of property or status to impede the couple. Likewise, there is a period when the young and wealthy wife's instability and love of pleasure threaten the household she has joined, but this episode is a reflection upon bourgeois life and the moral education of women; it is not a function of the size of her dowry relative to the wealth of the house, nor of an imbalance in reputation. The surface similarities conceal fundamental differences between a cosmopolitan and a local perspective, and the latter is completely missing from Bordeu's novel.

The charm of his book lies in its elegiac and nostalgic tone, linking morality and peace to an ideal of stable residence, and mourning their loss: 'A restless generation has replaced [the last]... Honour is a word devoid of meaning if men come and go, and die without taking root anywhere: if their memory, and respect for the dead, and the reputation gained for honest dealing, is no longer passed on, in a locality, to their children'.[84] It owes its reprinting to this tone, which can be mistaken for an appreciation of place ; the introduction notes, 'The richness of his thought is that of a true humanist, created for a locality'.[85] But this is an abstract desire for rootedness, a cosmopolitan humanism; it bears no relation to a particular place, in this case, to Béarn.

In Palay's novel, then, we are dealing with something quite different, an expression of local particularity. The same claim is made for Pierre Bourdieu's ethnographic writings concerning Béarn, the topic of the next chapter. In contrast to the novel, Bourdieu's work is well known and influential. Yet it offers parallels with it, drawing upon the same forms of life and describing their contestation and transmission in a prolonged encounter with an outside, metropolitan way of life. Moreover, through these encounters, such local experiences contribute to more widely held categories, in this instance shaping many features of Bourdieu's general sociology. If this at first sight appears an improbable claim, it is one Bourdieu himself makes. It allows my suggestion that his reflexive sociology be seen as a further expression of the life of property in Béarn. We began with Le Play's discovery of the Béarnais stem family, and its contribution to an understanding of French civil society; we conclude with another transformation of a similar kind, more than one hundred years later.

Notes

1. The novel was originally published in 1934 as *Lous tres gouyats de Bordevielhe*, employing the orthography adopted by the L'Escole Gastoû Febus. However, I have used the Per Noste edition, published in 1974 by Marrimpouey Jeune of Pau, which uses 'classical' orthography, a mark of the Occitan – as opposed to the Félibrige – movement. References are to this later edition (Palay 1974[1934]), and are cited in short reference form followed by page numbers.
2. With the exception of two letters cited, which are both in French (*Los tres gojats*, pp.86–89, 152), and the intervention of an agitator in a political meeting (ibid., p.182).
3. For this paragraph, see Darrigrand's preface to *Los tres gojats*; in additon, Lafont and Anatole (1970: 568-715), Clavé (1980: 255–259), Salles Loustau (1986), Sarpoulet (2005) and Grosclaude (1982).
4. *Los tres gojats*, p.25.
5. Sahlins calls comparable approaches in social anthropology 'despondency theory': a frame of mind which 'envisioned the inevitable collapse of indigenous cultures under the shattering impact of global capitalism' (Sahlins 1999: 401ff).
6. Cf. the essays in Poyatos (1988).
7. Palay (1900).
8. Le Play et al. (1994), Augustins and Bonnain (1981, 1986), and Bourdieu (2002a). On Bourdieu, see chapter 6.
9. Bourdieu (1972b).

10. See, e.g., Lefebvre (1990[1963]), Lynch (1992) and Thibon (1988).
11. See Bordeu (1970[1889]); cf. the sociological study of the end of a house in the Languedoc: Assier-Andrieu (1987).
12. For a sociological exploration of an Occitan novel, see Le Roy Ladurie (1982).
13. Cf. Lévi-Strauss's definition: 'la maison « consiste ... en un héritage spirituel et matériel, comprenant la dignité, les origines, la parenté, les noms et les symboles, la position, la puissance et la richesse »' (Lévi-Strauss 1991: 435, citing the medievalist Schmidt).
14. The use of such a feudal, Christian motif points towards Palay's Catholic social reform agenda, deriving from the evocation of the Middle Ages by such writers as Bonald and Lammenais.
15. The description of the building (*Los tres gojats*, p.27); single body with a single soul (ibid., pp.94–95); social integration (ibid., pp.114–115).
16. *Los tres gojats*, p.44. Note that the name by which it is known locally is not necessarily the name of the house.
17. Accurate location (*Los tres gojats*, p.113); without effacing distance or respect (ibid., p.47).
18. 'Bèra familha, de segur. Mès a l'epòca dont parlam de cap a 1840 – las leis navèras e l'anar de París que l'avèn un drin destroblada' (*Los tres gojats*, p.28).
19. I would want to modify that statement, with a proper modesty. But let Palay's simplification stand for purposes of exposition – see below; see also chapter 3.
20. 'Tant qui l'ainat, suivant la costuma, èra estat de dret l'aretèr la posicion de Bòrdavielha n'avè pas cambiat... Mès quan los ainats se trobèn a l'obligacion de har la legitima deus capdèths e de las capdètas, las maisons en Biarn qu'estén hèra segotidas e l'anar deus pèis que se'n trobà bèth drin cambiat' (*Los tres gojats*, pp.28–29).
21. 'En despeit de las leis navèras en lasquaus n'avè nada fe, lo pair, per testament, qu'at deishava tot a l'ainat dab las cargas ordenàrias. E tot-un que sabè que lo testament que podè estar atacat, mès segur en son amna e conciença que la costuma anciena qu'èra la bona, que deishava suu cap deu son permèr la carga de guardar sancèra la casa-mairau entà perpetuar lo lheit de la raça e sauvar l'acès de la familha; non s'avè pas volut dar tòrt ad eth medish en har lo partatge suvant lo lei civila de París; la costuma biarnesa qu'avè hèit las pròvas; que s'i tienè' (*Los tres gojats*, p.30).
22. 'Be voletz avoar, si disè lo gojat, qu'èm tots los vòstes hilhs, los capdèths com l'ainat! B'èm tots vaduts parièr, nuds mès deu medish sang e plens de la medisha vita? Davant Diu b'èm egals? (*Los tres gojats*, p.30).
23. 'Entà miélher assegurar l'anar deu monde, entà guardar la tèrra dab l'ordi qui hè besonh a la patz de tots, que n'i cau deus qui comandan e deus qui creden; ua familha tà estar cò qui déu ester, qu'a besonh d'un cap-maison. Lo mèste qu'averà los màgers besonhs, qu'ei juste, lavetz, qu'aja la maja part deus bens de casa. Son pair que'u déu hicar en man tot çò qui pòt, pusqu'ei eth qui déu assegurar la posteritat. La vertadèra familha, suvant la volentat de Diu, qu'ei la qui dura e qui dura unida tostemps e ligada a la tèrra deus ajòus com l'ongla e la carn' (*Los tres gojats*, p.30).
24. For a genealogy of French sociology of the family, see Bonald (1864[1800]), Le Play (1871); cf. Nisbet (1999[1968]). See also chapter 1.
25. The three brothers (*Los tres gojats*, p.37); good friends (ibid., p.29); Loïs a cipher (ibid., pp. 40–41).
26. From Pèira-clara (*Los tres gojats*, p.55); received in court (ibid., p.61); father impractical (ibid., p.56); head full of follies (ibid., p.59).
27. Andrèu's education (*Los tres gojats*, p.38); drawn to the town (ibid., p.39); rose late (ibid., p.51); dressed carefully (ibid., p.64); ability at conversation (ibid., p.70); interest in politics (ibid., p.61); family's anticipation (ibid., pp.131–132).

28. Latin thesis (*Los tres gojats*, p.64); definition of a lawyer (ibid., p.65); moral qualities (ibid., pp.67–68); threefold protection (ibid., p.89).
29. Universal disturbance of minds (*Los tres gojats*, p.29); desire to prove oneself (ibid., p.123); progress a form of restlessness (ibid., p.124).
30. Begins to gain notice (*Los tres gojats*, p.121–122); spoken of as future deputy (ibid., p.125); needs a wife (ibid., pp.127–128).
31. Raises question of will (*Los tres gojats*, p.37); Jan's renunciation (ibid., p.40); Andrèu sells share (ibid., p.42).
32. See Saint-Macary (1942); see also chapters 2 and 3.
33. *Los tres gojats*, p.94.
34. Mother's property: in reasons for Jan's renunciation (*Los tres gojats*, p.63); in listing of property (ibid., p.66); in legal document (ibid., p.72).
35. *Los tres gojats*, p.51.
36. 'Ad entorn de las duas meterias deu pè deus costalats que i avè juste dus casalars qui's valèn. Lo deu torn deu castèth qu'èra mei consequent, non pas tant per'mor de las tèrras mès per'mor de las bastissas' (*Los tres gojats*, p.66).
37. Money divided (*Los tres gojats*, p.66); local notary (ibid., p.70).
38. *La tèrra mairana* (*Los tres gojats*, p.53); measurements (ibid., p.54); Andrèu's disappointment (ibid., p.67).
39. *Los tres gojats*, p.127.
40. *Los tres gojats*, p.130.
41. Means at Andrèu's disposal (*Los tres gojats*, pp.133–135); Jan has saved enough (ibid., p.156); mother's contribution (ibid., p.161).
42. 'Qu'as rason de't voler maridar ... que's cau maridar joens tant qui òm pòt, a las condicions, tot-un, d'estar capable de har un pair de familha e un cap-maison segon la lei de Diu e deus òmis' (*Los tres gojats*, p.36).
43. Woman at Arbus (*Los tres gojats*, p.104); married elsewhere (ibid., p.107).
44. Difficulties in courting (*Los tres gojats*, p.93); need to return invitation (ibid., p.109); secrecy of meeting (ibid., p.140).
45. Camelat also hints at the repressive aspects of parental power in his poem *Belina* (Camelat 1978[1898]). Palay's omniscient narrator voice at this point may indicate a common focus in their modernist, regionalist agenda, in addition to its offering a local perception.
46. 'L'ainat qu'èra tròp seriós entà non pas aver sentit de tira que, shens lo pair, dont la ponha e lo capatge mestrejavan tot lo monde, Bòrdavielha non podè durar com èra' (*Los tres gojats*, p.29).
47. To assume such a responsibility (*Los tres gojats*, p.39); reasons against marriage, to remain unmarried is a sacrifice (ibid., p.63).
48. Jan's vocation to be an 'uncle' (*Los tres gojats*, p.40); praise for unmarried non-heirs (ibid., p.46).
49. Andrèu's taste for novelty and the town (*Los tres gojats*, pp.39–40); need for money, and marriage as a means (ibid., p.42); mother's expectations (ibid., p.60-1).
50. M. de Labatut conceives of marrying a daughter to the house (*Los tres gojats*, p.73); settles on the youngest (ibid., p.77).
51. The limits of arranged marriages etc. (*Los tres gojats*, pp.77–78).
52. M. d Labatut's local recognition (*Los tres gojats*, pp.79ff.); the family's similar hopes for Andrèu (ibid., pp.131–132, cf. p.153); limits with respect to moral force (ibid., p.78); gluttony (ibid., p.110).
53. Andrèu and Sorina meet (*Los tres gojats*, pp.79ff.); correspond (ibid., p.89); renew contact (ibid., p.98ff.); Loïs's observation (ibid., p.102); return invitation (ibid., p.110); brothers' visit to notary's household (ibid., p.114ff.); difficulties of such meetings (ibid., p.93); Andrèu's lack of present desire to marry (ibid., p.94); Jan's understanding (ibid., p.113).
54. *Los tres gojats*, pp.127–128, 134.

55. Impossibility of Jan visiting the Labatut house again (*Los tres gojats*, p.131); 'each for himself' (ibid.)
56. *Los tres gojats*, p.143. In this respect, Sorina shares the fate of other Occitan heroines; compare Mistral's *Mireille* or Camelat's *Belina*.
57. *Los tres gojats*, pp.141–142.
58. Mother informed of Andrèu's betrayal (*Los tres gojats*, p.147); her former approval of his plans (ibid., p.129); a timely excuse (ibid., p.149); suits our man's purposes (ibid., p.150).
59. Prepared to marry without dowry (*Los tres gojats*, p.161); two weddings contrasted (ibid., pp.165–166); Maria's lack of taste for social life (ibid., p.86); son (ibid., p.166); daughter (ibid., p.171).
60. See Goody (1975); cf. Hann (2008),
61. Goody (1975: 6).
62. Ibid: 8
63. Ibid.: 13.
64. Ibid: 13
65. Cf. Morgan (1871), cited in Goody (1975: 19). Such an account has been strongly challenged by, among others, Kuper (1988).
66. Bourdieu (1977b: 30–71).
67. Cf. chapter 1, which briefly discusses Balzac's registration of the same issue, and the evolution of his views.
68. *Los tres gojats*, p.149.
69. *Los tres gojats*, p.30.
70. Cf. Howe's general discussion of the importance of risk in the reinscription of social rules through ritual performance (Howe 2000).
71. Defence of thesis (*Los tres gojats*, p.86ff.); early successes (ibid., p.121); spoken of as potential deputy (ibid., p.125).
72. 'D'ua hutada, las solas paraulas entenudas au cafè que l'aven hèit entrar lo diable de la politica au cap' (*Los tres gojats*, p.127).
73. See Cobban (1961: 71–131) for this and the following two paragraphs.
74. Material on the elections of the period (*Los tres gojats*, pp.166–169).
75. *Los tres gojats*, pp.168–171.
76. Perpetual dissatisfaction (*Los tres gojats*, p.124); Loïs' admiration (ibid., p.40–41); accepts account (ibid., p.42); spreads views (ibid., p.172).
77. Pau follows Paris (*Los tres gojats*, p.173); dissemination of radical ideas (ibid., p.174).
78. Note the presentation of Andrèu as candidate to his public by the Count in the patois of Toulouse; cf. note 2.
79. 'aver tant hèit entà d'arrèn' (*Los tres gojats*, p.185).
80. Marx (1972[1852]: 10).
81. *Los tres gojats*, p.185.
82. Cf. chapter 2.
83. Bordeu (1970[1889]). This book may be equally or even more obscure than Palay's novel. J.-A. Catala claims, in the introduction to the 1970 reprint, that – other than an example in the Pau municipal library – the 1889 original edition had disappeared.
84. 'Maintenant une génération inquiète succède ... L'honneur est un mot vide de sens, si les homes vont, viennent, disparaissent et ne prennent racine nulle part: si la mémoire, le respect des morts, le renom de probité qu'ils acquirent n'est plus transmis sur place aux enfants' (Bordeu 1970, p.184).
85. 'sa richesse de pensée est celle d'un véritable humaniste, d'un humaniste fait pour un lieu' (Ibid, p.ii)

Chapter 6

BOURDIEU'S BÉARNAIS ETHNOGRAPHY

Seule l'attention aux données les plus triviales ... peut conduire à la construction des modèles empiriquement validés et susceptibles d'être formalisés.

— Pierre Bourdieu (2002a: 14)

I

The purpose of this chapter is to demonstrate through a close reading the contribution of indigenous Béarnais categories to shaping the thinking of a contemporary sociologist. We began with an earlier instance, Le Play's encounter with Pyrenean forms of social life, which led to a further exploration of these forms through archival and ethnographic materials; in the previous chapter, the active component in these categories emerged particularly clearly from consideration of Palay's novel. Just as the notarial documents outlined in chapter 3 indicate the continuation of these longstanding forms in the present so, in another, more abstract, plane, Bourdieu's work exemplifies the same lesson.

Pierre Bourdieu (1930–2002) was born in a market town in Béarn. His biographical experience forms a recurrent topic in his broad project, which he has termed a 'reflexive sociology'.[1] He conducted fieldwork in his home town, Denguin, in 1959 and 1960, publishing the results in an article on 'non-marriage and the peasant condition' in 1962.[2] He returned twice to that fieldwork article, offering an analysis of marriage strategies in 1972,[3] and a discussion of symbolic violence in 1989.[4] In the latter two articles, he developed several of the central concepts, concerns and approaches deployed in his major writings. In the last decade of his life, Bourdieu reflected increasingly on the place of biography in the reception and generation of social experience, and invoked his autobiography in expounding his ideas. More or less his last publication gathered his Béarnais papers together with an introduction[5] in which he claimed that the three articles constitute an account of the logic of research specific to the social sciences.[6] The Béarnais corpus represents, then, a privileged access at several levels to the link between biography and theory, as well as a means of grasping what is at stake in a reflexive sociology.

I shall use two terms to shape my investigation of the place of Bourdieu's biography in his work, which refer to two mutually implicated aspects of this return to his home town (disguised in the articles under the name of 'Lesquire'). The first is the intellectual 'synopsis' contained in Bourdieu's personal history: he embodies the transition from local to cosmopolitan, from the world of the patois to that of the French language, from traditional to modern. These are the oppositions of which he tried to give an objective account in 1962, and with which he traced a deepening engagement subsequently. The second is the emotional experience, or 'pathos', contained within this synopsis which, he claims, is almost completely excluded from the initial article. This pathos consists in pity for the objects of study, on the one hand, and a sense of guilt or betrayal, on the other. It was the motivation for his initial interest and the perspective he took, and its working-through provides the mainspring of his subsequent analyses.

We are not dealing with a simple biography and the charting of an emotional history, nor concerned with 'the facile delights of self-exploration'.[7] Bourdieu claims that the three successive treatments of the same problem – the failure of heirs to marry construed as a symptom of a crisis in the peasant condition – allow him simultaneously to develop a more general (or abstract) theoretical account and to come closer to experience. 'The more the theoretical analysis is extended, the closer it gets to the data of observation'.[8] A reflexive sociology is an exploration of the resources the social scientist brings to bear, allowing him or her to construct a social understanding which includes the location and motivations of the enquirer's mind. Bourdieu's articles contain, therefore, both a successive refinement of theoretical concepts and a corresponding growth in retrospective understanding of what was at stake in the initial encounter. In this way, the past is revised and recast: self-understanding is constructed against time. Bourdieu indeed suggests the trajectory of his research offers an 'intellectual *Bildungsroman*', the story of the transformation, both intellectual and emotional, of this 'phenomenology of affective life'. Experience of the 'pains and dramas linked to the relations between the sexes' is transformed into a more distanced and realistic account of the social world and of social practices.[9]

One can track his increasing emotional awareness through a series of articles, interviews and other writings.[10] In an interview in 1992 Bourdieu identifies for the first time the 'personal experience' that previously had been veiled behind neutral description.[11] He had attended a dance one Christmas Eve in a rural restaurant, where urban youths danced with local women and peasant bachelors looked on. The bachelors were Bourdieu's contemporaries and were, in the local view, fated never to marry. He concludes: 'I spent nearly twenty years trying to understand why I chose that village ball... I even believe – this is something I would never have dared to say even ten years ago – that the feeling of sympathy ... that I felt then and the sense of pathos that exuded from the scene I witnessed were surely at the root of my interest in this object'. This experience, he suggests in 2002, was concealed in the 1962 article behind a series of techniques aimed at providing an objective description. He elaborates on the 'emotional atmosphere' in which the enquiry took place. He recalls examining a class photograph with a former class mate, a young woman working in the neighbouring town, who classified half of the individuals as 'unmarriageable'. Then, he mentions the often painful interviews with old bachelors, in which he was assisted by his father's presence and interventions. He also outlines the path through life of an intelligent and sensitive contemporary who stayed on the farm. And he refers to his sense of committing an act of treachery, which underlay both the objective style of his presentation and his refusal until now to reprint the article, 'for fear of ill-intentioned or voyeuristic readings'.[12]

This complex experience could only be reconstructed and understood after the event, through the increasingly objective models produced. The more abstract the model, the more direct the access gained to the initial pathos or intuition, for the whole account had been present in the first description, but the truth only glimpsed.[13] This approach provides a vindication of the ethnographic method: other social sciences are constructed through an ignoring of the everyday in the name of a move to abstraction that is supposed to constitute the 'scientific' approach. In fact, this act of repression makes them incapable of achieving their objective. We might note how closely he links anthropological method and personal knowledge in this retrospective account, for his work does not always emphasize this connection.

The personal, by this token, cannot be excluded from social understanding. 'Progress in the knowledge of human matters cannot be separated from progress in understanding the subject who knows'. This understanding is developed through 'all the humble and obscure efforts by which the knowing subject frees himself from his unthought past, and immerses himself in the logic contained in the object to be known'.[14] By reflecting on his experience as socially constituted knowledge, the social scientist – over time and through hard work – becomes his own informant.[15] Bourdieu is thereby able to conclude that 'the author of the last article [1989] has been constructed through the effort of research that has allowed him to reappropriate the most obscure and the oldest part of himself, intellectually and emotionally'. In brief, this series of articles concerns the remembrance of thing past: the active construction of an understanding, through art and the recovery of the forces at work in the past, which permits situated (scientific) concepts to gain a certain generality.

I intend to explore this act of construction, seeking not to lose sight of the anthropological mode of understanding that lies at the heart of sociological knowledge. My aim in this chapter is twofold. First, I shall read the 1962 article to see how the motivating force of the pathos felt is expressed, particularly in terms of lacunae or limitations. For if Bourdieu's return to a rural childhood allows the eventual construction of theory-laden terms that can be applied more generally – terms such as habitus, strategy and interest, and symbolic domination (or violence) – the regret the writer felt also conditions the story he tells. This conditioning is expressed in such forms as the sense of an irreversible change having occurred around 1914; the selection of informants (principally old men and bachelors); the deployment of statistics; and, above all, the cryptic determinism that deprives the actors of all power of initiative, and therefore condemns them to defeat in advance. This argument is the heart of the chapter. Second, I shall read the later articles in the light of this analysis to determine whether the limitations perceived are transmitted through the concepts and models generated. This approach maintains the chronological distinction between the papers, even at some cost in elegance and concision of analysis; following in detail the play of ethnography and its progressive theorizing demands a certain discursive style of exposition. My concern is to trace the developments and transformations of Bourdieu's thinking over time, in this way pursuing a description of the processes to which he draws attention in his later reflections. I do not want to offer a critique of Bourdieu's work from some external position, but rather to apply what I have learnt from him to some of his own writings, partly in view of my own apprenticeship in Béarn. Bourdieu moves constantly between two systems of reading, which I shall trace, and criticism usually comes down to some fine tuning in emphasis, concerning how the two relate at a given point. This reading is not then critical, but rather an exemplification, most notably of the claim that it is in the small details that reliable knowledge emerges. By offering this detailed account, we can review both Bourdieu's interpretation of the local categories and their self-presentation – if that is not too anthropomorphic a term –

through his writing, identifying their characteristic combination of frankness and concealment which has been their trademark throughout this investigation.

II

Bourdieu's 1962 article, 'Célibat et condition paysanne', considers marriage in rural Béarn from the angle of a crisis, one affecting all the local institutions through the non-marriage of heirs and the consequent failure to transmit property. This approach, which views the crisis from the perspective of a change in the relations of authority within the family, and which sees the family as a key to the ordering of other social institutions, has a long tradition in French family sociology, going back to the work of Louis de Bonald.[16] Bourdieu portrays the crisis of non-marriage in Béarn as the collapse of a traditional world through the impinging of the values of modernity at all levels of the social order. The account captures a supposedly definitive and irreversible moment of transition and loss, conceived from within the family as an alteration in the mode of authority and from without as a form of moral anarchy, as the amorality of the market takes over.

These concerns structure the article, which begins with a description of the former system of matrimonial exchanges, grounded in particular relations of authority. A statistically based description of the current state of crisis follows, sketched in terms of marriage opportunities for men and women according to whether they originate from the local town or the isolated farms in the surrounding countryside. This division anticipates the third part, which offers an explanation of the crisis of authority in terms of a shift from rural to cosmopolitan values, acted out in the altering balance of power between the local centre and the hamlets. The last part elaborates on this shift in values which is encapsulated in the occasion of the Christmas Eve dance and incarnated in the peasant's body. A brief conclusion is followed by several appendices, including a bibliographical essay on sources concerning Béarn, and an attempt to extend the analysis by a comparison with non-marriage in a Breton case study.

The structure of the article repeats that adopted by Bourdieu with his Algerian materials, outlining first the previous system or order, and then the crisis of modernity that has overtaken it.[17] This is a common schema, which claims that anthropology comes first, to be replaced by history. We will investigate some of the problems it implies, but at heart they come down to this: there is a conflict between the active intelligence at work in the closed, anthropological phase, manifested in the manipulations and calculations of marriage exchanges, and the portrait of the peasant in the open, historical phase as an automaton, caught in habits that no longer serve him in the new situation and, indeed, accelerate his defeat. But before making detailed comments, I want to outline the argument concerning marriage and succession, for it exemplifies how, in Bourdieu's hands, the logic of anthropological categories shapes sociological concepts. This is a crucial component of the intelligence contained in Bourdieu's approach and so, although the detail is familiar from the earlier chapters, it is necessary here in order to see the work this logic performs in his writing.

Bourdieu describes the 'system of matrimonial exchanges in the society of former times'. 'Before 1914', he states, 'marriage was controlled by very strict rules'.[18] In offering this account, he relies principally on a single informant,[19] together with the various published works on marriage, dowry and inheritance in Béarn, which are listed in an appendix but not referred to in the text. Though the 'rules' are complex, we may offer the following summary, labelling the topics as house, single inheritance, authority, dowry, marriage contract, and the distinction between great and small houses. These six form a ring.

First, the principle 'actor' is collective, not individual. The 'house', conceived as family, household, property, means of production and reputation, is the focus; individuals have to be considered primarily as a function of their place within this collective entity.

Then, the principle aim of this entity is the transmission intact of the property in all its aspects between generations. This is expressed in the practice of single inheritance, usually primogeniture. The interests and identities of all parties concur in this aim, for they are defined by the house. Moreover, the whole local social order is implicated in this act of transmission, for the family is continually negotiating its worth – and being appraised – as an element within the hierarchy of houses, and the 'name' it perpetuates gains its value from this wider context.

Next, relations of authority within the house express this principle aim although, it is important to note, these various relations are not understood in functional terms, but are construed as the 'natural' values of peasant society. Bourdieu points to three such relations, the precedence of men over women, the heir over the others of his generation, and the authority of parents over children. The first is a function of the need for a man to manage the farming business, and also to represent the house and to maintain its reputation in the local order. In the second, the heir's privilege is a function of his belonging to the land, rather than vice versa.[20] Both of these relations however are subject to the demand of the overall aim; in the absence of a suitable son, a daughter may inherit; likewise, a younger child may be substituted for the eldest in case of incapacity or unwillingness. This power of substitution points to the third relation, the authority of parents over children, for the parents guide, and even determine, the destiny of their offspring. They institute the heir, or effect his substitution, and also grant to each non-heir their 'share' of the property at the point of transmission.

The notion of a share brings out a tension between the interests of the house, embodied in the heir and the authority of 'the master', and the interests of the individuals who compose the house, although they are not individuals in a modern sense. Authority as a precipitate of the house is by no means absolute, for non-heirs have rights over the property too. This is where the fourth topic appears: the 'dowry' may be construed simultaneously as the share an offspring is due, as the compensation paid for renunciation of an interest in the property, and as the holder's principal means of marriage. Bourdieu emphasizes the compensatory face of the dowry, pointing out that in practice division (*partage*) is a disaster, to be avoided by any means, including payments made over a period, and mortgaging land. He nowhere mentions that the amount due to each offspring is fixed by the Civil Code.[21]

The dowry articulates several different constraints, particularly in a society lacking ready cash. So, while an individual's chances of marriage depend on a number of factors – the status and wealth of the house, gender, birth rank and the number of siblings – they are summed up and brought to a common measure in the dowry. At the same time, the dowry continues to belong to the house of origin. Although under the management of the new family, it is for the support and protection of the spouse who marries in, and only passes at her death to the children of the marriage. If she dies childless – or if she is widowed – the dowry must be returned; given this possibility, it constitutes not just potential wealth but also a threat to the receiving household.

The business of the dowry brings us, next, to marriage considered as an occasion bringing these issues to the fore, for the first marriage in the generation, usually the marriage of the heir, is linked to the 'division' of the inheritance. It is then that the heir is installed and the compensation to be paid each non-heir specified. This is how the event is seen from within the family. At the same time, the dowry coming into the house through the heir's marriage is crucial to the settlement, often being the means by which the siblings' shares are paid. But considered as a matter between families, the dowry consists both in the material wealth the bride brings and the reputation she bears, both being functions of the house from which she comes. So marriage is controlled not only by the internal factors we have mentioned, but is also a moment of calculation between the houses in terms of economic interests and honour, embodied in the exchange. Both aspects, division and exchange, are effected through the dowry, and are given form in the marriage contract.

Sixth and last, there is a crucial local distinction between 'big' houses and 'little' houses, or great and small, which is also manifested at marriage. The distinction reflects both economic wealth and reputation, and lies behind the concept of a 'good' marriage, by which a family improves its place in the local hierarchy and so consolidates its name.

Through these topics, which can readily be understood in terms drawn from his later work – such as habitus and dispositions, strategy and interest, field and symbolic capital – Bourdieu reconciles the demands of objective social structures with the autonomy of mental categories, focusing upon the role representation plays in the reproduction of social order. There is a sophisticated practical logic at work, even if at an early stage of sociological articulation.

On the basis of this indigenous logic, Bourdieu offers two kinds of explanatory description. The first concerns the constraints on marriage, exercised through the judgement and authority of the parents, which weigh in particular on the heir. This authority can be expressed pathologically, indeed, in the non-marriage of the heir. In brief, marriage normally takes place between houses of equal status, for two reasons, both expressed negatively. First, because of the threat repayment of the dowry represents, a house cannot accept a sum above its means. And second, if an incoming wife has, owing to the wealth she brings, too high a status relative to the receiving house, the male authority of the husband on which right order is based is threatened, and this can undermine the house. Accordingly, within a narrow band, men tend to marry down, taking a good wife who will not upset the status quo.

Within the same logic and constraints, women tend both to move on marriage, and to marry up. Women therefore are more capable of perceiving and responding to new influences; they are more adaptable. This is an important point, to be invoked in subsequent analyses.

The second explanatory description concerns the fate of non-heirs and the place of non-marriage in the 'system'. It is possible to run through the permutations of marriage, of a younger son to an heiress, and the difficult alliances of younger sons and younger daughters, who lack means of support. Here again there is a strong distinction to be made between the fate of the sexes. Families wish to marry off their daughters; they go to other farms, or to the towns. An unmarried adult daughter is a burden on a farm, not extra labour, and also carries, in her supposed vulnerability, a risk of damage to the house's reputation. Dowry is the price that has to be paid to avoid this, and so numerous daughters can spell disaster for a house.

The options for younger sons are distinctive: in addition to marriage with an heiress, or marrying and leaving to seek employment elsewhere, they can remain in the countryside unmarried, working either on their farm of origin or as hired labour. If they remain unmarried, they contribute their labour and their earnings, while renouncing their share of the inheritance, contributing by their sacrifice to the integrity of the house. They represent the limits of the social logic; 'the non-marriage of some is integrated in the coherence of the social system and by this fact has an eminently social function'.[22]

The entire system, therefore, manifests the aim of maintaining the property intact, and the various forms of authority to which the actors subscribe – what they can do and what they cannot, including whether they marry – are functions of this aim and of nothing else. Bourdieu ends this account by reflecting on the importance that indigenous conceptions and categories play in sociological explanation, pointing to the significance of status rather than class; to the limitations of any notion of economic determination of social facts; and to certain demographic features: late marriage, low birth rate, few children, and the non-marriage of younger sons. All these features are functions of the local ambition to preserve the permanence of the house.

III

Despite its sensitivity to the role that native categories play in sociological explanation, we may criticize Bourdieu's account for its creation of an ethnographic – peasant – world isolated from history. There is no indication, for example, of the negotiations over time with outside forces that lie behind the formation and perpetuation of the farms and the forms of devolution and marriage settlement that are described. Yet these have their histories: they are not natural, autochthonous ways of life; they are being continually recreated. The omission of any reference to the Civil Code as the source of the formula for division is characteristic in this respect. Nevertheless, by this silence, Bourdieu seeks to bring out the self-regulation of the peasant world and its relative autonomy.

The remainder of his article seeks to contrast the present with this autonomous past. There has been a break: the peasant-focused system has been overthrown, or is in the last stages of its existence. And the symptom of this break is that the non-marriage of men, which had been an integral part of the system (even if as a limiting case), is now seen not to safeguard but to threaten the social order. 'Submission to the rule' is now seen as 'the breakdown of the system, or anomie'.[23]

In describing this break, Bourdieu employs a different source: the past can be recorded through informants, but to record the present and the changes it contains he has recourse to statistics, using census data to present an objective account. Yet enumeration is first of all a function of classification, and Bourdieu has a thesis. His aim is to show that, while bachelors formerly lived where their place in the social hierarchy dictated, now they are distributed across geographical space, being found in the scattered populations of the hamlets rather than in the concentrated populations of the market towns.

His conclusions from the data assembled may be summarized as follows. First, the former logic still pertains in the hamlets: marriage chances continue to be related to age, sex, birth order and status (whether a proprietor or not, and the size of the farm in question). Nevertheless – and second – men's marriage chances have become less closely linked to the socio-economic system than formerly.[24] The privilege of the proprietor and of the eldest son are threatened and, although the head of a house marries more easily than a farm hand or an agricultural labourer, he often remains unmarried, while the younger sons of small families, contrariwise, can find wives.

But third, these rural contrasts pale into insignificance when set against those between the inhabitant of the market town and the rural peasant. Bourdieu concludes that the chances of marriage are seven times greater for a man of the younger generation (31 to 40 years old) living in the *bourgs* than for one living in the hamlets. The disparity for the younger women (those between 21 and 40 years old), although far smaller, is also marked: the chances of marrying are twice as great in the *bourgs* as in the hamlets.[25]

On the basis of this account, Bourdieu argues for a crisis in peasant values, whereby the logic of matrimonial exchanges now prevents exactly what it sets out to achieve – the marriage of heirs. I have two reservations about this argument from statistics. In the first place, in transcribing census categories we have moved away from the indigenous categories. We find not the local division of 'great' and 'small' houses, but the listing of large, medium and small properties according to the area farmed, with arbitrary transition points between the classes. And among the non-property-owning classes – agricultural workers, sharecroppers and tenant farmers, *domestiques* and *aides familiaux* – younger brothers and eldest sons are not, of course, identified. Bourdieu does his best, but it is difficult to compute from the tables to the text.

In the second place, without denying the thesis Bourdieu proposes, another story can be told, many indications of which appears in the margins of his text. The contrast in the figures for male non-marriage between the hamlets and the market town can in large part be accounted for by a specific change in the demand for farm labour.

There are at least two factors in play. First, the post-Second World War period was one of improvements in agricultural techniques – the introduction of tractors, fertilizers, new crops and irrigation – bringing changes in the need for auxiliary labour. Bourdieu's article is contemporary with Mendras's classic account of 'the end of the peasants'.[26] Bourdieu scarcely registers the change in his text, although he mentions new forms of peasant economic organization – the *syndicats* and co-operatives, and the Crédit Agricole. Second, there are new local forms of industrial employment emerging in this period, notably the oil field at Lacq. These have the potential to reverse the rural exodus, which Bourdieu considers in Appendix II.[27] There have always been local or regional factories, but these can now be reached by car or bicycle from the farm; outside employment does not necessarily involve leaving the countryside. Bourdieu does not mention these factors either.

It is possible to give an alternative description of the period: while there is a change affecting surplus labour on the farms, involving a steep reduction in farm hands and home helpers, this does not necessarily represent a crisis affecting the survival of the farms. Certainly, amalgamating all the categories of employment in order to make a contrast between the market town and the hamlets in terms of possibilities of marriage distracts attention from discerning the fate of the farms, concerning which the numbers are rather small to lend themselves to statistical analysis. Indeed, it is more than a distraction, it is a function of Bourdieu's model.

Despite its claim to deal in specifics, Bourdieu's model involves the introduction of an idea from without, the discernment of a moment of irreversible change. The use of statistics serves not to introduce history into the analysis, but to conjure it away. A description of the farms in 1960, including their relationships with the town, is certainly needed. In addition to changes in agricultural techniques and associated labour needs, the threshold of viable farm size shifted upwards, reflecting the costs of investment in mechanization, and affecting the smallest farms (where most of the statistical tables' non-marrying proprietors are found). These farms have always been vulnerable to fluctuations in the threshold of viability; their failure provides land for other farms to grow, the other side of the coin. Then, the largest farms also have their own characteristic forms of crisis, expressed through non-marriage and the division of property, but these failures are both rare and not specific to the particular moment.[28] Last, there are other contemporary factors affecting the non-marriage of heirs, including the kind of phenomena Bourdieu has in mind. In the age group under consideration, one might add the crucial wasted years of the Second World War. But they are not decisive, in the sense of bringing the system to an end.

Bourdieu has read continuity through mutation and adaptation as crisis; he imposes the notion of a break, the ending of a way of life, when he might in fact be dealing with its perpetuation. By doing so, he abandons the ethnographic approach. Recourse to statistics allows a reading in terms of a narrative of loss in place of careful attention to local life and its (often painful) relation to time and change. The symptom of this substitution is the way he employs informants' accounts: in contrast to the first part, where an indigenous logic is carefully elucidated, here we are offered the uncritical reproduction of that part of local opinion which matches the model. In particular, we are presented with received opinion concerning male non-marriage and the reasons people have for leaving the land: the demanding physical work; the excessive power of parents (and parents-in-law); and the attraction women feel for the life and values of the town, despising their brothers and admiring men from the city. The indigenous logic is left unarticulated in this narrative, and we never hear the voices of those who leave. For this reason, we need to be particularly cautious of Bourdieu's explanations with respect to women, who are 'muted'[29] in these accounts.

IV

The approach this criticism draws on springs, of course, from Bourdieu's own work.[30] How might he reply? That the homogenization of which I complain – the ironing out of the local perspective – represents the truth of the historical moment. Modern, universalizing values invade and flatten ethnographic distinctions into statistical differences. The reason, however, why I point to the continuing force of local categories, attitudes and practices with some confidence is that one can find parallel accounts of the disappearance of local society under the pressure of modernity at any moment in the last two hundred years, starting from Bonald's version. This phenomenon was discussed above (in chapter 3): Weber suggests the crucial date of the transformation is 1870;[31] Mendras puts 'the end of the peasant' ninety years later; Le Play describes the collapse of the local system of inheritance in 1857; Bourdieu gives the vital date as 1914; Etchelecou's recent study[32] puts the failure of the system of successions in the 1960s; I myself have watched the failure of an important house to find an heir in the next generation in the 1990s. Bourdieu believes his fieldwork enabled him to grasp the logic of a local system on the brink of disappearing. Yet the evidence of the literature suggests that the system in fact survives in part by presenting itself to an outside gaze in the form of 'being about to disappear'. In practice, as argued in the previous chapter, local ways of life co-exist with metropolitan concerns by evolving strategies whereby they offer some aspects of themselves to outside interests, while concealing other aspects behind these offerings. There is a matching of expectation and revelation.[33]

In this part of his work, Bourdieu exemplifies the characteristic anthropological stance of ethnographic 'salvage'. In this instance, the stance owes a good deal to Le Play, whose discovery of the Béarnais family is a version of Bonald's account of the crisis induced in the family by legislation.[34] Bourdieu cites Le Play, but fails to give him his due.[35] Le Play's account also has two distinct moments, anthropological and historical respectively, describing a particular way of life – the Béarnais 'stem family' – as under threat of dissolution because of the compulsory egalitarian division of inheritance prescribed by the Civil Code.

This is not to argue for direct literary influence. Le Play articulated a widely shared ideology that has permitted the matching, in Béarn, of a cosmopolitan, sociological point of view with local opinion. First, he described a break: the end of a way of life, realized in patterns of marriage and inheritance. And second, he offered narrative detail that was shared not only by Bourdieu but also by his informants. When Bourdieu considers 'the factors overthrowing the system of matrimonial exchanges',[36] he cites the effects of inflation on dowries, with the consequent contesting of succession settlements and the undermining of parental authority, through the collapse of the dowry system and the loss of the power to disinherit. He also points to the impact of education and new ideas in the rise of individualism, reflected in the loss of a local focus, local institutions and a way of life, and expressed in the devaluation of the peasant, as social style becomes more important than economic worth. Above all, he emphasizes the part that women play in this new, unstable situation, for they adapt to the new values more than men do. The exodus principally involves women, who are predisposed to want to abandon peasant life, for they are educated to be adaptable, outward looking and socially mobile; they readily give up the rural world with its hard work and the authority of the parents-in-law, being drawn to salaried employment and the comforts of the town.

This description derives from informants, nearly all old men, who offer Bourdieu an 'official' account, to use his term. This is a shared ideology, which would have its part to play in any investigation of the indigenous critique of authority, working conditions and isolation, not to mention the settlement between the sexes, and which would serve as part of an inventory of the local resources generating change. But it is not the whole story. In particular, the voices of two groups are missing, those of the younger women and of the younger farmers. In French peasant society it is certainly difficult for a man to talk to women. However, while he mentions the young farmers' efforts at adaptation (see below), Bourdieu does not investigate them either; he sticks to his father's contacts.

On the basis of this shared, Le Playsian account, Bourdieu offers an explanation of the crisis in the marriage system. He suggests that the former logic – built on the distinction between the eldest and the others, and between great houses and small – has been replaced by another, based on the distinction between town and hamlets. In the context of this change, the survival of old values is destructive: considerations of honour are counter-productive, and economic contrasts prevent marriage rather than identifying partners. A conceptual scheme that is no longer relevant, focusing around the idea of the dowry, persists in particular in rural men; women, however, escape from the constraint of local values. It is worth underlining the role ascribed to mothers in this distribution of responses, for they transmit these contradictory aims to their sons and daughters – a good marriage or none for the heir, marriage and departure for the daughter. (The mothers' voices are also missing from the account.) For each actor, the ethnographic categories are reactive; they are adhered to in spite of the situation. The only power of initiative granted the ethnographic subject in this historical world is stubbornly to pursue his or her own defeat.

V

These reservations must be evaluated as precisely as possible if Bourdieu's work is to be given its due. Just as the anthropological account overstates the isolation of the peasant world, so the statistical account overstates the helplessness of that world in its engagements with the outside. Both lack a sufficient account of the indigenous relation to history. The peasant world has been actively constructed in interaction with the wider society, and has had continually to make sense of changing conditions that are not of its making. The latter can be as diverse as economic inflation of prices on the one hand, and the promotion of an ideology of equality on the other. Bourdieu examines the effects of these factors on such indigenous institutions as the payment of dowries and authority within the household, but he appears to lack awareness, first, that these factors will be read and coped with on the basis of local categories and, second, that these categories will bear in them the marks of previous, comparable encounters in which they were forged.

In such a light, we might note that there has been the potential for the breakdown of marriage settlements and the contesting of successions since the formation of the 'system', and, moreover, it is in the memory of these 'crises' that the system is in part transmitted.

Likewise, the dowry is a means for achieving certain defined ends within this same system; its discontinuation is not to be identified with the disappearance of the system, though – because of the Civil Code rather than despite it – local practices of division continue to replicate its function. And while a rise in individualism clearly changes the resources open to the 'individuals' within the system – the non-heirs who marry away or who do not marry – their potential to respond is defined by their place in the system, rather than by their individuality.

In short, the practical logic continues to operate. Bourdieu is right to point out that some indigenous responses will be destructive in their effects, but he appears to be blind to the potential of human intelligence to adapt. In adopting this point of view, he expresses an opinion appropriate to a marginal status within the system.

Bourdieu abandons ethnographic description when he turns to sociological myth, introducing, in essence, the story of a social mechanism (of marriage exchanges) that has been placed in a new environment. It is a myth because it excludes history, so that time becomes a function of the structure, and the persons become stereotypes, supported by informants' accounts. These idealized forms populate the accounts Bourdieu gives of the now destructive logic of misalliance and of the declining frequency of marriage between peasants and town dwellers, where the same pattern emerges.[37] Bourdieu's analysis in the latter case depicts decline: fewer peasants marry women from the local town than before; there are still strong social constraints operating with respect to a peasant's choice of wife; and there is the loss of those 'backward' areas whence peasants formerly took wives. The unasked question concerns initiative: what is the developing pattern of marriage, employment and residence in the hamlets and, in particular, on the farms? In addition to an account of passivity faced with decline, there needs to be a complementary investigation of initiative and adaptation in order to give a complete account. Yet the latter is missing.

This figure of the passive ethnographic subject beset by active, anonymous, historical forces structures the subsequent analyses of the opposition between the market town and the hamlets and of the peasant's body. It operates at either scale. In each case, the facts assembled are instructive and the analysis valuable, but running through each is this flaw, perhaps best described as the author's withholding from the actors the capacity to act and to understand.

Bourdieu correlates the restructuring of the system of matrimonial exchanges with the restructuring of the global society around the opposition between the market town and the hamlets – which is itself the product of a process of differentiation tending to give the town the monopoly of urban functions.[38] He describes the relation between the two prior to 1914, when farming preoccupations predominated even in the town, reflected in its architecture, uses of land and sources of wealth. In this period, too, there was greater social density in the countryside, with collective work patterns and associated entertainments, places to gather – inns and skittle alleys – and shops and businesses. In more recent times, both have altered. The town has gained the monopoly on places to gather, eat or be entertained; it has also concentrated the businesses and shops. It has gained an independent professional class, made up of state functionaries, doctors, teachers and the like. It has consequently changed in terms of ethos, becoming less oriented to the surrounding countryside and more of a relay for metropolitan ideas and values. This shift is expressed in language use, for French has replaced Béarnais in the town. Bourdieu reflects that the town still exists as a tertiary sector to the countryside, but this dependency is no longer perceived. Instead, the town has become an alien place for the peasant, on which he is nevertheless dependent in order to find mediators for dealing with the market and the state. This dependency is reflected in the distribution of elected offices: town people have the political power.

In concluding this section, Bourdieu makes two contrasting points. The first concerns the physical sense of alienation that peasants experience in the town, their unease being given expression in such intimate ways as language use, the clothes they wear, their posture and gait.[39] This anticipates his final section (on the Christmas dance). The second is a brief consideration – in the concluding paragraph[40] – of the emergence of 'a new rural elite' from the ranks of the middle ranking and smaller farm proprietors, which forms a potential opposition both to the former peasant leadership, the 'big' farmers, and to the town-dwelling *notables* who currently hold political power. He refers to the initiatives these younger farmers have undertaken – rural centres, CUMAs (co-operatives for sharing equipment), centres for the improvement of agricultural techniques[41] – and hints at their power to renew the rural economy.[42]

Here, clearly, are some seeds of future development. But instead, he elaborates on the first point in discussing the Christmas Eve dance, taken as the moment of interiorization of the scheme of contradictions in the peasant's body. This analysis introduces the notion of habitus for the first time in Bourdieu's work,[43] conceived in the limited form of bodily hexis. The physical and mental incapacity of the peasant to dance is an instantiation of the shift from local to cosmopolitan values, from a world where the choice of a marriage partner is the product of a collective calculus to one where the individual must use his own initiative to find a wife.

The dance is a privileged occasion, then, to grasp the root of the tensions and conflicts, for it is 'a clash of civilizations',[44] when the urban world, with its cultural models, music, dances and bodily techniques, irrupts into the peasant world. The peasant habitus – the old dances, rhythms, music, words – has gone, and the corresponding bodily hexis – the marks of his work and environment, his clothes, attitudes and expressions – is devalued. Here again, the role of women is crucial, for they constitute the section of the local population that has adopted urban values, and it is through their response to him that the peasant learns to interiorize the image others have of him; he becomes aware of himself as a 'peasant' through his awareness of his body and its alienation.

This is a brilliant analysis, which deepens the psychological description given earlier of the contemporary logic at work in the choice of marriage partners; there are two incompatible models, and a differing penetration of the urban cultural frame of reference according to sex. It is still worth remarking, however, that there are fragments of evidence that suggest this account of male peasant anomie may not be the whole story. The principal informant for this section ('P.C.') is a man of thirty-two, resident in the market town and an employee (*cadre moyen*), not a peasant, who shares the sociologist's perspective of decline and provides much of the opinion leading to the account of the peasant's 'unhappy consciousness' of self.[45] One might question such an informant's insight or agenda, or at least be cautious. Moreover, he also provides some counter-evidence, for he refers to some of 'the most active and able' farmers who 'dress well, [and] go out a good deal. They have introduced new methods, new crops. Some have modernized the house'.[46] Despite this testimony, the informant concludes they are 'unmarriageable'.

Bourdieu similarly incorporates this rural elite within his framework, though perhaps with a note of doubt; 'modernization in the technical domain, while it confers a certain prestige, does not necessarily favour marriage'. Formerly, he adds, only married men exercised public authority, for example, serving on the town council; now, leadership is not a matter of status but of personality. Non-marriage, he concludes, is a focussed way of experiencing the poverty (*la misère*) of the peasant condition. The peasant projects this experience, saying 'the land is no good (*fichue*)', when he means even the best cannot assure the continuity of his line.[47] We might wonder whether the pity that Bourdieu experienced at the Christmas Eve dance is not projected in a similar way when he says 'the peasant is finished'.

VI

How do the synopsis and pathos contained in the first article play out in the later ones? To sum up the argument from the first article, Bourdieu uses two distinct approaches, employing different evidence with different implications. On the one hand, he gives priority to certain indigenous practices and orderings, and derives a series of powerful sociological concepts on the basis of this practical logic. On the other, he imposes an externally conceived narrative on these practices, in the form of a statistical analysis which denies any power of adaptation or initiative to the actors, who then play out the parts allotted to them in the story.

Each approach contains its limitations and its insight; the issue lies in the way these two perspectives – anthropologically isolated and historically conditioned – are portrayed as successive rather than as simultaneous, co-existing forms. Bourdieu's account of the 'economy' between these two conditions, one replacing the other over time, draws on a sociological tradition (Bonald, Le Play) which corresponds at particular points to various popular conceptions, notably concerning the place of women with respect to change.

Although he twice revisits the article, Bourdieu does not alter the temporal framework adopted; rather, he strengthens the power of the second moment. The 1972 paper develops the anthropological logic contained in the first section of the earlier article, maintaining that account's indifference to questions of the conditions for the system's formation, transmission and adaptation, and freeing it, too, from any explicit consideration of its demise, although we shall find the marks of that anticipated end in the formalization of the model.

In 2002, however, Bourdieu claims that the bibliographical appendix to the 1962 article[48] prepared the way for a 'proper, that is, historicized understanding of a world that is breaking apart'. He also points to the intellectual context in which the 1972 article was written, as a 'break with the structuralist paradigm', marked by 'the move from rule to strategy, from structure to habitus, and from system to socialized agent'. Yet, though the account departs from structuralism's objective, impersonal stance with respect to rules, it maintains the latter's 'synchronicity'.[49]

The 1972 article represents a formalization of the 'system of matrimonial exchanges' at a higher level of abstraction, capable therefore of a greater generality. At the same time, Bourdieu emphasizes the significance of generating sociological concepts from indigenous practices. He employs local materials to cause him to think, in a dialectic with formal sociological concerns. It is the latter emphasis that constitutes the paper's innovation.

There is then a polemical aspect, for Bourdieu defines his approach against a family of sociological practices that generate their own descriptions: these all share the notion of 'following a rule'. Bourdieu condemns any analysis, whether ethnographic or juridical (or popular), which supposes informants execute a plan, whether consciously or unconsciously held, formalized or customary. In every case, the notion of rule-following supposes a distinction between theory and practice, or plan and realization, which Bourdieu rejects in his notion of practices. An outsider presumes you have to master the rules. An insider has unconscious mastery of everyday practices; he or she presumes the familiar. This familiar Bourdieu terms habitus: 'the system of dispositions inculcated by the material conditions of existence and by familial education'.[50] These dispositions are the generative principles that unify practices and give rise to the actors' strategies. Rather than following rules, the insider uses all permitted means to achieve a desired outcome, which is defined in local terms. This Bourdieu identifies as the safeguarding or increase of economic and symbolic capital.

Bourdieu derives this loose set of terms[51] – practices, habitus, strategies and symbolic capital – using the specifics of the Béarnais materials, whilst at the same time revising his original analysis. The notion of practices is glossed as that 'by which Béarnais peasants try to assure the reproduction of the lineage at the same time as reproducing its rights over the instruments of production'.[52] These practices may be expressed as regularities because habitus consists not in end-oriented rules but in 'schemes which guide choices without ever being open to complete ... explanation'.[53] This latter notion has changed its scope, from the set of guises, postures and so forth of embodied peasant culture, to such matters as the unquestioned relations of authority, which in turn express the 'natural' primacy of the group and the importance of preserving its identity in the form of the house. Habitus enables the choices made by the actors in pursuit of their ends to result in the reproduction of the social structures. In this fashion, Bourdieu reintroduces the primacy of meaning whilst simultaneously escaping from objective determinism and without falling into subjective intuitionism.

Strategies by this token reproduce but do not reflect social structures. The strategies of the Béarnais aim at assuring the integral transmission of the inheritance whilst maintaining the family's place in the social and economic hierarchy, and marriage is a function of these ends. The fact that these interiorized principles create typical solutions, which can be named by tradition, is not the same thing as there being rules.

VII

Bourdieu no longer defines the aims of each family in a marriage in terms of reputation and honour, but rather as the management of symbolic capital, pointing to the calculations and exchanges that underlie a family's laying out of its local forms of wealth in order to accumulate. This shift resolves the earlier discussion of the limits of economic determinism by assimilating the vocabulary of honour to that of the economy.

This is a significant move. Initially, Bourdieu likens marriage strategy to playing a hand of cards, combining necessity and skill. But he quickly turns to the economic model, the word 'capital' allowing him to introduce a series of related terms in his detailed redescription of marriage exchanges. He can offer the following 'translation': 'given matrimonial strategies always aim, at least in the best-placed families, to make a "good" marriage ... in other words, to maximize the profits and/or minimize the economic and symbolic costs of the marriage considered as a transaction of a particular type, they are controlled in each case by the material and symbolic value of the inheritance at stake in the transaction',[54] as well as, he continues, the mode of transmission which defines the interests of the various parties.

There are two problems concerning this translation of marriage exchanges into an economic vocabulary. The first is whether we are dealing here with a more profound description of indigenous realities, including motivations, or with an automatism of language, whereby the vocabulary employed generates its own associations and effects that come to substitute for the reality being described.

Second, this vocabulary lends itself to focusing the description of the interests of the family in terms of the importance of the dowry, for the dowry is the mechanism that allows the commensurability of the different imperatives contained in the generative structure. It is analogous to the power of money, allowing different values to be compared. Yet the key feature of the Béarnais world articulated around the dowry is that it is 'an economic universe dominated by the scarcity of money'.[55] Inflation and the penetration of modern values, essentially the cash economy, will in due course undermine the dowry. The adoption of an economic vocabulary allows modernity to penetrate into the heart of the description of an isolated anthropological world. Its fate is anticipated, as are the terms in which that fate will be explained.

The redescription of the logic of marriage strategies contains several important refinements. First, Bourdieu emphasizes that, because marriage affirms the respective places in the social hierarchy of the families concerned, it at the same time confirms that hierarchy. It serves both as a driving force behind the whole social structure and as a stabilizing influence.[56] Then, he elaborates the notion that each family has a 'matrimonial history', so that each marriage takes into account the significance of previous exchanges. This perspective also reflects the importance of wives/mothers in determining future unions, and the interest of marrying where a wife has been found before. Together, these conclusions suggest that 'the sociology of the family ... could only be a particular instance of political sociology'.[57] Third, he introduces the concept of 'strategies of fecundity' as, in the last instant, determining marriage strategies, as peasant families balance the respective demands of biological and social reproduction.[58]

Last, he discusses in greater detail how the dispositions of agents are adjusted to objective structures. The self-evidence of habitus to the participants conceals conflicts of duty and feeling, reason and passion, collective and individual interest. Participants never discuss the contradictions generated by the structure to which they are subject, but simply articulate the recommendations and precepts of the ethical and pedagogical discourse of local society,[59] which lend themselves to the reproduction of the system. The earlier discussion of authority is transformed into the notion of legitimacy, taken as the expression of symbolic power or domination. This concept is the focus of his contemporary *Esquisse d'une théorie de la pratique*,[60] and will reappear in his major works describing the role of education in the reproduction of social order.

This last discussion is simultaneously an expansion of the field of habitus and a closure. The field expands so that all the various strategies – whether marriage, succession, fecundity, instruction or other – combine to inculcate a set of values that are incarnated by the agents and serve to reproduce the system. We are dealing with a 'total social fact',[61] a classic anthropological locus. Yet at the same time, habitus has altered its emphasis, from generating solutions to encompassing a closed cultural set of possible responses, and this is because concealing the mainsprings of motivation is now its principal feature. However sophisticated the solutions enacted on this basis, this principle of concealment has eliminated intelligent initiative from the anthropological system, which is thereby reduced to a finite set of recombinations. Awareness of the truth of the historical situation is confined to the anthropologist, who knows that at the heart of the system lies the dowry, with its future dissolution inscribed in it.

VIII

In the 1989 article, Bourdieu develops the second, historical moment (which has already made its mark in the first, anthropological world through the notion of symbolic capital), to give an account of 'the symbolic dimension to economic domination',[62] which culminates in a theory of 'symbolic violence'.

The crux of this redescription lies in the notion of 'conversion': conversion from a closed world to one open to global influences, drawing on Polanyi's account of 'the great transformation' from isolated, regulated markets to the self-regulating market economy.[63] The group loses control of the mechanisms of exchange, and can no longer offer resistance to outside values. Formerly, resistance was a function of a related set of conditions and mechanisms. Bourdieu cites geographical isolation and poor transport, together with slight dependence on the market and the values of consumption. These in turn reinforced a culturally isolated social world centred on production, in which local marriage and dependence on traditional values went unquestioned. These were the objective and subjective conditions of a form of cultural particularism, which was locally focused and which determined the representation and reception of cosmopolitan values, subjecting even economic value to its cultural norms.

The collapse of this world is described in terms of the unification of the market of economic and symbolic goods. Peasant values cease to be different and, to a degree, controlling, and become instead 'other', recognized by all concerned as dependent.[64] Bourdieu describes the economic aspect of this unification as the integration of agricultural production into the market through dependence on industrial products (machinery and chemicals), the need for credit, and the consequent pressure to produce crops for cash. The farmer becomes caught up in the agricultural industry, the food industry, and commercial markets. Bourdieu outlines the political options open to peasants who have become salaried workers but who perceive themselves as owners, and who regard their work as regulated by nature and not by the market. He then links this economic integration to a parallel unification of the market of symbolic goods, which undermines the peasants' ethical autonomy and rots their capacity to resist.[65] Within this symbolic field there is a collective conversion, whereby the peasants are brought from being independent of the town to, first, comparing rural and urban life within a single frame and then, second, believing in the superiority of the latter. This restructuring of perceptions takes place in a way organized by the old order, with women serving as the key point for the entry of modern values. 'The women who, as symbolic objects of exchange, circulate upwards and, by this fact, are spontaneously open to being impressed by and compliant to the slogans and seductions coming from the city, are, with the younger sons, the Trojan horse of the urban world'.[66]

This is a Copernican revolution, whereby the former centre of local space – the heir – now finds himself isolated in a vast universe. He is no longer singled out but is amalgamated into a dominated class: he is insignificant and devalued.

I offer the following observations. First, 'conversion' allows the matching of Bourdieu's autobiography with the processes he describes; there is a perfect fit of the conversion of peasants into Frenchmen in the individual and the collective case. He makes this clear in an initial discussion, where he describes the development between the first two articles as a theoretical progress associated with the conversion of the subjective relation of the researcher to his object. This conversion is from a relation of exteriority to a 'theoretical and practical proximity which favours the theoretical reappropriation of the indigenous relation to practice'.[67]

Second, the myth of a closed peasant world perpetuates the story told by Le Play and many others. The peasant world has never been an isolate, and has had sufficient autonomy – though that may not be the right word – to make its own assessment of outside forces and respond to them. This may be the single most important lacuna in Bourdieu's approach: we are not dealing with isolates that meet, even if one of them is universalizing, but rather with boundaries that generate differences – or blindness and insight – on either side. Interfaces, not entities, are primary.

Third, and following on from this, Bourdieu reads his model onto the material, as when he revisits the statistical analyses, recalculating the figures on the basis not of residence but of the fate in 1970 of the cohort born in the commune before 1935. This return confirms his earlier results and, he claims, points to the unification of the market of symbolic goods, to the force of the attraction of urban realities that this unified field makes possible, and to the differential perception, appreciation and response to that attraction, defined as inertia, felt by the differently placed agents. This analysis simply prepares the way for the theory of unification. He does no further fieldwork on peasants' responses and peasant leadership, nor on women's attitudes and experiences. As we shall see, the economic language in which he describes the world of meaning also increasingly works its effects.

IX

The marriage market constitutes a particularly dramatic moment for peasants to discover the transformation of exchange values and the fall in the social price they command. The Christmas Eve dance makes this change clear: 'the *bal* is the visible form of the new logic of the matrimonial market'.[68] This dance was the starting point for Bourdieu's research and it encapsulates the complete logic of a complex process, which was available only in the first instance to a sympathetic intuition.[69]

The economic (determinist) vocabulary has full play in this description. The previous monopoly the heir had enjoyed in the protected market is lost as he is subjected to competition in the open market, suffering a brutal devaluation in all those values that he represents and that sustain him.[70] As in the first article, the ethnographic subjects only employ their native categories to their own despite; ethnography appears as immobile, leading to its own defeat, in the anarchy of the modern marketplace.

This symbolic domination is now described as symbolic violence[71] when it applies to the internalization of contradictions. It is particularly focused in the role of the mother, with her contradictory desires for her sons and daughters. Bourdieu develops this account of self-destruction in terms of an analogy with the processes of inflation, where 'each family or agent contributes to the depreciation of the group as a totality, which is [nevertheless] the principle of its matrimonial strategies'. The symbolically dominated group conspires against itself. It adopts externally generated values – 'the city image of the peasant is imposed on the peasant's consciousness'[72] – giving rise to an internal sense of defeat and isolated acts of treason, as the individualism of the market leads to those undesired results, the departure of women and the non-marriage of men.

This account is close to the thesis of internal colonialism: the interiorization by a dominated class of dominant categories. Bourdieu elaborates by describing how peasants have come willingly to participate in the education system, which is the principal instrument of urban symbolic domination. The peasant hopes through schooling to gain the means to compete in both the economic and symbolic markets; yet through adopting the values of French and of calculation he contributes to the conquest of a new market for urban symbolic products. The school offers the promise of mastery while in fact inculcating recognition of the legitimacy of this culture and of those who have the means to appropriate it. The education system accelerates the process of devaluation and inflation, completing the circle of Bourdieu's lived experience.

He concludes his account of the processes of interiorization with a description of the peasants' pessimism and demoralization, who express their dominated position in self-fulfilling prophecies of imminent disappearance. In this perspective, the pity Bourdieu felt, his original intuition, is absorbed into the peasant interiorization of their objective future and the dominant representation of it.[73] As Bourdieu says, economic and political competition between classes includes the symbolic manipulation of the future. In their unhappy pessimism, the peasants' actions threaten their reproduction, and Bourdieu's unhappy intuition apprehends this moment. Synopsis and pathos meet in the concept of symbolic violence: the peasant's interior submission to domination, and the intellectual's potential to offer liberation from it.

The intellectual is introduced as an actor only at the end of this depressing sequence, suddenly appearing to raise the possibility of a way out. At the last minute, Bourdieu can offer one small element of hope, this time in a footnote.[74] There he mentions, in contrast with the politics of demoralization, of flight (nostalgia) or racism, movements 'based soundly in symbolic reason', such as 'linguistic struggles, certain feminist demands ... and forms of regionalist claims'. However, he does not develop this theme and, indeed, defends his account of internalized violence and collapse against any suggestion of the 'emergence of a new peasant elite'.[75]

In sum, he offers a sophisticated theory of a moment of irreversible historical change in terms of symbolic domination, elaborated as symbolic violence through concepts of interiorization and demoralization. He also elaborates an economic vocabulary to describe these symbolic processes, allowing education to play its vital part, which was quite absent from the first paper. He concludes with a warning aimed at the world of education, in this case, the sociologists who attempt to impose a division of the economic from the symbolic or the infrastructure from the superstructure: they are concurring in the mystification of symbolic violence. This warning is indeed elaborated in the postscript,[76] where he links poor social science which uncritically transmits dominant categories with the bourgeoisie crushing the peasant. The only actor capable of acting for the liberation of the peasant – or posthumously, of recognizing his pain – is the intellectual who has mastered his trajectory.

X

If the 1972 article contains the formalization of a series of terms that Bourdieu employs widely in his work, the significant feature from our perspective is the introduction of an economic vocabulary into the symbolic realm, allowing the anticipation of a shift in the locus of initiative and understanding. This vocabulary also underlies the theory-dense notions of conversion and symbolic violence in the 1989 article. And because they correspond to aspects of the author's life, identified earlier as synopsis and pathos, they provide the means by which the sociologist achieves a critical understanding, through what we have termed a reading against time, the reversal of autobiography.

In a characteristic later interview,[77] Bourdieu discusses his 'social conversion' as he came from outside the system to gain a place in the French elite educational establishment. He describes the price paid in this process of education in terms of the renunciation of early solidarities, of unhappiness and shame.[78] He also claims that through sociological reflection on that upward trajectory – in which the 1962 article played a particular role – he has been able to become reconciled to his primary experiences and to take responsibility for them. Further on, he talks about the literary techniques, direct and indirect speech in particular, needed to transcribe these kinds of experience of the contradictions of the social structure. He points out how these techniques appear spontaneously in documents produced in the field – in transcripts of interviews, for example – as informants attempt to convey their own experience of and involvement in social life, in terms of what they suffer and what they achieve. Finally, referring to the task of the sociologist as he seeks to transform into science the social conditions that produce the writer, and so convert self-therapy into tools that may be of use to others, he employs two terms that correspond to those of suffering and achievement. Reflexive sociology, he says, will never be free of all unconscious elements, but when it succeeds in being reflexive, it will be free of resentment (he uses the term *ressentiment*) and it will be generous, in the sense of giving freedom.

Having traced Bourdieu's trajectory both forwards and backwards in time, these terms offer an appropriate means of summarizing the issue at the heart of his Béarnais ethnography. He has been motivated by a certain pathos to discover, articulate, formalize and develop a series of theory-laden concepts contained synoptically in his own autobiographical experience. To what extent has he succeeded in freeing himself from resentment and offering freedom? For this trajectory is constructed around the tension between the force at work in the subjects and the forms imposed upon them. Rather than reduce this tension to a simple opposition between actions and passions (or anthropology and history), it is better to conceptualize these moments as two kinds of interaction, the one permitting an increase in the parties' capacity to act and to understand, the other causing it to decrease. These interactions would correspond well to generosity and resentment respectively.

Bourdieu is moved to pity by his encounter. He identifies the pity that he feels with the pain that he supposes his subjects feel. This attribution is permitted by the coincidence of, or misfit between, habitus and structure; it permits scientific understanding; and it is expressed in the idea of symbolic violence. At the same time, it may be asked whether the pity he feels diminishes his own capacity to understand and to act, and so colours his interpretation. This diminution is given expression in the marginalization of peasant initiatives in his account, and his recourse to theoretical constructions rather than empirical enquiry.

From this angle, we can see why Bourdieu can be read as pessimistic, a vulgar Marxist, neglecting the category of gender, and so forth.[79] This is the face of his project which, rather than put power in the hands of the actors, returns to one of the dominant myths of sociology: an episode of irreversible change that happens, fortuitously, to have been witnessed by the author, who alone holds the truth of the moment. To this reading we can oppose a series of features, drawn equally for the most part from Bourdieu's study. First, the repeated experience of the 'disappearance' of the peasant. Then, evidence of the adaptability of the peasant in the face of outside pressure. Third, crediting the peasant with a certain responsibility in the generation of modernity, and not simply with reacting to it. And last, an appreciation of the role of self-presentation to the outside, and self-concealment, in the act of offering to an external gaze what is expected.

A description of this second aspect of Bourdieu's work might be that the mixture of social bodies – urban and rural – in some cases creates new possibilities, rather than one simply destroying the other and imposing its perspective on it. Whilst in the latter instance, the affective attitude of the sociologist who understands may be pity, in the former it may be something akin to joy. Such a positive solidarity would correspond closely to the moment of generosity described in the interview: it gives a certain detachment and a critical judgement. Rather than simply seeing the misery of the world, the sociologist looks to a new kind of involvement, ridding him or herself of resentment in order to see clearly, with a wide sympathy.

In the Béarn work, the relevant figures are present but underplayed. The analysis needs to include the new peasant elites as well as the defeated bachelors, and the regionalist movements in addition to the conservative or even reactionary elements of local politics. These omissions are the product of the strong time frame adopted, whereby the two series – solidarity/ethnographic analysis/sociological insight on the one hand, pity/statistical analysis/sociological story on the other – succeed one another, rather than forming part of a single picture. Bourdieu's own categories should be applied more thoroughly to his understanding of time, in order to develop an account of history. This limit point, where he takes part of the story for the whole, may be a function of the pain which, while it provided the mainspring for his work, he never fully came to terms with.

These two interrelated moments, of transition and loss on the one hand and of creative reinterpretation on the other, are expressed in Bourdieu's work both at the level of the theoretical categories of historical change and anthropological initiative, and through the experienced emotions of pity and even resentment which are contrasted with those of attraction and joy. These oppositions are a transformation of the indigenous resources of the local society rather than simply their narration, a writing-out embodying the complex local equilibrium between history and modernity: in short, an expression of the life of property in Béarn.

Notes

1. See Bourdieu and Wacquant (1992).
2. Bourdieu (1962a). This article has never been translated. For the sake of completeness, we should mention the contemporary article (Bourdieu 1962b) which is made up of extracts taken from the longer paper, focusing on the relations between the sexes.
3. Bourdieu (1972a). This article was translated (Bourdieu 1977a), and the analysis is included in a condensed and slightly recast form in Bourdieu (1980b) as a case study illustrating a 'practical logic'.
4. Bourdieu (1989). While Bourdieu includes analysis of 1968 statistics – and refers, in Bourdieu (1972a), to field visits in 1970 and 1971 (see Bourdieu 2002a: 177, n.6) – there is no evidence from new informants taken into account; this is a re-analysis of the 1962 article. He also draws on a series of discussions published in *Actes de la recherche en sciences sociales*: see Bourdieu (1980a, 1982b, 1983) and Bourdieu and Boltanski (1975); the first two of these are reprinted in Bourdieu (1982a). These articles all mention Béarnais materials, but do not refer to any new research.
5. Bourdieu (2002a). This volume contains an introduction (pp.1–14) plus reprints of Bourdieu (1962a, 1972a, 1989).
6. Ibid.: 13.
7. Bourdieu (2003: 282).
8. Bourdieu (2002a: 9).
9. Ibid.: 9–10.
10. See, e.g., Bourdieu (1989, 1993, 2001, 2002a, 2004) and Bourdieu and Wacquant (1992).
11. Bourdieu and Wacquant (1992: 162–164).
12. Bourdieu (2002a: 12).
13. Ibid.: 13.
14. Ibid.: 14.
15. See also Jenkins (1994), which discusses Bourdieu (1977b).
16. Louis de Bonald's pamphlet, 'Du Divorce' (Bonald 1864a[1800]), was written during debates about the framing of the Civil Code. See also his 'De la famille agricole, de la famille industrielle, et du droit d'aïnesse' (Bonald 1864b[1826]). For discussion, see Nisbet (1952); cf. chapter 1.
17. See Reed-Danahay (2004) for a discussion of the relation of the Béarnais and Kabyle materials.
18. Bourdieu (2002a: 19).
19. J.-P.A., born in 1875, contributes the substance of the account, although P.L., born around 1882, adds some astute remarks on relations of authority within the household.
20. Following an observation of Marx, cited Bourdieu (2002a: 169).
21. Though notice Bourdieu's concluding remarks in Appendix I, that the nature of the commune as a neighbourhood with collective rights holds the key to Béarnais custom surviving the Civil Code (ibid.: 141).
22. Ibid.: 50.
23. Ibid.: 56.
24. He uses the censuses of 1881, 1911 and 1954.
25. Bourdieu (2002a: 62).
26. Mendras (1976[1961]).
27. The population of the commune halved between 1836 and 1954. Bourdieu transcribes a local narrative of the reasons invoked, together with some sociological interpolations: crop failure and drought in the late nineteenth

century; the effects of the First World War; a lower birth rate, combined with the attractions of the town, and repulsion at the hard work country life represented for labourers and women alike, after the Second World War.

28. They are remembered locally, for they hold an exemplary value; Bourdieu cites a case from the 1830s (Bourdieu, 2002a: 27; repeated 182).

29. The term is Edwin Ardener's: see 'Belief and the Problem of Women', in Ardener (1989: 72–85).

30. See Bourdieu (1972b, 1980b).

31. Weber (1977).

32. Etchelecou (1991).

33. Cf. Herzfeld (1987). The same kind of arguments are taken up in Sahlins (1999) and Kirsch (2001).

34. The argument for the importance of Le Play to the subsequent ethnography of Béarn needs to be substantiated. I offer a preliminary sketch in chapter 1.

35. Bourdieu accuses of Le Play of presenting a mystificatory representation of kinship relations, taken from the indigenous subjective account and ignoring their ambiguous, even exploitative, aspect (Bourdieu 1980b; 1990: 159).

36. Bourdieu (2002a: 63ff.)

37. For a different approach, one may consult the contemporary account in Pitt-Rivers (1960).

38. Bourdieu (2002a: 86).

39. Ibid.: 107–108.

40. Bourdieu has two notable literary characteristics concerning novelty. First, he introduces important new distinctions often either in a footnote (*bourg*/hamlets – Bourdieu 2002a: 56, n.33) or in a summary of a section (marrying up/down – ibid.: 28). Second, he adds material that could cause a major revision of the analysis in a final paragraph (as here), sentence (see note 21, above), or even a footnote (see ibid.: 243).

41. He mentions, in a footnote, the role of Catholic social organizations in these developments.

42. Bourdieu (2002a: 108–109).

43. It is taken from Mauss's essay on body techniques (Mauss 1950b[1936]).

44. Bourdieu (2002a: 113).

45. Ibid.: 117.

46. Ibid.: 124.

47. Ibid.: 126.

48. Reprinted in part as an appendix to Bourdieu (1972a).

49. Bourdieu (2002a: 12).

50. Ibid.: 171.

51. They overlap and in many places substitute for one another.

52. Bourdieu (2002a: 169).

53. Ibid.: 171–172.

54. Ibid.: 176.

55. Ibid.: 177.

56. Ibid.: 180.

57. Ibid.: 196.

58. See ibid.: 191, 200, 202.

59. Ibid.: 202.

60. Bourdieu (1972b).

61. Cf. Bourdieu (2002a: 205).

62. Ibid.: 213.

63. Polanyi (1974[1957]); Bourdieu (2002a: 229).

64. Bourdieu (2002a: 222–223); Bourdieu introduces the Platonic opposition of 'enantion' to 'heteron', 'which', he claims, 'should serve to clarify a good many confused discussions on "popular culture"' (ibid.: 223).
65. Ibid.: 225.
66. Ibid.: 227.
67. Ibid.: 216.
68. Ibid.: 219.
69. Ibid.: 219, n.9.
70. Ibid.: 230–231.
71. Ibid.: 236.
72. Ibid.: 237.
73. Ibid.: 241.
74. Ibid.: 242–243, n.19.
75. Ibid.: 243.
76. A republication of Bourdieu (1977c).
77. Bourdieu and Wacquant (1992: 204–212).
78. See also his autobiographical fragment on his schooling (Bourdieu 2002b).
79. For a brief summary, see Mottier (2002).

Chapter 7

THE LIFE OF PROPERTY

When investigating a rural society in Western Europe, the overwhelming temptation is to suppose it to be on the point of extinction. The investigator imagines himself to be the witness to a way of life that is undergoing such radical change, as modern, urban, metropolitan values impinge, that he will be the last visitor to find it. On my first visit to Béarn in 1977 I saw a man ploughing with a single ox, a sight I have not seen repeated in thirty years. Yet on further acquaintance it becomes clear that there are continuities, resources in the local society that allow it to adapt and develop, and that we may say two things about these creative resources. First, that they may allow the local forms of life to present themselves to an outside gaze under the aspect of 'being about to disappear'; and second, that they contribute to shaping the outside gaze in unanticipated ways. They in part generate the forms that, in a partial apprehension, appear to be consuming them; it is therefore less surprising that the results of these encounters between the local and modern life appear to lead to prolongations of local life rather than its obliteration. This account is not to deny change, even radical change, but it is a claim concerning the forms that change takes.[1] This curious enduring existence is what has been termed the life of property. I wish to make four points to summarize the argument.

In the first place, a distinction should be made between a local way of life and its representation offered by outside interests. In the case of Le Play, the type of the family found in the Pyrenees contributed to a national – or metropolitan – debate about the forms of civil society. It may be suggested that broad matters of politics and government, economy and culture will always be discussed in narrower terms that draw in part on metaphors that play upon kin and alliance, as modelling involuntary and chosen solidarities. Intimately known domestic practices will be used to make sense of less-well understood social processes. In the case of the 'stem family', there are features which lend themselves to the task, for the family form is already mixed with matters of authority and wealth, the division of labour and political power, and such aspects of local culture as reputation and language. The discovered form brought out the interdependence of social institutions and their potential for integration even in a society with such highly differentiated institutions as mid-nineteenth-century France. This is a general characteristic of ethnographic cases: they offer themselves to reflection upon the potential of the metropolitan society, potential conceived in terms of polity, order, interdependence and flourishing, which are experienced largely in terms of their perceived absence or loss from that wider society.

The first point leads to the second, concerning the detailed evidence for this form of life identified by Le Play. Archival material allows the description of a long-lived co-existence of two distinct kinds of relation to property – concerning two conceptions of inheritance and of marriage, of authority within the family and of individual initiative – which have legal expression. Indeed, the evidence suggests a series of encounters between feudal governmental techniques and local life may have generated these two models of organizing social life, to be appealed to according to context, models expressed in the innumerable ordinary events of marriage, succession to property and office, and death. A seemingly archaic form exists alongside a seemingly more modern form, and their co-inherence permits a distinctive, flexible and complex social life. Many readings of this complex social life make two complementary errors: they tend on the one hand to take a single aspect of the complex, be it family, household, land or law, as determinant of the others, and on the other hand tend to read as a succession what is in fact a simultaneity, so that one form of life is seen as giving way to the other. Either account is misleading because the balance between these two conceptions lies in the mental preference for the first in the appropriate circumstances on the part of those who share these complex social categories of thought, the preference or evaluation being part of the categories and the actors' situation with respect to them, so that, whilst 'modern' options will be pursued when relevant, their success may lead to positions in which preferred 'traditional' options can operate. Hence the latter way of life can exist and be perpetuated under the guise of being about to disappear: it is both contained in and permits what appears to deny it. It is worth repeating that, on the one hand, the testimony of certain local actors – non-inheriting younger sons, the less wealthy proprietors of small farms and, more rarely, a defecting large farmer – lends plausibility to the partial, outside interpretation of the evidence and, on the other hand, that local categories actively defend themselves through playing on such a misinterpretation, so that in conversation continuities are habitually unremarked and so disguised, while disruption is emphasized.

The claim is then double: first, that this complex of possibilities is transmitted not through any single institution – the house, the distinction between great houses and small, authority within the family, single inheritance and the compensation of non-heirs, the marriage contract and its legal form – but through the combined strands and the pattern between them, so that individual institutions may transform or cease to operate without the complex structure of co-inhering contrary possibilities being destroyed. And second, this flexible way of life has been sufficiently enduring to receive the impact of outside events, giving a certain local order and continuity to the turbulences of wider history. Local resources can generate different accounts of time, personality, transmission and authority, shaping encounters with the outside; these encounters are the forms in which local life is adapted and prolonged. The test case for this assertion is the introduction of the Civil Code, the encounter which structures the 'discovery' of the Béarnais family by Le Play and which begins our particular segment of the story, but it can also be explored in the contemporary forms of value, legitimacy and authority that operate in the region, as well as in the reception of innovation in agricultural practices. The novel by Palay offers an unusually detailed indigenous account of these processes. It is framed by a series of crises – 1789, 1805, 1848, 1870, 1914, 1933 – and presents a representation of the multiple and conflicting resources that local categories offer to meet periods of turbulence. This account spells out the relationship of the life of property to history: the simultaneous generation of the new and its being read and conformed in terms deriving from the past, using categories that are prolonged through their employment in this fashion. This evidence also illustrates the wider point that social facts, the most enduring – and therefore the most real – aspects of a form of social life, are also the most intangible facts and the least susceptible to processes of recording. Social reality at this level consists neither in the transmission of an essence, nor in the invention of the new, but has a third form of existence. It is neither simply present nor absent, but has to be reconstructed in the light of events, so that motivations and the meaning of acts can only be comprehended retrospectively. The preceding chapters offer illustrations of this process.

The third point is a development of the second; if we are concerned with the capacity of local life not only to suffer but also actively to shape encounters with the outside, a small but important part of that encounter concerns the contribution local thought makes to wider metropolitan categories. In the case both of Le Play and of Bourdieu, their central sociological categories include transformations of apprehensions of local life: sociology exemplifies the wider practices of which it speaks. But this feature is also expressed in the hints that Le Play drops, that modern citizens have to come from some local setting. In this sense, metropolitan life is bound in some respects both to apprehend provincial life in terms coloured by local experience, and to be engaged with by persons exploiting aspects of local knowledge. This process is explored in Bourdieu's conception of a reflexive sociology; there is an intimate connection between national categories and local life, for the wider categories both emerge from, and have to make sense to, people with a particular history.

In brief, this ethnographically-focused account of the life of property in Béarn places some power of initiative in the hands of local actors, without making any strongly conservative or nostalgic claim. Modern life is more complex for this reason than many descriptions would allow; this approach questions accounts that see anthropology simply as a meditation upon force, that separate too distinctly institutions such as the family and culture from politics and economics (and usually make the last determinant), and that portray local life as at best forms of resistance that must be eroded by contact with cosmopolitan forms of life. Thereby, this approach links up with a good deal of contemporary writing on the informal economy, local theories of the state and of political action, and accounts recasting kinship and the family.

There is a last point to raise concerning what are the specific features of the way of life identified that have permitted it to make the contribution it has to the wider context. We may suggest it is because it cross-cuts standard categories derived from forms found elsewhere which have lent themselves to clearer formulations than those permitted by the life of property in Béarn of the separation of institutions and of unidirectional causalities between them. It is in this sense a mixed social form which brings out ambiguities in the standard formulations that might otherwise remain hidden, formulations whose limitations are felt particularly in times of crisis. European thought concerning property from Locke onward has divided broadly into two traditions, the one termed 'instrumental', in which the justification for property turns upon the need to reward men for undertaking the work required to serve human ends, the other called 'self-developmental', in that labour is seen as an intrinsically worthwhile activity, and there is a substantial bond between a man and property as the medium for his self-realization.[2] Each tradition makes claims as to the proper description of society, economic activity and political action, and offers differing diagnoses of social disorder and ways forward. They are, in the last analysis, theodicies: accounts of the causes of men's ills and the possibility of their flourishing. The account of property derived from Béarn mediates between these two dominant traditions, allowing the occasional insufficiencies of each to be supplemented by drawing together concepts that are usually separated and reintegrating social life. It contains to an unusual degree what Proust in a remarkable passage calls 'the wisdom not of nations but of families', wisdom inspired by 'a Muse ... which has collected up everything ... that is simply contingent but which also reveals other laws: the Muse of History'.[3]

Notes

1. Cf. the similar concerns, though expressed through very different materials, in Gow (2001). Gow too deals not only with how an indigenous people (native Amazonians) react to European colonial expansion, but also seeks to demonstrate how the successive forms of the encounter arise in large part from the active employment of native categories.
2. See Ryan (1984); cf. Hann (1998).
3. Proust (1954: 357); see Epigraph.

BIBLIOGRAPHY

Abélès, Marc. 1984. 'Pouvoirs dans la commune, pouvoirs sur la commune', *Études rurales* 93/94: 325–329.

——— 1986. 'L'État en perspective', *Études rurales* 101/102: 9–17.

——— 1991[1989]. *Quiet Days in Burgundy*. Cambridge: Cambridge University Press.

Amann, Peter. 1990. *The Corncribs of Buzet: Modernizing Agriculture in the French Southwest*. Princeton, NJ: Princeton University Press.

Ardener, Edwin. 1989. *The Voice of Prophecy and Other Essays*. Oxford: Blackwell.

Arensberg, C.M. and S. Kimball. 2001[1940]. *Family and Community in Ireland*. Ennis: CLASP Press.

Aron, Raymond. 1954. *Histoire de Vichy 1940–1944*. Paris: Fayard.

Assier-Andrieu, Louis. 1981. *Coutumes et rapports sociaux: étude anthropologique des communautés paysannes du Capcir*. Paris: CNRS.

——— 1984. 'Le Play et la famille-souche des Pyrénées: politique, juridique et science sociale', *Annales ESC* 39: 495–512.

——— 1986b. 'Coutume savante et droit rustique. Sur la légalité paysanne', *Études rurales* 103/104: 105–137.

——— 1987. 'Maison de mémoire: structure symbolique du temps familial en Languedoc: Curnis', *Terrain* 9: 10–33.

Assier-Andrieu, Louis. (ed.) 1986a. *Le droit et les paysans*, special issue of *Études rurales* 103/104.

Augustins, Georges, 1989. *Comment se perpétuer?* Nanterre, Société d'ethnologie.

Augustins, Georges, and Rolande Bonnain. 1981. *Les Baronnies des Pyrénées. Tome I: Maisons, Mode de vie, Société*. Paris: Éditions de l'École des Hautes Études en Sciences Sociales.

——— 1986. *Les Baronnies des Pyrénées. Tome II: Maisons, Éspace, Famille*. Paris: Éditions de l'École des Hautes Études en Sciences Sociales.

Bailey, F.G. (ed.) 1971. *Gifts and Poison: The Politics of Reputation*. Oxford: Blackwell.

Banfield, Edward. 1958. *The Moral Basis of a Backward Society*. Chicago: Free Press.

Barraqué, Jean-Pierre, and Thibon, Christian. 2004. *Le discourse régionaliste en Béarn*. Orthez: Éditions Gascogne.

Berkner, Lutz, 1975. 'The Use and Misuse of Census Data for the Historical Analysis of Family Structure', *Journal of Interdisciplinary History* 4: 721–738.

Bernot, L. and R. Blancard. 1953. *Nouville, un village français*. Paris: Institut d'Ethnologie.

Bidot-Germa, Dominique. 2008. *Un notariat medieval. Droit, pouvoir et société en Béarn*. Toulouse: Presses Universitaires du Mirail.

Bidot-Germa, Dominique, Michel Grosclaude and Jean-Paul Duchon. 1986. *Histoire de Béarn*. Denguin: Edicions Per Nostre.

Blaxter, Lorraine. 1971. '*Rendre service* and *jalousie*', in F.G. Bailey (ed.) *Gifts and Poison: The Politics of Reputation*. Oxford: Blackwell.

Bonald, Louis de. 1864a[1800]. 'Du divorce', in *Oeuvres complètes de M. de Bonald*. Paris: J.P. Migne.

——— 1864b[1826]. 'De la famille agricole, de la famille industrielle, et du droit d'aïnesse', *Oeuvres complètes de M. de Bonald*. Paris: J.P. Migne.

Bonnain, Rolande. 1986. 'Les noms de maison dans les Baronnies, 1773–1980', in Georges Augustins and Rolande Bonnain, *Les Baronnies des Pyrénées. Tome II : Maisons, Éspace, Famille*. Paris: Éditions de l'École des Hautes Études en Sciences Sociales.

Bonnin, Philippe. 1992. 'La maison rurales et les structures de l'habiter', *Études rurales* 125/126: 153–166.

Bordeu, Charles de. 1970[1889] *Le dernier maître*. Pau: Marrimpouey Jeune.

Bourdieu, Pierre. 1962a. 'Célibat et condition paysanne'. *Etudes rurales* 5/6: 32–135; reprinted in Bourdieu (2002a: 15–166).

——— 1962b. 'Les relations entre les sexes dans la société paysanne', *Les Temps Modernes* 195: 307–331.

——— 1972a. 'Les stratégies matrimoniales dans le système de reproduction', *Annales ESC* 27: 1105–1125; reprinted in Bourdieu (2002a: 167–210).

——— 1972b. *Esquisse d'une théorie de la pratique*. Geneva: Librairie Droz.

——— 1977a. 'Marriage Strategies as Strategies of Social Reproduction', in R. Foster, R. Ranum and O. Ranum (eds), *Family and Society: Selections from the Annales*. Baltimore, MD: Johns Hopkins University Press.

——— 1977b. *Outline of a Theory of Practice*, trans R. Nice. Cambridge: Cambridge University Press.

——— 1977c. 'Une chose objet', *Actes de la recherche en sciences sociales* 17/18: 2–5.

——— 1980a. 'L'identité et la representation: éléments pour une réflexion critique sur l'idée de région', *Actes de la recherche en sciences sociales* 35: 63–72; revised and reprinted in Bourdieu (1982a: 135–148).

——— 1980b. *Le Sens pratique*. Paris: Editions de Minuit.

——— 1980c. 'Le nord et le midi: contribution à une analyse de l'effet Montesquieu', *Actes de la recherché en sciences sociales* 35: 21–25.

——— 1982a. *Ce que parler veut dire: l'économie des échanges linguistiques*. Paris: Fayard.

——— 1982b. 'La formation des prix et l'anticipation des profits'. In Bourdieu (1982a).

——— 1983. 'Vous avez dit "populaire"?' *Actes de la recherche en sciences sociales* 46: 98–105.

—— 1989. 'Réproduction interdite: la dimension symbolique de la domination économique', *Etudes rurales* 113/114: 15–36; reprinted in Bourdieu (2002a: 211–247).

—— 1990. *The Logic of Practice*, trans R. Nice. Cambridge: Polity Press.

—— 1991. *Language and Symbolic Power*. Cambridge: Polity Press.

—— 1993. *La misère du monde*. Paris: Editions de Seuil.

—— 2001. *Science de la science et réflexivité*. Paris: Raisons d'agir.

—— 2002a. *Le bal des célibataires: crise de la société paysanne en Béarn*. Paris: Éditions du Seuil.

—— 2002b. 'Pierre par Bourdieu', *Nouvel Observateur*, 21 January 2002.

—— 2003. 'Participant Objectivation', *Journal of the Royal Anthropological Institute* 9: 281–294.

—— 2004. *Esquisse pour une auto-analyse: ou, ceci n'est pas une autobiographie*. Paris: Raisons d'agir.

Bourdieu, P. and L. Boltanski, 1975. 'Le fétichisme de la langue', *Actes de la recherche en sciences sociales* 4: 2–32.

Bourdieu, P. and L. Wacquant, 1992. *An Invitation to Reflexive Sociology*. Cambridge: Polity Press.

Brun, Auguste. 1923. *L'introduction de la langue française en Béarn et en Roussillon*. Paris: Champion.

Cadier, Léon. 1979[1888]. *Les Etats de Béarn depuis leurs origines jusqu'au commencement du xvie siècle*. Marseille: Lafitte Reprints.

Camelat, Miquèu. 1978[1898]. *Belina: Poèma de tres cants*. Tarbes: Nosauts de Bigorra/Institut d'Estudis Occitans.

Carsten, Janet, and Stephen Hugh-Jones (eds). 1995. *About the House*. Cambridge: Cambridge University Press.

Cazaurang, Jean Jacques. 1968. *Pasteurs et paysans béarnaise*, vol. 2. Pau: Marrimpouey Jeune.

Cazaurang, Jean Jacques, et al. 1978. *Maisons Béarnaises*, vols 1 and 2. Pau: Musée Béarnais, Imprimerie Tonnet.

Chenu, Alain. 1994. 'La famille-souche: questions de méthode', in Frédéric Le Play et al., *Les Mélouga: Une famille pyrénéenne au XIXe siècle*. Alain Chenu (ed.). Paris: Éditions Nathan.

Clavé, Paul. 1980. *Prosateurs béarnaise*. Pau: Per Noste et Marimpouey Jeune.

Claverie, Élisabeth and Pierre Lamaison. 1982. *L'impossible mariage: violence et parenté en Gévaudan 17e, 18e, 19e siècles*. Paris: Hachette.

Cobban, Alfred. 1961. *A History of Modern France, Volume 2: 1799–1871*. Harmondsworth: Penguin.

Collomp, Allain. 1983. *La maison du père: Famille et village en Haute-Provence aux XVIIe et XVIIIe siècles*. Paris: Presses Universitaires de France.

Connerton, Paul. 1989. *How Societies Remember*. Cambridge: Cambridge University Press.

Déchaux, Jean-Hughes. 1991. 'Structures de parenté et sociétés paysannes: deux points de vue et des suggestions pour une sociologie de la parenté dans les sociétés urbaines', *European Journal of Sociology* 10: 153–171.

Desplat, Christian. 1986. *Le For de Béarn d'Henri d'Albret (1551)*. Pau: Librarie Marrimpouey.

Di Méo, Guy, 1987. 'Stratégies foncières et processus d'urbanisation dans les petites villes', *Revue économique du Sud-Ouest* 4: 97–132.

—— 1996. *Les territories du quotidian.* Paris: L'Harmattan.

Di Méo, Guy, and R.Guerrero. 1985. 'La périurbanisation dans l'agglomeration de Pau: mutations foncières et resistances des agriculteurs' *Revue économique du Sud-Ouest* 2: 25–51.

Dinguirard, Jean-Claude. 1976. *Ethnolinguistique de la Haute Vallée du Ger.* Dissertation: University of Lille III.

Dumont, Louis. 1951. *La Tarasque: essai de description d'un fait local d'un point de vue ethnographique.* Paris: Gallimard.

Dupont, G. 1914. *Du régime successoral dans les coutumes du Béarn.* Dissertation: University of Paris.

Durkheim, Émile. 1988[1894]. *Les règles de la méthode sociologique* Paris: Flammarion.

Etchelecou, André. 1991. *Transition démographique et système coutumier dans les pyrénées occidentales.* Paris: Presses Universitaires de France.

Faillie, Marie-Henriette, 1968. *La femme et le Code civile dans la Comédie humaine d'Honoré de Balzac.* Paris: Didier.

Fardon, Richard (ed.) 1990. *Localizing Strategies: Regional Traditions of Ethnographic Writing.* Edinburgh: Scottish Academic Press.

Fauve-Chamoix, Antoinette. 1984. 'Les structures familiales au royaume des familles-souches: Esparros', *Annales ESC* 39: 513–528.

Favret-Saada, Jeanne. 1980[1977]. *Deadly Words: Witchcraft in the Bocage.* Cambridge: Cambridge University Press.

Foster, George. 1965. 'Peasant Society and the Image of Limited Good', *American Anthropologist* 67: 293–315.

Geertz, Clifford. 1961. 'Studies in Peasant Life: Community and Society', *Biennial Review of Anthropology* 2: 1–41.

Gilmore, David. 1982. 'Anthropology of the Mediterranean Area'. *Annual Review of Anthropology* 11: 175–203.

Goode, W.J. 1970[1963]. *World Revolution and Family Patterns.* New York: Free Press.

Goody, Jack. 1973. 'Bridewealth and Dowry in Africa and Eurasia', in Jack Goody and S.J. Tambiah, *Bridewealth and Dowry.* Cambridge: Cambridge University Press.

—— 1975. *Production and Reproduction: A Comparative Study of the Domestic Domain.* Cambridge: Cambridge University Press.

—— (ed.) 1971. *The Developmental Cycle in Domestic Groups.* Cambridge: Cambridge University Press.

Gow, Peter. 2001. *An Amazonian Myth and its History.* New York: Oxford University Press.

Grosclaude, David. 1982. *Une tentative de presse régionaliste en Béarn au début du siècle 'La bouts de la tèrre'.* Orthez: Per Noste.

Halbwachs, Maurice. 1952. *Les cadres sociaux de la mémoire.* Paris: Presses Universitaires de France.

—— 1968[1950]. *La mémoire collective.* Paris: Presses Universitaires de France.

Hann, C.M. 1998. 'Introduction: The Embeddedness of Property', in C.M. Hann (ed.) *Property Relations: Renewing the Anthropological Tradition.* Cambridge: Cambridge University Press.

—— 2008. 'Reproduction and Inheritance: Goody Revisited', *Annual Reviews of Anthropology* 37: 145-58.

Hellman, John. 1993. *The Knight Monks of Vichy France: Uriage 1940–1945.* Montreal: McGill-Queen's University Press.

Hertz, Robert. 1983[1913]. 'St. Besse: A Study of an Alpine Cult', in S. Wilson (ed.) *Saints and their Cults*. Cambridge: Cambridge University Press.

Herzfeld, Michael, 1987. *Anthropology through the Looking-glass: Critical Ethnography in the Margins of Europe*. Cambridge: Cambridge University Press.

—— 1992. *The Social Production of Indifference: Exploring the Symbolic Roots of Western Bureaucracy*. Chicago: University of Chicago Press.

Ho Tai, Hue-Tam. 2001. 'Remembered Realms: Pierre Nora and French National Memory', *American Historical Review* 106: 906–921.

Howe, Leo. 2000. 'Risk, Ritual and Performance', *Journal of the Royal Anthropological Institute* 6: 63–79.

James, Wendy. 2003. *The Ceremonial Animal: A New Portrait of Anthropology*. Oxford: Oxford University Press.

Jeanjean, Henri. 1992. *De l'utopie au pragmatisme? Le mouvement Occitan 1976–1990*. Perpinyà: Libres del Trabucaire.

Jenkins, Timothy. 1981. 'A Social Anthropological Study of Occitan Identity in Modern France: The Case of Béarn', unpublished report to the Social Science Research Council (U.K.)

—— 1994. 'Fieldwork and the Perception of Everyday Life', *Man* 29: 433–455.

—— 1999. *Religion in English Everyday Life: An Ethnographic Approach*. Oxford: Berghahn.

Jones, P.M. 2003. 'Recent Work on French Rural History', *The Historical Journal* 46, 4: 953-961.

Kirsch, Stuart. 2001. 'Lost Worlds: Environmental Disaster, "Culture Loss" and the Law', *Current Anthropology* 42: 167–198.

Klinck, David. 1996. *The French Revolutionary Theorist Louis de Bonald (1754–1840)*. New York: Peter Lang.

Kuper, Adam, 1988. *The Invention of Primitive Society: Transformations of an Illusion*. London: Routledge.

Laborde, J.-B. and P. Lorber. 1932. *Histoire du Béarn*, Tome 1. Pau: Lescher-Moutoué.

Laborde, Laurent. 1909. *La dot dans les Fors et Coutimes du Béarn*. Bordeaux: Cadoret.

Lafont, Robert and Christian Anatole. 1970. *Nouvelle histoire de la littérature Occitane*. Paris: Presses Universitaires de France.

Lamaison, Pierre. 1979. 'Les strategies matrimoniales dans un système complexe de parenté: Ribennes en Gévaudan (1650–1830)', *Annales ESC* 34: 721–743.

Lamarche, H., C. Karnoouh and S.C. Rogers. 1980. *Paysans, femmes et citoyens: luttes pour le pouvoir dans un village Lorrain*. Le Pardou: Actes Sud.

Laslett, Peter. 1965. *The World We Have Lost*. London: Methuen.

Latour, Bruno. 1991. *Nous n'avons jamais été modernes: Essais d'anthropologie symmétrique*, Paris, Éditions La Découverte.

Laughland, John. 1997. *The Tainted Source: The Undemocratic Origins of the European Idea*. London: Little, Brown.

Layton, Robert. 2000. *Anthropology and History in Franche-Comté*. Oxford: Oxford University Press.

Lefebvre, Henri. 1990[1963]. *La vallée de Campan: Etude de sociologie rurale*. Paris: Presses Universitaires de France.

Le Play, Frédéric. 1855. *Les Ouvriers européens: études sur les travaux, la vie domestique et le condition morale des populations ouvrières de l'Europe, précédées d'un exposé de la méthode d'observation*. Paris: Imprimerie Impériale.

—— 1870. *L'organisation du travail, selon les coûtumes des ateliers et la loi du Décalogue, avec un précis d'observations comparées sur la distinction du bien et du mal dans le régime du travail, les causes du mal actuel et les moyens de réforme, les objections et les réponses, les difficultés et les solutions*. Tours and Paris: Mame et Dentu.

—— 1871. *L'organisation de la famille, selon le vrai modèle signalé par l'histoire de toutes les races et de tous les temps*. Paris: Bibliothécaire de l'Oeuvre Saint-Michel.

—— 1875[1864]. *La Réforme sociale en France, déduite de l'observation comparée des peuples européens*. Tours: Mame.

Le Play, Frédéric, et al. 1994[1857]. *Les Mélouga: Une famille pyrénéenne au XIXe siècle*. Alain Chenu (ed.) Paris: Éditions Nathan.

Lerat, Serge. 1963. *Les Pays de l'Adour, structures agraires et économie agricole*. Bordeaux: Union Française d'Impression.

Le Roy Ladurie, Emmanuel. 1975. 'De la crise ultime à la vrai croissance', in Georges Duby and Armand Wallon (eds), *Histoire de la France rurale. II, De 1340 à 1789*. Paris: Editions du Seuil.

—— 1982. *Love, Death and Money in the Pays d'Oc*. Harmondsworth: Penguin.

Lévi-Strauss, Claude. 1983[1979]. 'The Social Organisation of the Kwakiutl', in *The Way of the Masks*. London, Cape.

—— 1987[1984]. *Anthropology and Myth*. Oxford: Blackwell.

—— 1991. 'Maison' in Pierre Bonte and Michel Izard (eds), *Dictionnaire de l'ethnologie et de l'anthropologie*. Paris: Presses Universitaires de France.

Levy, Jonah D. 1999. *Tocqueville's Revenge: State, Society, and Economy in Contemporary France*. Cambridge, MA: Harvard University Press.

Le Wita, Béatrice. 1994[1988]. *French Bourgeois Culture*. Cambridge: Cambridge University Press.

Loubergé, Jean. 1958 'Villages et maisons rurales dans la vallée moyenne du gave de Pau', *Revue de géographie des Pyrénées et du Sud Ouest* XXIX: 21–50.

—— 1986. *La maison rurale en Béarn*. Nonette: Éditions CRÉER.

Luc, Pierre. 1943. *Vie rurale et pratique juridique en Béarn aux xive et xve siècles*. Toulouse: Imprimerie F. Boisseau.

Lukács, Georg, 1989[1937]. *The Historical Novel*. London: Merlin Press.

Lynch, Edouard. 1992. *Entre la commune et la nation: Identité communautaire et pratique politique en vallée de Campan (Hautes Pyrénées) au xixe siècle*. Toulouse: Université de Toulouse II/ Tarbes: Archives des Hautes-Pyrénées.

Macfarlane, Alan. 1984. 'The Myth of the Peasantry: Family and Economy in a Northern Parish', in Richard M. Smith (ed.) *Land, Kinship and Life-cycle*. Cambridge: Cambridge University Press.

Marca, Pierre de. 2000[1640]. *Histoire de Béarn*, tomes 1 and 2. Pau: Princi Néguer.

Marx, Karl. 1972[1852]. *The Eighteenth Brumaire of Louis Bonaparte*. Moscow: Progress Publishers.

Mauss, Marcel. 1950a[1924]. 'Essai sur le don: forme et raison de l'échange dans les sociétés archaïques', in *Sociologie et anthropologie*. Paris: Presses Universitaires de France.

—— 1950b[1936]. 'Les techniques du corps', in *Sociologie et anthropologie*. Paris: Presses Universitaires de France.

Mazure, A. and J. Hatoulet. 1841–1843. *Fors de Béarn*. Pau: Vignancour.

Mendras, Henri. 1976[1961] *The Vanishing Peasant*. Cambridge, MA: MIT Press.

M.G.N. [Nogues]. 1837[1760]. *Les coutumes de Barège et du Pays de Lavdan*. Bagnères.

Moen, Phyllis, and Elaine Wethington. 1992. 'The Concept of Family Adaptive Strategies', *Annual Review of Sociology* 18: 233–251.

Montesquieu. 1989[1748]. *The Spirit of the Laws*. Cambridge: Cambridge University Press.

—— 1993[1721]. *Persian Letters*. Harmondsworth: Penguin.

Morgan, Lewis Henry. 1871. *Systems of Consanguinity and Affinity of the Human Family*. Washington, D.C.: Smithsonian.

Mosko, Mark. 2000. 'Inalienable Ethnography: Keeping-while-giving and the Trobriand Case', *Journal of the Royal Anthropological Institute* 6: 377–396.

Mottier, V. 2002. 'Masculine Domination: Gender and Power in Bourdieu's Writings', *Feminist Theory* 3: 345–359.

Nisbet, Robert. 1952. 'Conservatism and Sociology', *American Journal of Sociology* 58: 167–175.

—— 1999[1968]. *Tradition and Revolt*. New Jersey: Transaction.

Nora, Pierre (ed.) 1981–1992. *Lieux de mémoire*, 3 vols. Paris, Gallimard.

Ott, Sandra. 1993[1981]. *The Circle of Mountains: A Basque Shepherding Community*. Reno: University of Nevada Press.

Ourliac, Paul. 1979[1956]. 'La famille pyrénéene au moyen age', in Paul Ourliac, *Études d'histoire du droit médiéval*. Paris: Picard.

Ourliac, Paul and Monique Gilles. 1990. *Les Fors anciens de Béarn. Edition et traduction*. Paris: Éditions du Centre National de la Recherche Scientifique.

Palay, Jan. 1977[1900]. *Coundes biarnes*. Pau: Bibliothèque de l'Escole Gastou Fébus.

Palay, Simin. 1974[1934]. *Los tres gojats de Bòrdavielha*. Pau: Marrimpouey Jeune.

Papy, Michel. 1995. 'La famille-souche revisitée', *Etudes rurales* 135: 89–94.

Phillips, Roderick. 1988. *Putting Asunder*. Cambridge: Cambridge University Press.

Pitt-Rivers, Julian. 1960. 'Social Class in a French Village', *Anthropological Quarterly* 33: 1–13.

Polanyi, Karl. 1974[1957]. *The Great Transformation*. Boston: Beacon Press.

Pottage, Alain, and Martha Mundy (eds). 2004. *Law, Anthropology, and the Constitution of the Social: Making Persons and Things*. Cambridge: Cambridge University Press.

Poumarède, Jacques. 1972. *Les successions dans le sud-ouest de la France au moyen âge*. Paris: Presses Universitaires de France.

Poyatos, Fernando (ed.) 1988. *Literary Anthropology: A New Disciplinary Approach To People, Signs and Literature*. Philadeplhia, PA: John Benjamins Publishing Co.

Raymond, Paul. 1873. *Le Béarn sous Gaston Phoebus: Denombrement des maisons de la vicomté de Béarn* (Extract from tome VI of *Inventaire sommaire des Archives*). Pau: Archives des Basses-Pyrénées.

Redfield, Robert. 1960. *Peasant Society and Culture: An Anthropological Approach to Civilization*. Chicago: University of Chicago Press.

Reed-Danahay, Deborah. 2004. '*Tristes Paysans*: Bourdieu's Early Ethnography in Béarn and Kabylai', *Anthropological Quarterly* 77: 87–106.

Riles, Annelise (ed.) 2006. *Documents: Artefacts of Modern Knowledge*. Ann Arbor: University of Michigan Press.

Robisheaux, Thomas. 1989. *Rural Society and the Search for Order in Early Modern Germany*. Cambridge: Cambridge University Press.

Rogé, P. 1908. *Les anciens Fors de Béarn: Études sur l'histoire du droit béarnaise au Moyen Age*. Toulouse: Privât.

Rogers, Susan Carol. 1991. *Shaping Modern Times in Rural France*. Princeton, NJ: Princeton University Press.

—— 1995. 'Natural Histories: The Rise and Fall of French Rural Studies', *French Historical Studies* 19, 2: 381–397.

—— 2001. 'Anthropology in France', *Annual Review of Anthropology* 30: 481–504.

Rohlfs, Gerhardt. 1977[1935]. *Le Gascon: Etudes de philologie pyrénéenne*. Pau: Editions Marrimpouey Jeune.

Ryan, Alan. 1984. *Property and Political Theory*. Oxford: Blackwell.

Sabean, David. 1990. *Property, Production and Family in Neckerhausen, 1700–1870*. Cambridge: Cambridge University Press.

Sahlins, Marshall. 1999. 'Two or Three Things I Know about Culture', *Journal of the Royal Anthropological Institute* 5: 399–421.

Sainte-Beuve, C. A. 1867. *Nouveaux lundis, tome 9*. Paris: Michel Lévy Frères.

Saint-Macary, Jacques. 1939. 'La désertion des campagnes en Béarn et dans le Pays Basque'. Pau: Lescher-Moutoué.

Saint-Macary, Jean, 1942. *Les régimes matrimoniaux en Béarn avant et après le Code civil*. Pau: Marrimpouey Jeune.

Salles Loustau, Jean. 1986. 'Langue et littérature d'expression occitane', in Pierre Tucoo-Chala et al. (eds), *Béarn*. Paris: Christine Bonneton Editeur.

Sarpoulet, Jean-Marie. 2005. *Les débuts des* Reclams de Biarn e Gascougne: *revue occitane en Gascogne (1897–1920)*. Pessac: Presses Universitaires de Bordeaux.

Scott, James C. 1976. *The Moral Economy of the Peasant*. New Haven, CT: Yale University Press.

Segalen, Martine, 1985. *Quinze generations de Bas-Bretons: parenté et société dans le Pays Bigourden sud, 1720–1980*. Paris: Presses Universitaires de France.

—— 1986[1981]. *Historical Anthropology of the Family*. Cambridge: Cambridge University Press.

Shanin, Teodor. 1990. *Defining Peasants: Essays Concerning Rural Societies*. Oxford: Blackwell.

—— (ed.) 1971. *Peasants and Peasant Societies*. Harmondsworth: Penguin.

Silver, Catherine Bodard. 1982. *Frédéric Le Play on Family, Work and Social Change*. Chicago: University of Chicago Press.

Stein, Peter. 1999. *Roman Law in European History*. Cambridge: Cambridge University Press.

Thibon, Christian. 1988. *Pays de Sault. Les Pyrénées audoises au xixe siècle: les villages et l'Etat*. Paris: Éditions du Centre National de la Recherche Scientifique.

Tilly, Louise A. and Joan W. Scott. 1987[1978]. *Women, Work, and Family*. New York and London: Methuen.

Tisset, Pierre. 1959. 'Mythes et réalités du droit écrit', *Études d'histoire du droit privé, mélanges Pierre Petot*. Paris: Éditions Domat-Montchrestien.

Tucoo-Chala, Pierre. 1956. 'Les institutions de la Vicomté de Béarn (xe-xve siècles)', in F. Lot and R. Fawtier, *Histoire des institutions au Moyen Age. Tome 1: 'Les Institutions seigneurales'*. Paris: Presses Universitaires de France.

—— 1961. *La vicomté de Béarn et le problème de sa souveraineté des origins à 1620*. Bordeaux: Bière.

—— 1970. *Histoire du Béarn*. Paris: Presses Universitaires de France.

Verdier, Yvonne. 1979. *Façons de dire, façons de faire: la laveuse, la couturière, la cuisinière*. Paris: Gallimard.

Verdon, Michel. 1979. 'The Stem Family: Towards a General Theory', *Journal of Interdisciplinary History* 10: 87–105.

Vialles, Noëlie. 1994[1987]. *Animal to Edible*. Cambridge: Cambridge University Press.

Viazzo, P.P., and K.A. Lynch. 2002. 'Anthropology, Family History, and the Concept of Strategy', *International Review of Social History* 47: 423–452.

Weber, Eugen. 1977. *Peasants into Frenchmen: The Modernization of Rural France, 1870–1914*. London: Chatto and Windus.

Weiner, Annette. 1992. *Inalienable Possessions: The Paradox of Keeping-while-giving*. Berkeley: University of California Press.

Wolf, Eric. 1966. *Peasants*. Englewood Cliffs, NJ: Prentice Hall.

Wylie, Laurence. 1964[1957]. *Village in the Vaucluse*. Cambridge, MA: Harvard University Press.

Young, Arthur. 1929[1792]. *Travels in France during the years 1787, 1788 & 1789*, abridged edn. Cambridge: Cambridge University Press.

Yver, Jean. 1966. *Egalité entre héritiers et exclusion des enfants dotés: Essai de géographie coutumière*. Paris: Sirey.

Zink, Anna. 1993. *L'héritier de la maison: Géographie coutumière du Sud-Ouest de la France sous l'Ancien Régime*. Paris: Éditions de l'École des Hautes Études en Sciences Sociales.

—— 1997. *Clochers et troupeaux. Les communautés rurales des Landes et du Sud-Ouest de la France avant la Revolution*. Bordeaux: Presses Universitaires de Bordeaux.

Zonabend, Françoise. 1984[1980]. *The Enduring Memory: Time and History in a French Village*. Manchester: Manchester University Press.

—— 1985. 'Du texte au prétexte: la monographie dans le domaine européen'. *Études rurales* 97/98: 33–38.

INDEX